AF539847

QUALITY SCHOOL EDUCATION

ENCYCLOPAEDIA OF SCHOOL EDUCATION - 4

QUALITY SCHOOL EDUCATION

By

Dr. Marlow Ediger
M.S. Education, Ph.D.
Professor Emeritus in Education
Truman State University
Box 417, 201 W, 22nd St
North Newton KS 67117
United States of America

&

Dr. Digumarti Bhaskara Rao
M.Sc., M.A., M.A., M.Ed., Ph.D.
Reader & Research Director
R.V.R. College of Education
Srinivasa Nagar Colony
Guntur–522 006
(India)

DISCOVERY PUBLISHING HOUSE PVT. LTD.
NEW DELHI-110 002

First Published - 2005

Reprinted - 2018

ISBN: 978-93-5056-599-5 (Set)

ISBN: 978-81-8356-022-1

Quality School Education

Published by:

DISCOVERY PUBLISHING HOUSE PVT. LTD.

4383/4B, Ansari Road, Darya Ganj
New Delhi-110 002 (India)
Phone: +91-11-23279245, 43596064-65
Fax: +91-11-23253475
E-mail: discoverypublishinghouse@gmail.com
sales@discoverypublishinggroup.com
web: www.discoverypublishinggroup.com

Printed at:
Infinity Imaging Systems
Delhi

Dedicated
To
The Affectionate Administrator

Mr. M. Vasudev
Regional Director
National Council for Teacher Education
Bangalore

Dr. Digumarti Bhaskara Rao
greeting
Mr. M. Vasudev

Preface

School education across the world has gained special significance as it makes its students acquire adequate knowledge in various disciplines and decide the future course of action in education.

Several individuals and national and international professional organisations are suggesting various measures to enhance the status of school education in all its dimensions. As a part of it, several things need to be taken care of.

This book, on quality in school education, discusses many things to be taken care of, to be worked out, and to be implemented. This book will be of great use to all the people concerned to and personnel involved in school education.

Marlow Ediger

Bhaskara Rao

Contents

Preface

1. What Makes for Quality Teaching? 1
2. Who Should Determine the Curriculum? 9
3. Objectives, Learning Activities and Assessment: *(Which of the Three is Most Important)* 17
4. Special Education Students and Mandated Objectives 25
5. Problems in Implementing No Child Left Behind 32
6. Testing and Predictions of Pupil Success 39
7. Absolute Standards Versus Value Added Criteria 47
8. Meeting Student Needs 52
9. Connecting the Home and the School 58
10. Community Service and the Schools 66
11. The Competent Teacher in the Classroom 73
12. Assisting the New Teacher to do Well 81
13. Teacher Education at its Best 88
14. Teaching Vocabulary Development 95
15. Speaking, Listening and Writing: *The Forgotten Language Arts Areas* 101
16. Listening in the Language Arts Curriculum 109
17. Identification of New Words in Reading 116
18. Analysing the Goals of the National Reading Panel 123

19. How Often Should Students Be Tested in Reading? 129
20. Reading and the Internet 136
21. Writing in the Mathematics Curriculum 142
22. Writing in the Science Curriculum 149
23. Writing in the Social Studies 154
24. Reading, Writing and Relevancy in Mathematics 160
25. Developing Enthusiasm for Mathematics 169
26. Learning Opportunities in Science 177
27. Current Events in Science 184
28. Science Learning and the Student 189
29. Guidelines for Teaching Social Studies 194
30. Teaching History in the Classroom 202
31. Themes to Emphasise in the Geography Curriculum 211
32. Notebooks in the Social Studies 218
33. Citizenship Education in the Social Studies 226
Additional Reading 233

1

What Makes for Quality Teaching?

Good teachers are needed to staff the public schools and assist students to achieve as optimally as possible. Much has been written in providing guidelines for teaching excellence. One guideline is very salient and that is to provide for individual differences among students. Thus, selected students posses more academic abilities than do others; some are faster in responding to the teacher's questions, while others have more interest in an ongoing lesson or unit of study. Students then do differ from each other in intelligences possessed, learning styles exhibited, motivation possessed to pursue, learn, grow and achieve. Good teaching is cognizant of the multiple ways in which students may differ from each other and make provisions in learning opportunities for these differences. What then is done to emphasise quality teaching.

Providing for Individual Students

The good teacher does stress the importance of student meaning in learning. Rote learning and memorisation are not adequate in learning. Why? So often, students do not understand that which was memorised. Thus, meaning needs to be stressed in student learning. What is learned must make sense. Students need to understand in-depth, subject matter and skills acquired. To reveal comprehension, the student might say orally in his/her own words what has been learned. If students do not comprehend that which was taught, they need to have additional learning opportunities which clarify and make meaningful subject, matter learned. The same may be said about skills not mastered; the student needs to have additional information and demonstrations to attach meaning to a skill. To reveal what has been learned, the student needs to show others how to do the skill. Meaningful learnings need to be emphasised in the curriculum.

Second, learning opportunities experienced by students need to be challenging and yet realistic. To have learning opportunities which are too difficult make for student failure. The opposite case has its detrimental effects also. That would then stress learning opportunities being too easy whereby student boredom sets in. This is a critical part of teaching in that learning opportunities not being too complex or too easy. The classroom teacher then must do the best professional job possible in having tasks for which are just right in complexity so that successful learning is possible. Success is a motivator for students in being ready for the next challenge in learning. A successful teacher is able to do this (Malini, 2002).

Third, students should have some opportunities to choose what they wish to learn within a unit of study. In a unit taught on the Middle East, a set of students may wish to develop a products map of that area of the world. The map needs to be planned carefully. Each committee member with teacher guidance is involved in planning the map. After careful planning, the committee may decide on which member does what on the products map. An actual product, such as rice on a nearby small table, may be linked with yarn to the place on the map where it is grown. The map, when completed, needs to be neat, clear, meaningful, and tidy. Each student may tell classmates what was learned about the product in the country it was produced. Students from other classrooms may be invited to view the exhibit. When students are involved in selecting learning opportunities, they feel energised because they had a voice in curriculum development. Then too, if students choose tasks to pursue, they tend to select those which are achievable.

Fourth, the teacher as well as students need to have high, but reasonable, expectations for learners. High expectations mean that the teacher does not accept sloppy and erroneous work from students. The quality of student work should harmonise with the optimal capabilities of the learner. It may be necessary to scaffold the work of the student so he/she may achieve as optimally as possible. Each student is important and needs guidance and assistance to learn as abilities permit. The assistance may come in the form of encouragement. Effort might then be put forth by the student to do well in ongoing lessons and units of study (Ediger, 2003, 5-9).

Fifth, the teacher needs to provide a positive atmosphere for learning. Too frequently, students feel negatively about the school curriculum. They feel they can't do well, therefore they minimise what can be accomplished. The classroom environment needs to emphasise that students can succeed if they try. The learning environment and climate must be positive and optimistic; otherwise low levels of achievement will be in evidence. "You can, if you try", is a good motto to follow when challenging objectives are in the offing.

Sixth, students need to be recognised for doing well in the classroom. The recognition assists in meeting esteem needs of students. A smile or saying, "You did well", can do much to spur students on to greater efforts. The words used to reward should be varied and said in a sincere manner. Students do have needs to receive recognition for something well done (Mohanty, 2003).

Seventh, resources should be organised to facilitate student learning. Thus, the following resources should be available for teaching students in order to attain the objectives of instruction:

- basal textbooks, library books, encyclopaedias, and other verbal materials;
- audiovisual aids, such as films, filmstrips, slides, video tapes, CDs, DVDs, and cassettes;
- written work including the writing of reports, summaries, conclusions, outlines, plays, poems, stories, among others;
- oral communication activities such as reading aloud, oral reports, debates, explanations and directions given,

public speaking experiences, dramatic activities, peer teaching, and dimensions;

- listening to records, tapes, the spoken voice, and conversion.

The resources listed above become learning opportunities for students to achieve objectives of instruction. The teacher needs to sequence these activities appropriately and provide for each learner's optimal achievement (Mayer and Sims, 1994).

Eighth, cooperative and individual endeavours need to be implemented. There are students who prefer to work together in ongoing lessons and units of instruction. They might be able to achieve at a higher level using collaborative endeavours. This is a preferred method of learning for these students. Toward the other end of the continuum, there are students who prefer to work by the self. Thus the teacher must plan to satisfy both styles of learning be it cooperative work or by the self (Searson, and Dunn, 2001).

Ninth, the teacher needs to monitor student achievement continuously or as often as possible. Teacher observation can be a good approach to use in monitoring learner achievement. Quality criteria used to evaluate which harmonise with teacher observation may do a good job of monitoring progress of students.

Tenth, students should receive regular feedback from the teacher on how well they are doing individually and collectively. With feedback, students may learn subject matter and skills sequentially. Diagnosis and remediation are necessary in the evaluation process.

Teacher Qualities in Student Learning

Teachers bring the total self to ongoing classroom instruction. They bring more to the instructional arena than academic knowledge. Thus, teachers need to be caring individuals. They care for each student so that the latter learns, grows, and achieves. Thus, teachers encourage students to achieve in all curriculum areas. Teachers are willing to assist students in the curriculum. Students can rely upon the teacher to offer needed assistance.

The teacher plans each lesson thoroughly to incorporate questions which stress higher levels of cognition. Problem solving, critical and creative thinking, inferential thinking, and probing are essential student skills to develop. Students with teacher guidance also need to use logic when feasible in the curriculum. Planning daily lessons and units of study is a complex matter and incorporates not only subject matter to master but also diverse thinking skills.

The teacher needs to use commercially developed materials satisfactorily as well as those which are made to assist students in cases where learning problems exist. Home made materials can be used readily to meet student needs. There are a plethora of games, for example, which teachers can make inexpensively which assist students to overcome problems in learning.

Homework assignments given to students need to meet appropriate criteria such as being:

- meaningful and understandable;
- purposeful and interesting;
- sequential and worthwhile;
- moderate in amount, not of excessive length nor too brief.

Students should be actively involved in classroom discussions. They need to be well prepared for interaction with others. Active student involvement is preferable to passive recipients of knowledge. Thus students need to be fully engaged in learning. The use of inquiry learning aids in furthering the goals of quality discussions and questions. Inquiry learning stresses that:

- students are questioned in-depth with probing questions and problems;
- students are assisted to develop quality generalisations;
- students listen to interesting lectures and arrive with their own concepts and generalisations through an inductive procedure;
- students have much freedom in coming up with valid and reliable information;

- students may work in small groups so that more frequent participation by each member is possible;
- the student is responsible for active involvement in inquiry teaching and the encouragement of others to do likewise;
- respect for the thinking of others is invited and acknowledged.

Evaluation of Student Achievement

Student achievement needs to be evaluated thoroughly so that diagnosis and remediation is possible and continuous progress being in evidence. A variety of procedures need to be used. State mandated testing is required of all students. The teacher needs to use the objectives provided by the state in teaching students. These objectives and their use should assist students to do better on state mandated tests. Tests are valid if what is tested upon has been covered in diverse units of study. All tests taken by students should be valid (Ediger, 2001, 61-66).

Teacher written tests may be used to measure intermediate gains of students since state mandated tests are given once a year in grades three through eight and grade ten. On type of teacher written test is the multiple choice kind. Multiple choice tests need to contain four distractors or choices for students to make in responding to a test item. Each response of the four needs to be plausible so that clues are not given as to which is correct. If a stem exists for the multiple choice test item, the stem and each of the four distractors should be grammatically correct. The four distractors should be similar in length. Thus, no clues should be given as to which is the correct response.

True/false test items may provide relevant information pertaining to student responses. Each test item needs to be clearly written. Vague wording should be avoided. Thus, the answer should clearly be either true or false. It is true Thai students may guess correctly fifty per cent of the time when responding to true/false tests. The guessing factor may be minimised if students are required to write what is true in a test item which is false. The incorrect part may then be crossed out and the correction written directly above a true/false test item.

Matching tests may be used to obtain knowledge of relevant facts obtained by students. One of the two matching columns should contain more items than the other so that the process of elimination may be minimised when students respond to a matching test.

Completion test items may also provide the teacher with feedback in terms of what students have learned. Enough information needs to be provided in the completion test item so that students know what is wanted in the response. The following example indicates that basic information is lacking: The ----, ----, and ---- are in the Western hemisphere.

Certainly, the above completion test item needs clarification so that one knows what is wanted.

Essay test items can be excellent to use to evaluate student responses in not only knowledge that has been acquired by students but also spelling, punctuation, and the other mechanics of writing, Essay test items need to:

1. be written with clarity so that students know what is wanted in terms of responses;
2. adequately delimited so that a whole book cannot be written as an answer nor should they be so delimited that a single word or fact provides the answer;
3. encourage higher levels of cognition such as analytic thinking, synthesising, problem solving, and assessment of ideas presented;
4. emphasise high validity in test what is tested upon has been covered in class in a unit of study or lesson;
5. stress reliability in that the text measures consistently;
6. ideas presented are first in importance followed by proper grammar, usage, and the mechanical aspects of written work;
7. stimulate learner skills and attitudes.

In addition to testing, students with teacher guidance may also develop portfolios individually to show actual class work done on a daily/weekly basis. The portfolio needs to contain the following student work in a representative sampling manner:

1. written work such as summaries, conclusions, reports, poems, plays, outlines and impressions;
2. cassette recordings of speaking activities such as oral reports, read alouds, dramatic experiences, committee deliberations, and oral conferences with the teacher;
3. art products as they relate to ongoing units of study including murals, pencil sketches, water colouring, and drawings;
4. photos of dioramas, construction work, creative and formal dramatisations, making of bulletin board displays, and the development of puppets.
5. self evaluation reports based on quality criteria (See also National Science Teachers Association, 2001).

The above named items may be viewed by responsible persons such as parents, and the school principal.

REFERENCES

Ediger, Marlow (2003), *"Challenge in Children's Literature"*, Journal of Research in Education, 2 (2), 9-13.

Ediger, Marlow (2002), *"Assessing Student Progress in Science"*, School Science, 39 (1), 61-66.

Malini, J. Sujatha (2002), *Competencies Required for Primary School Teachers tc Handle Learning Difficulties in Children*. Karaiku, India: Alagappa University.

Mayer, R.E. and V.K. Sims (1994), *"For Whom is a Picture Worth a Thousand Words? Extensions of a Dual Coding Multi Media Theory of Learning"*, Journal of Educational Psychology, 86, 389-401.

Mohanty, Jagannath, *"Education in Transition"*, Edutracks, 3 (3), 16-21.

National Science Teachers Association (2001), Classroom Assessment and the National Education Standards, Washington, DC: The Association, NSTA.

Searson, Robert, and Rita Dunn (2001), *"The Learning Styles Teaching Model"*, Science and Children, 38 (5), 22-36.

2

Who Should Determine the Curriculum?

There are a plethora of ideas on who should make curricular decisions. Each has a rationale for its determination. Diversity of philosophies need to be analysed. After analysing each school of thought, decisions may be made on which plan or combination thereof should be adopted in the school setting.

Student Centred Views

Student centred views generally put the learner at the centre of instructional decision making. The student then should be heavily involved in determining what to learn with teacher guidance. Student/teacher planning of the objectives, learning opportunities, and assessment procedures might then be in the offing. This takes time to plan a quality curriculum, but a student centred curriculum also stresses the importance of cooperative decision making. Making choices, from among alternatives, is highly significant in school and in society. There are always choices to be made in almost every aspect of life. Student/teacher planning may take several forms among the following:

1. students choosing, from among alternative tasks, at different learning stations. At each station, in an ongoing unit of study, students may choose which task to work on and which to omit, and still stay optimally busy;

2. students may select sequential library books to read in an individualised reading programme. There must be ample genres as well as reading levels of books when students make choices. A conference with the teacher may be conducted following the library book reading. The conference is an informal evaluation of student needs and progress. The Drop Everything and Read (DEAR) plan of student choices of reading materials, during a special segment of the school day, does not have an evaluation session, but otherwise is closely related to the individualised reading programme;
3. student chooses a project to complete for an ongoing unit of study. The project then involves student's individually or committee wise in developing a purpose for the project. Planning needs to be thorough to achieve the goal in doing the project. Carrying out the plan and then evaluating the quality of the project using desired criteria are musts.

Teacher Centred Plans of Instruction

In moving away from a student centred curriculum, the teacher, in a more hierarchical approach, may determine the curriculum. Here, the teacher selects the objectives, learning activities, and appraisal techniques in teaching situations. This may be indicated with the following scenarios:

1. the teacher selecting basal textbooks for the class;
2. the teacher assigning lessons to students;
3. the teacher selecting questions for discussion to check student comprehension and progress on a daily basis;
4. the teacher asking questions, during summative evaluation sessions. These tend to require right responses from students;
5. the teacher testing student achievement frequently, using different kinds of teacher written test items.

District Wide Determination of the Curriculum

School districts may determine the curriculum in selected ways. District wide tests to ascertain student achievement may well emphasise that decision making has gone beyond that of the students and the classroom teacher. The school district then has selected objectives for the teacher to attain in teaching students. District wide curricular decisions centralise decision making to the central office. The thinking here is that:

1. better curricular decisions can be made at the apex of the school district than at lower levels in the hierarchy;
2. the school district is set up to deal with the curriculum directly such as the offices of assistant superintendent in charge of the curriculum, the system wide curriculum director, and other capable personnel;
3. the central office has the advisors and secretarial help necessary to further efforts in the environment of the curriculum. Leadership then may come from the central office in working toward the best curriculum possible for students.

The State Level in Affecting Instructional Endeavours

The state level has had much influence over educational decision making. State mandated objectives, as the name indicates, are developed by each state in the union. These objectives have been written to indicate the basics which students are to learn. Ideally, they have bee pilot tested to secure validity and reliability. Kinks need to be taken out of any assessment device written and used. Worthwhile knowledge and skills need to be measured, not trivia. There are issues which need to be addressed pertaining to state mandated objectives:

1. Which types of test items should be used to assess student achievement? Multiple choice test items are generally used since, among other reasons, they are easy to score with computerised services.
2. What should be the scope of items on the test? Reading and mathematics are two required areas. Selected states have gone beyond this to incorporate since and social studies.
3. How should test items be sequenced?

The Federal Level

The federal level and the Secretary of Education and heavily involved in decision making within the curriculum. The federal level has determined that the former Elementary and Secondary Education Act (ESEA) should incorporate the features of the No Child Left Behind Act (NCLB) to include the following in order to receive federal moneys:

1. required testing of students in grades three through eight for promotion purposes. Required testing of students in grade ten is required to indicate proficiency to receive a high school diploma;
2. a school meeting adequate yearly progress (AYP) as determined by each state. If a school/school district has not met AYP for two years in a row, they are categorised as "needing improvement". With five years of Needing improvement, the state may step in to redo that school/ school system.

Methods of Teaching

There are selected methods of teaching which need to be implemented in order that students achieve desired objectives. The teacher needs to engage learners in teaching and learning situations. Students need this engagement if they are to attend carefully to the ongoing lesson or unit of study. Wasted teacher and student time will lower the efficiency rate of learning. Interesting procedures of instruction, as well as materials of instruction, will assist in optimising learning. Instructional procedures used is an art whereby creativity is involved to encourage student learning.

Purpose must be emphasised in student learning. With purpose involved, the student will perceive reasons for achieving. Perceiving purpose will guide the learner to achieve that which is worthwhile. If the objectives to be achieved are considered to be menial in value, the student may fail to put forth effort in achieving. Purpose within students for learning may be developed through the teacher stating reasons for the value of the subject matter to be learned. This is a deductive approach. The teacher may also use induction to assist student achievement. A questioning procedure is then used to help students accept purpose for achieving.

Meaning theory must be used in the instructional arena. If meaning is omitted, the student will not make sense out of the knowledge and skills to be encountered. With meaning, students understand that which is taught. Too frequently, students, if coerced to learn, might memorise content for a test if meaningless materials are being emphasised.

Individual differences need adequate provision in the classroom. One size does not fit all in teaching and learning situations. Each student is unique and desires to have his/her needs met. Using a variety of teaching materials in order that individual needs are met is important. The teacher may need to diagnose student achievement of objectives in order that weaknesses may be uncovered and remedied.

Learners possess multiple intelligences in the curriculum. These intelligences include:

1. verbal intelligence. Students possessing verbal intelligence prefer reading and writing activities in the curriculum, above others;
2. logical reasoning which is common to mathematics, but is valuable in any curriculum area. The ability to reason logically provides a salient effort to think things through;
3. objective thought, as used in science, is extremely valuable in coming up with truth:
4. musical/rhythmical as in setting words to music, and/or dance activities;
5. intrapersonal in which the student achieves more optimally an individual basis;
6. interpersonal emphasising committee or group work in which the student achieves well:
7. bodily/kinesthetic whereby the student does best in hands on approaches in learning (See Gardner).

The preferred intelligence of the student needs to be sought and emphasised in teaching and learning situations. It is important to use the talents of a learner. Student performance should increase in the curriculum when possessed intelligences are being identified and implemented.

Personal Needs of the Student

Each student has personal needs which should be met, if at all possible. Proper fitting, appropriate clothes need to be worn by students. Shabby, unclean clothes will not do. To feel well about the self, the student must have clothing which harmonises with the present temperature readings of the season. The clothing should be neat and free from obnoxious odors.

The school environment must be free from human made annoyances. Bullying is not good for the bully, nor for the one being bullied. Generally, one or more bullies will gang up on a student who is vulnerable to something. That student may be ridiculed due to speech habits and patterns. He/she may also be bullied due to the kind of clothing worn, religious beliefs, physical appearance, and/or behaviour. It is very uncomfortable to be bullied and hinders social interaction with others as well as in academic achievement. Teachers and principals must work with students and have strict guidelines to prevent bullying.

Ample, nutritious food should be available for each student. Hungry students can not achieve well in school. Three meals a day, seven days a week must be served to each student or the learner may achieve at a very low level.

A safe, school environment is needed for all learners as well as for adults involved in the educational process in school. Murders of individuals in school has been written about in detail such as in Columbine High School in Littleton, Colorado in the 1990s. These are extreme cases, and do breed fear in schools far away from Littleton. Selected school buildings are old and susceptible to provoking injuries to students, such as slate shingles from a roof sliding down en mass from the roof or plaster falling from the classroom or hallway ceiling. Mold and mildew circulating through the furnace has made for illnesses and even hospitalisation of students. Bad odors and things which do not work need repairs, such as toilets which do not flush properly. Certainly, students required to attend school should have a safe place to be in teaching and learning situations. States and school districts need to budget adequate moneys to pay for upkeep and repairs as well as build new buildings as needed.

Psychological needs of students must be met. Each student desires to be accepted and belong to a group. Shunning and ridiculing need to be eliminated from a teacher's repertoire. Students need to be taught to respect each other and learn to live harmoniously, students should learn to offer assistance to each other as curricular needs demand. A democratic atmosphere needs to be in the offing.

Esteem needs of each learner must be met. Students individually are important and should be recognised for achievements made. Every student then has opportunities to be recognised for contributions made. Belittling and talking down to a student should be omitted from the curriculum.

The student needs to be able to optimise achievement with teacher guidance. No one should be left behind from achieving optimally!

REFERENCES

Cuddeback, Meghan, and Maria A. Ceprano (2002). *"The Use of Accelerated Reader with Emergent Readers"*, Reading Improvement, 39 (2), 89-95.

Ediger, Marlow, and D. Bhaskara Rao (2003), *Improving School Administration*. New Delhi, India: Discovery Publishing House, 141 and 142.

Ediger, Marlow and D. Bhaskara (2003), *Language Arts Curriculum*. New Delhi, India: Discovery Publishing House, Chapter Thirteen.

Ediger, Marlow (1988), *The Elementary Curriculum, 2nd Edition*, Kirksville, Missouri: Simpson Publishing Company, Chapter Seven.

Epstein, Joyce (1995), "(1995), *"School/Family/Community Partnerships,"* Phi Delta Kappan, 76: 704.

Gardner, Howard (1993), *Multiple Intelligences: Theory into Practice*. New York; Basic Books.

Friedrich, L.E. (1983), *"The School Budgeting Cycle,"* Winneconne, Wisconsin.

Paris, Scott (2002), *"Centre for Improvement of Early Reading Achievement,"* Reading Teacher, 55 (2), 170.

Richard, Alan (September 4, 2002), *Florida Sees Surge in Use of Vouchers"*, Education Week, 1, 34.

Risko, Virginia J., et. al. (2002), *"Preparing Teachers for Reflective Practice: Interactions, Contradictions, and Possibilities"*, Language Arts. 82 (2), 134-144.

Tyler, Ralph (1949), *Basic Principles of Curriculum Construction*. Chicago: University of Chicago Press.

Objectives, Learning Activities And Assessment
(Which of the Three is Most Important?)

Which is most important in teaching—objectives, learning activities, or assessment procedures? Perhaps, the reader will say they all are important, and they definitely are. There is an interrelationship between the objectives and learning activities. The learning activities are there for students to achieve the stated objectives. The assessment procedures have as their role to evaluate if the objectives have been achieved. But, the writer feels that major attention in educational manuscripts and speeches at conventions is focused on assessment. Thus, state mandated assessment and The National Assessment of Educational Progress focuses upon test scores and results. With state mandated testing, the emphasis is upon.

1. testing students in grades three through eight and grade ten;
2. the number of schools which will be in the "needs improvement" category;
3. the number of students who fail the graded standards;
4. the number of students from "needs improvement" schools who will be able to transfer to satisfactory schools which have met state standards;

5. the elimination of social promotion.

Should more attention be paid to the objectives of state mandated tests and/or learning activities?

State Mandated Objectives

Much attention should be given to the quality of state mandated objectives. Each objective needs careful consideration in having much worth. This is a highly salient task. Many terms have been given to salient objectives such as being relevant, important, significant, and being meaningful. When an entire state chooses its final objectives, careful consideration needs to be given to the overall importance of its goals for all schools within its borders. The areas covered in a state mandated test will, no doubt, receive the most instructional time. Many educational articles have been written lamenting the excessive instructional time spent on what will be tested and that being reading and mathematics. Is this adequate when considering the scope of the curriculum?

Objectives for mandation should cover the scope of what is taught in the public schools within a state. This should then cover content in basal texts used in teaching, different syllabi for a grade level being taught in diverse schools, and recommended psychologies of instruction in reading and in mathematics. Scrutiny of objectives needs to be continuous and ongoing. Emphasis must be placed upon relevancy of subject matter in objectives for student attainment.

The final set of objectives for reading and for mathematics should be readily accessible to teachers and administrators. The objectives need to be:

1. clearly stated so that teachers understand what students are to learn;
2. stated as precisely as possible so that little interpretation is involved as to their meaning. Vague objectives need to be rewritten;
3. broad in scope to cover vital goals in reading and mathematics;

4. challenging but achievable. This is a difficult situation when all students in a grade level are to achieve these objectives. This means that the gifted and talented as well as special education students should achieve the same objectives as measured by the same test.

Learning Activities to Achieve Objectives

Learning activities for students has received much less attention in the educational literature as compared to the objectives, and *much* less as compared to the testing facet of the curriculum. And yet, it is the learning activities which propel achievement. Subject matter and skills taught are actually an integral part of the curriculum, but need to be treated separately to indicate their importance. Learning activities chosen by the teacher should provide for individual differences among students in the classroom. When twenty to twenty five students per classroom, the teacher indeed has a difficult task in selecting and implementing learning activities. Ability and interest differences among students truly do present problems in making adequate provision for individual differences. There is a plethora of learning activities available such as concrete, semi-concentrate, and abstract experiences. These activities should:

1. engage students fully in learning;
2. assist students to perceive purpose or reasons for learning;
3. help students to become motivated individuals. Preferably, intrinsic motivation should be emphasised;
4. develop interest for learning;
5. be used to scaffold learnings for students when needed;
6. guide students to perceive meaning and understanding;
7. permit students to choose, periodically, if individual or committee endeavours are desired as methods of learning;
8. use learning stations to enrich student experiences;

9. have students engage in self selected activities as well as those stressing teacher direction;
10. emphasise student self assessment as well as teacher directed assessments of learner progress.

Learning activities are actually the heart of the curriculum since the objectives provide direction as to what students are to learn and the assessment portion stresses the determination of what each student has learned. It is the learning activities which energises accomplishment. Students are actually doing things in order to achieve. Thus, students are involved in:

1. listening, speaking, reading and writing to achieve objectives;
2. interacting with concrete, semi-concrete, and abstract learning opportunities;
3. inferring, predicting, generalising, summarising, and concluding;
4. thinking critically and creatively, as well as engaging in problem solving;
5. meeting in large groups, small groups, and in doing individual tasks;
6. learning by doing as well as learning from print materials;
7. using one or multiple intelligences;
8. choosing sequential tasks to complete at different learning stations as well as working on assigned activities;
9. stressing inductive as well as deductive learning;
10. assisting others to achieve and developing a caring, humane feeling toward others.

There are multiple learning activities for students. Computer use has further increased the number of activities available for students such as using the internet, web site, word processor, CDs, and DVDs. Computer work may also involve doing spread sheets, painting, drawing, presentations, and data base use.

Assessment Procedures

State mandated testing has placed major emphasis upon evaluation rather than the objectives, and learning activities in the curriculum. Test results of students then predominate in importance. Increased concern then should be shown toward the quality of tests. All state mandated tests need to be pilot tested to take out kinks such as weak, vague test items. Tests also need to asses validly. Thus, they need to cover what has been taught. This goes back to the statements of objectives in that they are clear and in the hands of all teachers to use as guidelines for teaching. The tests when administered should cover what has been taught providing that each teacher has truly followed the state's clearly stated intents.

Each test item must be clearly written. If multiple choice test items are used, then one of the four distractors is clearly the correct choice. The other three, however, are plausible. Recommended standards for writing multiple choice test items must be used. Reliability data on each state mandated test should provide information and indicate that it does measure consistently.

Computer glitches have been reported somewhat frequently. It is a shock to the student and parents when the offspring is reported to have failed the state mandated test for a grade level, but reassessment indicated the learner has passed very favourably! This makes for much anxiety and tension which need not be there. Computer scoring must be accurate or the lay public will lose interest in the accuracy of testing.

Grade level testing is *summative* in nature. Changes then cannot be made in the course of instruction, because the student either passes or does not pass onto the next grade level. Thus, *formative* assessment by the teacher must also be in evidence.

The teacher may also write valid and reliable test items to measure student growth, formatively, to notice if instruction being provided is leading students to achieve state mandated objectives. The following guidelines are salient for teachers to follow in writing their own tests to notice if students are achieving favourably:

1. use the type of test item format as is used on the state mandated test;
2. provide directions for test taking as are provided for state mandated testing;
3. use test results diagnostically to notice what is lacking in learner achievement;
4. based on diagnosis, help students to learn what is needed to be successful;
5. use teacher observation, in addition to the formative test, to provide for individual differences among students.

Guidelines for Teaching

Each school/school system needs to develop guidelines for three generalised parts of the curriculum—the objectives, learning activities, and assessment procedures. They are interrelated and integral parts of the curriculum. Each is very important. Teachers need to have aims to guide instruction. These aims are transferrable to objectives for student achievement. The objectives, by themselves, have little value unless there are learning activities to operationalise instruction. Little is known about the quality of instruction unless there are appropriate assessment procedures used to ascertain what students have learned. There are additional ingredients which need to be stressed in curriculum development.

It is important to sequence the learning activities appropriately. There may be a student centred sequence such as in Drop Everything and Read (DEAR) whereby the student selects literature to read and orders his/her very own achievement. Or, it may be a teacher centred sequence in which the teacher chooses the objectives, learning activities, and evaluation techniques. With the latter procedure, students might raise salient questions and thereby help to sequence ideas intrinsically.

There might be flexible grouping in a classroom such as in large group, small group, and individualised instruction. Or, in the case of learning centres, the student may select ordered tasks to pursue from the different centres. Grouping procedures used may also be more formal in which students are seated in rows and columns, and yet the instructional quality may be quite stimulating, inviting learner interaction. Within the latter plan of grouping for instruction, the teacher may idividualise by having committees at work in a problem solving experience, related to the ongoing learning activity.

Methods of Instruction

The methods of instruction used varies from teacher to teacher and yet quality instruction might well be a by product. Generally, each approach comes in degree. The following may stress good teaching, even though they are emphasised on a continuum:

1. inductive versus more of deductive learnings for students;
2. student/teacher planning versus more of teacher determination of the curriculum;
3. student selection of seating arrangements as compared to more of the teacher deciding how students are to be seated. The heterogeneous versus homogeneous controversy continues as a debate on grouping students for instruction purposes;
4. textbook procedures of instruction as compared to increased emphasis upon multi media methods;
5. project methods of instruction as compared to more stress being placed upon the basics.

REFERENCES

Aiken, Adel G., and Lisa Bayer (2002), *"They Love Words"*, The Reading Teacher, 56 (1), 68-75.

Astleitner, Herman (2002), *"Teaching Critical Thinking Online"*, Journal of Instructional Psychology, 29 (2), 53-76.

Chappuis, Stephen, and Richard J. Stiggins (2002), *"Classroom Assessment for Learning"*, Educational Leadership, 60 (1), 40-41.

Ediger, Marlow, and D. Bhaskara Rao (2000), *Teaching Reading Successfully*. New Delhi, India: Discovery Publishing House, Chapter Eight.

Ediger, Marlow (2002), *"Developing a Reading Community"*, Edutracks, 1 (4), 16-19.

Ediger, Marlow (2002), *"Social Studies and the Guidance Counsellor"*, Experiments in Education, 30 (9), 176-181.

Ediger, Marlow (2002), *"Improving Spelling"*, Reading Improvement, 39 (2), 69-70.

Gardner, Howard (1983), *Frames of Mind*: The Theory of Multiple Intelligences. New York: Basic Books.

Maslow, A.H. (1954), *Motivational and Personality*. New York: Harper and Row.

Meyer, Richard J. (2002), *"Captives of the Script: Killing us Softly with Phonics"*, The Reading Teacher, 79 (6), 452-461.

Searson, Robert, and Rita Dunn (2001), *"The Learning Styles Teaching Model"*, Science and Children, 38 (5), 22-36.

Special Education Students And Mandated Objectives

There certainly is a major problem in having special students meet state mandated objectives. Special education students here will refer to the handicapped, English language Learners (ELL), English as a Second Language (ESL), and students from minority groups. These students are to meet state mandated objectives as are the regular students in the classroom. Special education students have not had the opportunities that other learners have experienced. And yet, they are to achieve as well as others. When viewing state mandated test results, the special education students are viewed in separate categories to notice if they, too, are meeting mandated standards.

Should They be Assessed in the Same Manner?

Special education students have lacked opportunities which other learners have had, such as in the following ways:

1. handicapped students include the visually and hearing impaired as well as the mentally retarded;
2. ELL students who are learning the English language presently but are being tested in the English language;
3. ESL students who speak another language much more fluently as compared to English;

4. minority students due to experiencing poverty have not had the chances to achieve due to limited financial resources.

It hardly seems fair to assess special education students with the same standards as those who are more favoured with having grown up speaking the English language as well as having more beneficial ability and economic resources. But, they do need to be assessed in some manner to determine educational achievement. The best objectives, learning opportunities to achieve the objectives, and assessment procedures need to be available to special education students.

The playing field is not level, by any means, when testing normal students with those in special education categories. Special education students may be helped with high quality developmentally appropriate learning opportunities whereby concrete, semiconcrete, and abstract learnings are provided on their present level of achievement. Sequentially, students need to achieve as optimally as possible. Assessment procedures include not only state mandated testing but also teacher developed informal evaluations. State mandated testing is terminal whereas teacher developed tests are formative, assisting students along the way to do better on state mandated tests.

Absolute Versus Value Added Assessments

Special education students have been required to achieve absolute standards. The state mandated tests, being terminal, are used to ascertain if students should be promoted in grades three through eight and grade ten. With summative evaluation, a student either does or does not pass the mandated test. There are no exceptions made. All students in a grade take the same test and are provided with the same directions for test taking. No allowances are made for special education students in test taking. When giving a teacher written test, allowances may be made in terms of time limits, pronouncing unknown words, and even ways of responding to a test item. When responding to a teacher written test item, the test taker would not need to fill in a bubble, punch a computerised card, or take the test online. With teacher written tests, the student may draw a picture, a diagram, or make a chart to indicate what has been learned. What does a test measure if:

1. a student cannot read in the English language?
2. a student lacks needed abilities in reading?
3. a student has not had opportunities to learn which suburban learners have had?

In measuring adequate yearly progress (ayp), those schools having the most ELL, ESL, minorities, and handicapped students will do worse than schools from very favourable home and school environments. Also, those schools having fewer than thirty students in any one category, will not be considered when determining the ayp.

Having all special education students achieve value added standards would make more sense. With value added, each special education student is measured against his/her previous test performance, not against absolute standards. Measuring a student's progress from previous to present times would indicate the amount of achievement made, be it individually to be promoted from one grade level to the next or to be incorporated into the ayp. For any one student, what has been achieved from one measurement to the next is what is salient. Absolute standards may be too easy for some and too difficult for others. Value added standards then measure:

1. to notice achievement of a student as a result of instruction;
2. to notice the amount of student achievement in yearly testing;
3. to notice how value added instruction affects ayp;
4. to better diagnose and remedy individual student progress as a result of value added testing;
5. to notice how valued added testing compares with absolute standards of measurement.

Value added testing makes comparison of the individuals present achievement as compared to an earlier measure. Absolute standards make comparisons among individuals as to how well each is doing. Absolute standards makes comparisons of how well a student is achieving the predetermined state mandated objectives, as revealed through testing. Absolute standards in determining ayp compares this year's students with those of last year. Cohort groups are then used in making these comparisons since last year's and this year's comparison groups are not the same students.

Additional Accepted Approaches in Assessments

No school or school system should conceive of state mandated testing as being the only way of assessment. Teachers may also write tests which are valid and reliable. When using face validity, the teacher may write a test item which relates directly to what just has been taught. By doing this, the teacher does not forget what has been taught when writing a test items. Notes may be made or a check placed on the lesson plan on what has been taught. After school or during break time, the teacher may write the test item and also preserve test security. If test items are written very clearly by following recommendations of measurement specialist, reliability might well be more in evidence than would otherwise be the case. The teacher cannot give the same test to the same students to ascertain test/retest reliability, but he/she may use split half reliability. Split half reliability requires giving the test once only. Then split half reliability may then be determined.

Too frequently, only multiple choice test items are used on state mandated tests. With teacher written tests, there is a better chance of using essay tests measuring higher levels of cognition. Essay tests, well written and edited, might well measure skills in problem solving, as well as critical and creative thinking. To assess essay test results more objectively, the teacher may develop and use a rubric. The rubric pinpoints what the teacher is looking for in essay test results. Thus, it objectifies what is being evaluated. All tests have elements of subjectivity involved. State mandated tests then have standard errors of measurement which indicate margin of error. It indicates the range within which any student score may fall. A student, for example, received a score of sixty on a test. The standard error of measurement, statistically arrived at, may reveal three score points. The student's true score may then be in the range of 60 + 3 and 60 - 3. Errors in test construction make for a statistically computed standard error of measurement.

State mandated testing involves summative evaluation. The test score for the student represents the end for the instructional year. Teacher written tests generally emphasise formative evaluation, unless it is given at the end of an instructional sequence or unit of study. With formative evaluation, the teacher receives feedback from the student as to what has/has not been learned. What has not been learned provides information to the teacher as to what still needs to be taught and retaught. In addition to essay tests and multiple choice test items, the teacher needs to use observation of daily student performance. Here, the teacher notices problems which students have in learning and achievement. Diagnosis and remediation might then be in the offing.

Recommendations on State Mandated Testing

There are a plethora of recommendations which might be made in improving evaluation of student progress.

First, there needs to be accommodations for special education students. These accommodations may pertain to the difficulty of the test, the length of the test, and assistance given during test taking.

Second, additional procedures of assessment need to be in the offing other than a single test score to determine promotion from one grade level to the next and for receiving a high school diploma. Portfolios, projects completed, and teacher recommendations should also be a part of the assessment procedures.

Third, high validity and reliability for state written tests need to be in the offing, otherwise the test may have little value in ascertaining learner achievement. Thus, thorough pilot testing is recommendable, resulting in the kinks being taken out of the test.

Fourth, accuracy in computer scoring needs to be assessed so that student irregularities of results do not occur. There have been too many nightmares about computer scoring errors.

Fifth, the length of a state mandated test needs to be such as to avoid student fatigue in test taking. Sixth, state mandated tests need to be diagnostic in nature so that teachers may receive feedback on how to assist students in learning.

Sixth, students should receive necessary accommodations which harmonise with disabilities involved.

Seventh, directions given for test taking should be very clear. Vague directions for test taking do not help in ascertaining how much students have learned.

Eight, experimentation should be done to find multiple ways for students to respond to test items. Multiple intelligences theory indicates that each student has a preference in indicating what has been learned. Not all responses should involve filling in a bubble to show what has been learned. Art work, making a diagram, or pointing to an answer should also be an alternative.

Ninth, styles of learning might well provide additional information to determine under which conditions students learn best. There are students who work best individually whereas others prefer are students who work best individually whereas others prefer cooperative endeavours. Selected evaluations may include student preference in learning be it intrapersonal versus interpersonal.

Tenth, state mandated, as well as other forms of evaluation, should include items and observations including the following:

(a) caring for others;

(b) working harmoniously with others;

(c) thinking critically and creatively;

(d) solving identified problems;

(e) assisting peers when needed;

(f) modelling good study habits;

(g) preservering through difficulties.

(h) cultivating good listening habits;

(i) speaking clearly so all can hear;

(j) doing neat school work and stressing neatness in all significant endeavours;

(k) being able to do school work well which is developmentally appropriate.

Conclusion

Special education students need a developmentally suited curriculum whereby sequential progress might well be in evidence. Suitable objectives, learning activities which make for success in learning, and assessment procedures which are valid and reliable make for a successful special education curriculum.

REFERENCES

Cuddeback, Meghan, and Maria, A. Ceprano (2002), *"The Use of Accelerated Reader with Emergent Readers"*, Reading Improvement, 39 (2), 89-95.

Ediger, Marlow, and D. Bhaskara Rao (2003), *Improving School Administration*. New Delhi, India: Discovery Publishing House, 141 and 142.

Ediger, Marlow and D. Bhaskara Rao (2003), *Language Arts Curriculum*. New Delhi, India: Discovery Publishing House, Chapter Thirteen.

Ediger, Marlow (1988), *The Elementary Curriculum*, 2nd Edition. Kirksville, Missouri: Simpson Publishing Company, Chapter Seven.

Epstein, Joyce (1995), *"School/Family/Community Partnerships"*, Phi Delta Kappan, 76: 706.

Friedrich, L.E. (1983), *"The School Budgeting Cycle,"* Winneconne, Wisconsin.

Paris, Scott (2002), "Centre for Improvement of Early Reading Achievement," Reading Teacher, 55 (2), 170.

Richar, Alan (September 4, 2002), Florida Sees Surge in Use of Vouchers", Education Week, 1, 34.

Risko, Virginia J., et. al. (2002), *"Preparing Teachers for Reflective Practice: Intentions, Contradictions, and Possibilities"*, Language Arts, 82 (2), 134-144.

Tyler, Ralph (1949), Basic Principles of Curriculum Construction. Chicago: University of Chicago Press.

5

Problems in Implementing No Child Left Behind

There are a plethora of problems involved in implementing "No Child Left Behind (NCLB)". NCLB was signed into US law in 2002 and, no doubt, took more time to implement as compared to its beginning during the 2004-05 school year. There are many facets of this law which will require modification and change. The National Education Association and the American Federation of Teachers have both been strong critics of NCLB, as are others in society. The membership in these organisations consists of classroom teachers, largely. Which are major criticism of this law?

Testing in Selected Grades

Students are to be tested using state mandated tests in grades three through eight, as well as in grade ten. If a student fails to meet standards for any of these grades levels, he/she will be held back from promotion until mastering the requirement. Social promotion is not to be emphasised. Thus, a student may be left behind in a grade level due to failing a test while his/her peers are promoted to the next grade level. Being completely unsuccessful is never a pleasant thing to experience. A major problem here has been that too many students fail and are held back a grade level. What happens if too many fail to pass a state mandated test? There will be an excessive number of students then in selected classrooms. Special classes, tutoring, more teachers, and summer school, among other approaches, may then need to be increased in number more thoroughly than ever before.

If a student fails the exit test in grade ten, he/she may then not receive a high school diploma. A state may permit retesting of course, on all mandated grade levels of testing. In the meantime, a failing student loses feelings of an adequate self concept.

Testing in Reading and Mathematics Only

With state mandate testing in reading and mathematics, only, the other curriculum areas receive short schrift. News reports indicate that reading and mathematics receive much of the attention during the school day. What is tested upon will be strongly emphasised in teaching and learning situations. Much time has been spent on drilling student for test taking on areas of mandated testing. Science is to be incorporated in 2007 for mandated testing. That still leaves social studies, art, music, and physical education on the periphery of curriculum areas. A balanced school curriculum should make for a well rounded individual in all academic disciplines. Multiple intelligences Theory (Gardner) states that there are a possible eight or nine intelligences which individual difference must provide for. Reading and mathematics are basics in the curriculum. All students need to develop literacy and numeracy skills to function well personally and in society. However, the curriculum, indeed, becomes narrow in scope when two academic areas are paramount in the school day.

One Size Fits All

All students take the same test on the mandated grade levels, somewhat toward the end of the school year. Different classifications of students are also tested on the same subject matter. No allowances are made in difficulty level of subject matter tested on their grade for the following classification of students, among others:

1. the mentally retarded;
2. English as a second language (ESL students);

3. English language learners (ELL students);
4. Minority groups of students.

South Dakota, has experimented with adaptive testing whereby a student's level of achievement is determined and then developmental test items follow in sequence. The thinking, here, has been that it does no good to test a student who responds incorrectly to all or almost all test items. Rather, the attempt is made with adaptive testing whereby the student's present level of achievement is found and then sequential items are tested upon. The printout from the computer may then indicate at what level the student can achieve. There is considerable pupil input using this procedure. Thus, if a ELL student has very little knowledge of the English language, he/she will do very poorly on a graded level state mandated test. And yet, the ELL student is held to the same standard as are all students taking the state mandate test.

A Single Mandated Test As An Absolute

One single test result is to determine if a student is to be promoted in grades three through eight as well as in grade ten, as an exit exam from high school. This puts much pressure upon the student to do well on a *single test* to determine how well he/she is doing in school. It also places, much responsibility upon the teacher to have students pass tests. The following are questions which may be raised about state mandated tests:

1. Are the test items valid an reliable?
2. Are the test items salient in terms of what the student needs personally an in society?
3. Are the test items written in a meaningful manner?
4. Are the test items arranged sequentially from the easiest to those gradually more complex?
5. Are the test items written on the reading level of the involved test taker?

There are additional methods of ascertaining student achievement. The following may be used also as evaluation techniques to determine student progress:

1. teacher written tests to include essay, multiple choice, true/false, matching, completion, and short answer;
2. portfolios to include a random sampling of student products.

Punishment to Motivate Achievement

State mandated testing emphasises punishment as a way of holding schools and teachers accountable for student achievement. The following punishments may then be meted out for undesirable student achievement:

1. A school which does not meet adequate yearly progress (ayp) for two years in a row, as determined by each state, is labelled as "needs improvement". Students then may opt out of the failing school to one deemed successful.
2. A category of students such as the mentally retarded must also meet the ayp as do all categories of pupils so that the "needs improvement" label does not apply.
3. A school may be taken over by the state if it does not produce satisfactory results after five years of labelling.

These punishments are given at a time when school budgets are greatly lacking in finances. Teachers are custodians, among other support personnel, have lost their jobs as a result of insufficient funding. Quality schools require adequate funding to do well in all its expectations. They do not produce, profit, but educate all to become contributing members in society. There are states where a federal judge has declared that the present level of state funding is unconstitutional and does not provide an adequate education for all, especially minority groups.

Means of Scoring State Mandated Tests

Using computer scoring of mass numbers of tests has made for many errors. Students who passed a test have had failing scores. A few years ago, selected students in Minnesota received failing scores. The father of a student challenged her computed test results. The daughter had passed but computer glitches recorded her score as failing. Several states recorded computer glitches in scoring teacher entrance tests to teach within a state. Fortunately, the errors were corrected, but at a tremendous cost to the emotional health of the involved teachers. Recommendations to improve accuracy of computer test scoring are the following:

1. rescore a random sampling of tests;
2. emphasise a sunshine law whereby tests are open to viewing after their use, then too, the answer key is open also so that students and parents may hand score the former's test results, if desired;
3. notice how test results correlate with student grade point average;
4. use additional procedures to assess learner achievement other than state mandated testing.

Feedback From Test Results

Teachers need feedback from student test results to use in planning instruction. A single percentile pertaining to student's test score lacks specific information about what the teacher can dc to assist the student to achieve well in school. There is much which a teacher might use from student test taking feedback. Among other information as feedback, the teacher might use the following from the reading section:

1. deficiencies of student knowledge in phonics;
2. lack of student knowledge in syllabication, context clues, and identification of phonograms (onset and rimes) within a word;
3. failure in using comprehension skills such as critical and creative, thinking, problem solving, inferring, predicting, concluding and summarizing;
4. need to improve in using semantic and syntactic clues in reading;
5. improper reading of punctuation marks in reading.

From the mathematics section of the state mandated test, feedback from the student's test results to the teachers may include the following:

1. lack of knowledge of the basic addition, subtraction, multiplication, and division facts;
2. failure to carry in addition/multiplication as well borrow in subtraction/division (also referred to as renaming);
3. misunderstanding the system of integers and negative numbers;
4. not attaching meaning to the concept of "set" as well as combining disjoint set;
5. inability to use structural ideas in mathematics such as the commutative and associative properties in addition and in multiplication.

The teacher needs to use information from the feedback on state mandated tests to assist each student to achieve well. Errors made by students may become objectives for learner attainment. To achieve these objectives, the teacher needs to provide a variety of learning activities so that objectives may be attained. Frequent evaluation needs to be in the offing to notice success of each student in achieving objectives.

Attitudinal Objectives for Student Achievement

State mandated tests do not measure the attitudinal dimension of student learning. There are numerous attitudes which students need to achieve and these may be evaluated through teacher observation. Self appraisal by the student may also be used to assess if attitudinal objectives are being achieved. The following are worthwhile objectives for student attainment:

1. wanting to learn in reading and mathematics;
2. desiring to achieve optimally;
3. doing extra credit work at the enrichment centre;
4. assisting other students as needed in the classroom;
5. caring for the success of others;
6. working harmoniously with others in cooperative learning;
7. feeling positively toward all curriculum areas;

8. achieving in an optimal manner;
9. assessing the self continuously in ascertaining what has been learned and what is left to learn;
10. keeping a journal to record achievements and impressions of the curriculum.

The teacher must use quality criteria when evaluating student achievement in the attitudinal dimension. Quality student attitudes assist in doing better in reading and in mathematics than would less positive feelings about the curriculum. The teacher's role is to assist students to achieve as well as possible in the school curriculum.

REFERENCES

Ediger, Marlow (1994), *"Philosophy in Teacher Education Programmes"*, The Journal of Teaching Practice, 14 (2), 31-43.

Ediger, Marlow, and D. Bhaskara Rao (2001), *Teaching Social Studies Successfully*. New Delhi, India: Discovery Publishing House, Chapter Sixteen,

Ediger, Marlow, and D. Bhasakra Rao (2000), *Teaching Mathematics Successfully*. New Delhi, India: Discovery Publishing House, Chapter Nine.

Ediger, Marlow (2002), *'Writing Achievement in Technical Education"*, ATEA Journal, 29 (3), 20-21.

Gardner, Howard (1993), *Multiple Intelligences: Theory into Practice*. New York: Basic Books.

Olson, Lynn (February 20, 2002), *"A Proficient Score Depends Upon Geography"*, Education Week, 21 (23), pp. 1, 14, 15.

Searson, Robert, and Rita Dunn (2001), *"The Learning Styles Teaching Model"*, Science and Children, 39 (5), 22-26.

6

Testing And Predictions of Pupil Success

The revised Elementary and Secondary School Act (ESEA) of USA requires pupils to be tested annually in grades three through eight, as well as in grade ten. The purpose of these tests is to measure annual progress of learner progress. Then too, teacher accountability is in evidence. Pupils are to make annual progress on these tests to indicate how well teachers are teaching. The ultimate in accountability is the exit test. Thus, a pupil needs to pass the exit test to receive a high school diploma. Thus, a high school graduation diploma might be withheld from a pupil if the exit test is not passed. This is high stakes testing. There are selected problems here when using tests for pupil promotion consideration to the next higher grade level as well as for maintaining teacher tenure in the public schools (Ediger, 2003, 9-15).

Problems in Testing

There are immediate problems when using tests in a stringent manner to assess pupils and teachers. The following are vital questions to raise:

1. are these test items valid? Do they measure what they are supposed to measure? This brings up the question, "What should pupils know and be able to do as a result of school attendance?" With all the needs in society, there are a plethora of vocations for pupils to follow

ultimately. This includes the professions as well as highly skilled areas of work. Teachers are encouraged to teach the academics, but are there salient skills also needed in society, which do not consist of academic subject matter? Quality automobile mechanics, carpet layers, bricklayers, and carpenters, among other services, are indeed essential and academic subject matter knowledge for these workers is not exactly essential. It is good, however, to be well educated and have much subject matter knowledge;

2. are the test items reliable? Good test items should measure each pupil's test results consistently. If a pupil's score is on the fortieth percentile the first time and the ninetieth percentile the second time of testing, in test/ retest reliability, then one wonders what the percentile ranking of that child actually is in achievement. Certainly, consistency of test results is lacking. Sometimes, a test shows high reliability, but low validity. It is easier to obtain reliable test results as compared to valid results;
3. is it good to spend much time on pupils honing for good test results when there is much to learn in life? No occupation known tests the worker to determine how much he/she is skilled at in actual job performance. Should an automobile mechanic, medical doctor, or lawyer be tested with a paper/pencil test to ascertain what can be done skillfully? Each worker/professional, rather, shows at the work place what can be done capably by his/her duties performed. The knowledge will be inherent within the skill performed. Thus, knowledge acquired in school needs to be useful and not obtained for its own sake (See Education Week, 2002).

Predictive Tests

There are predictive tests taken on the high school level, for example, which do attempt to predict university coursework success. These predictive tests, even if the test results from a student are very satisfactory, has a measure of error. If a student then receives a score of twenty and the standard error of measurement is two points his/her score actually could vary from 18 to 22 score points. Thus, if nineteen points is needed for admittance to university, the student's score of twenty and its error of measurement may make for a score as low as 18. Hopefully, a university would not discard a student from attendance due to missing the passing mark by one point. There are a plethora of other factors than test scores which should enter in as admittance factors. Thus, the following are viable factors to consider on the student's part in university admittance:

- motivation and a desire to succeed. Wanting to learn and being willing to work hard certainly are valuable factors to consider;
- interest factors are significant when a student wishes to pursue a given area of specialisation. Interest can be part of motivation, but also can be developed in time;
- purposes held can be deciding factor to pursue a given area of specialisation. If a student can perceive much purpose or reasons for becoming a teacher, certainly, this should be helpful in being successful as compared to seeing little or no purpose in teaching;
- meaning in pursuing a goal. Some individuals cannot pursue meaning in following a particular objective in life. Of, they may not later on, at the work place, tend to perceive meaning on what is being done. Choices made at one time may change in time as to staying with a career.

Flexibility is a key concept when thinking of what areas of study should be available for public school pupils and which career choices should be made on the higher education level. Teachers, supervisors, and parents must keep options open for children in the public schools to pursue. Extra curricular activities whether offered in school or outside the school setting should be varied, open to those interested, provide for individual differences, and not closed to those who may lack financial means. Extra or co-curricular activities can assist many to make viable decisions presently as well as for the future (Allen, 2001).

State Mandated Objectives and Tests

State mandated testing has as its purpose to make certain that pupils achieve what is essential for live and living. That makes for a very broad set of guidelines in the writing of objectives and test items. Certainly, when pupils differ from each other in a plethora of ways, it becomes impossible to write and implement that which fits all in one size. However, states have attempted to do this with nearly each state in the union having their own tests and cut off points for pupil promotion. With a single test for all pupils on a selected grade level within a state, there are perhaps very few accommodations made for those who read very slowly, are mentally impaired, physically handicapped, among other difficulties. One variable, basically, is kept the same and that being the test items each pupil responds to.

There certainly are things to watch for when the current set of pupils is performing at the work place in different fields of endeavour. The core curriculum in school must then:

1. provide for all learners whatever the future will hold for these pupils. It is true that all need to learn, to read, compute, and write as basics, but the level of expectancy for each will vary and for some the variation will be great indeed;
2. provide subject matter as general education for all, such as in science, social studies, art, music, and physical education. General education, indicates the inherent subject matter is needed for enriching the self and for becoming a good citizen whereas the core pertains to that which all need to be successful as a minimal level at the work place;
3. explain if divisions between the core and general education is needed and rational. The future work place and good citizenship, no doubt, are done and cannot be separated from each other. With high stakes testing reading and mathematics might receive priority in the classroom due to being tested upon (Ediger, 2002, 90-95).

If pupils with heavy testing presently will become better readers in the future as compared to those in the elementary schools presently remains to be seen. The author was amazed one day when having his car being repaired by a mechanic. The car was a 1991 model and the mechanic faced a problem in doing the repair work. So, he went up the steps to the archives where there were repair manuals of older cars. He brought the manual down and read aloud from the needed section as to what to do. The content was very complex. The author complemented on his reading ability. He looked surprised and said his teachers had always been critical of his reading ability! What makes subject matter easy to read? No doubt, the mechanic was interested in reading about automobile repair work, even though the related script was indeed difficult. The familiarity of the ideas read made the act of reading easier. There still is the problem of why the mechanic in his public school years had been labelled a poor reader. Many labelled as good readers would, no doubt, be labelled as poor readers when reading the automobile repair manual. Good mechanics are certainly needed in modern society. Present day norm and criterion referenced tests make no leeway for those not inclined academically. The same can be said for other relevant trades such as carpenters, bricklayers, carpet layers, and plumbers. State mandated test and their results from pupils need consideration that not all important knowledge and skills are being measured. The question of validity comes up again in terms of which content should be contained on state mandated tests. Thus, what correlation will there be between state mandated test results and the future citizen at the work place (See Donaldson, 2001)?

Problems in Testing

In a third grade classroom, most students are at various points in Piaget's concrete operational stage of development. Milestone of development occur in one child or another almost daily. Often, they go unnoticed, until suddenly, something makes an observer say, "Wow!" Still the children have not become abstract thinkers. They learn and test best in a concrete, hands on mode. The curriculum framesworks for mathematics recognise in their opening section: "Students are active individuals who construct, modify, and integrate ideas in interacting with materials, the world around them, and their peers." This statement is especially true for third graders: they must construct and interact with materials if they are going to understand and learn. But, this test is an abstract, paper and pencil test. Very few manipulatives are supplied—and those only for mathematics. In the language arts section, there is nothing for the student to touch, to hold, or to move around (Gould, 2003).

There certainly are problems then in the academics versus pupil development. The tests used so frequently are not developmentally sound. If the stage of pupil development is the concrete operations, according to Jean Piaget, and the test items stress the abstract only, test results will not show what a pupil has knowledge of or can do.

In daily life, each person generally is given the time needed to complete a task, be it in the classroom or at the work place. However, testing situations tend to be standardised in that each test taker receives the same amount of time to complete the test. It certainly is true that not every one completes a task in the same amount of time, such as in a standardised test.

Then too, each one in a group setting is to read the same set of test questions. Reading skills differ much from one person to the next. Interest in content read also differs much. And yet each person is to read the same content. Background information for test items to be read may be totally lacking for some, but for others the content sounds familiar indeed. Selected pupils are more independent than others and are able to read and respond to test items independently whereas others need more encouragement to proceed sequentially. Test taking skills are more in the repertoire for some as compared to other pupils. Reading of test items is then important whereas other pupils like a hands on approach to learning. That cannot be a fair test to appreciate or evaluate reading progress (Ediger, 2002, ERIC ED 462401).

Remedies in Testing

There are no easy ways of documenting pupil achievement. Testing and measuring are still in their infancy. Much work remains to be done to document and use test results to improve instruction.

Computer adapted tests (CAT) have been tried out and have attempted to answer the problem of providing for individual differences. In CAT, if a pupil responds incorrectly to a few sequentially presented items, easier items are presented to respond to until the responder has a chance to show what is known. Too frequently, there are children who have a very complex test for their individual developmental level. They miss most of the test responses which they give. This then does not measure at their individual achievement level. Little, if anything is measured, if a pupil continually responds incorrectly to test items. Toward the other end of the curriculum, if a pupil responds correctly to all, or most, of the test items, CAT provides more complex test items. This is done to determine a present achievement level as well as provide information as to what a pupil needs to learn next. CAT then does make provisions for individual differences in that a leaner does not get all, or almost all items incorrect, or a pupil does not respond correctly to all, or almost all test items continuously. CAT items then:

1. might well vary, in complexity, from one child as compared to the other;
2. attempts to measure at a point and place where a pupil is presently achieving, not at too complex nor too easy a level;
3. makes adjustments for the test taker.

CAT attempts to minimise the criticism that "one size fits all," in test taking by pupils. These are still paper pencil types of tests and do not take into consideration those who prefer hands on approaches in testing

Another kind of assessment which could provide valuable information pertaining to pupils achievement orientated tests. Here, the school system or state gives a valid/reliable test at three intervals during a school year to notice pupil achievement and progress from one time to the next. Sequential progress might then be noticed with feedback provided on what a child needs to work on next. Much excess time might then be necessary to give these interval tests to notice achievement of each pupil.

In Conclusion

There are a plethora of differences among pupils which has in its infancy just been tapped. The following are problems and questions for pondering:

1. there are many kinds of futures for a child such as hands on jobs, such as carpentering with the mass number of houses being built continuously. Should possible pupil progress in these areas be measured? Certainly, many home repair skills are also needed by all pupils, regardless of job or profession followed, for future success;
2. there are many kinds of skills needed in the entertainment industry, such as those with musical intelligence. How can achieve be measured here?
3. leaders are always needed in different fields of work. What kind of evaluations should be developed to measure sequential skills in pupil leadership?
4. ethics in society is increasingly necessary. Measuring growth in ethics certainly is a vary valuable task;
5. group/committee as well as individual endeavours in the classroom are musts for the teachers to provide. How can state mandated tests measure pupil success in committee work?

REFERENCES

Allen, Rick (2001), *"Technology and Learning"*, Curriculum Update. Published by ASCD.

Donaldson, Gordan A. (2001), *"The Lose-Lose Leadership Hunt"*, Education Week, October 3, 2001). p. 42.

Ediger, Marlow (2003), *"Data Driven Decision Making"*, College Student Journal, 37 (1), 9-15.

Ediger, Marlow (2002), *"Assessing the School Principal,"* Education, 12? (1), 90-95.

Ediger, Marlow (2002), *Philosophy of Testing and Measurement*. ERIC, ED 462401.

Education Week (January 10, 2002), *Quality Counts*. Pew Charitable Trust Report on Education in the Fifty States.

Gould, Franklin (2003), *"Testing Third Graders in New Hampshire"*, Phi Delta Kappan, 84 (7), 509.

7

Absolute Standards Versus Value Added Criteria

There are a plethora of problems involved when having students achieve objectives. With absolute standards, the objectives may be set at an appropriate level of difficulty. Hopefully, the objectives will be challenging and yet achievable. With absolute standards, all students must achieve a predetermined level of achievement. This is true regardless of the category of students involved be it special education students, English Language Learners (ELL), English as a second language students (ESL), or students from poverty homes.

Value added criteria stresses the importance of achievement of each student above his/her pervious level of accomplishment. This would be true for all categories of students.

Absolute Standards

State mandated objectives, presently, emphasise absolute standards. Thus, there are state mandated tests which have set the standards well ahead of time when these tests will actually be administered to students. The No Child Left Behind Low of 2002 mandates that the tests be administered in grades three through eight and in grade ten. The cut off point has been made as to which students will pass and which will fail the next grade level. No exceptions are to be made for any category of student including the mentally retarded. All students in a grade level are to meet the minimum standard for passing to the next higher grade level.

State mandated tests have become standardised in that:

1. the time limit for test taking is the same for all; no adjustments are made for any category of students;
2. the test items are the same for all students in the grade level being tested;
3. the conditions for test taking are the same with no adjustments made for any category of student;
4. the same scoring key is used for all students;
5. tests and machine scored. There have been computer glitches which have been costly to students emotionally.

There are bound to be certain categories of student who are very vulnerable to failing a test such as the student who comes from a poor home economically, those who are below average in intelligence, and those who speak/read English poorly. Students from suburban areas will tend to do well on state mandated tests. These students come from a favoured environment.

All answers will be scored as being either right or wrong. There are no responses by students to questions which require critical and creative thinking, as well as life like situations problem solving. Higher levels of thinking tend to be minimised in standardised testing. It would be very expensive to grade essay tests requiring higher level of cognition. These would need to be hand scored and inservice training would be necessary for evaluators. Quality rubrics then need to be developed and used in the appraisal process. Hopefully, increased reliability would be in the offing with high interscorer reliability. All of these items would raise the cost off state mandated testing.

Schools need to meet the adequate yearly progress (ayp) standards. Each state sets their own ayp. If a school does not meet the ayp standard two years in a row, then that school is listed as "needing improvement". A student may then transfer out of that failing school to one which has been rated as being satisfactory. Cohorts are being compared in a failing school. With the two years of achievement, comparisons comparing different sets of students, not the same students during the two year interval to determine ayp.

Value Added Standards

With value added standards, student growth in achievement is determined with the same students being compared from one year to the next. From the state mandated tests, the assessor looks at achievement of the same students from and for successive school years. The question to be answered then would pertain to, "Are these students as a school unit and individually making progress?"

Value added emphasises the following:

1. comparing the student's progress presently with that of last year;
2. noticing if students make adequate progress with no precise predetermined standard being used;
3. comparing each category of student with his/her past school year of measured achievement. Thus, each of the following would be evaluated in terms of having made adequate progress over his/her previous school year:
   (a) the special education student;
   (b) the English Language Learner (ELL);
   (c) English as a Second Language (ESL);
   (d) each category of minority student. This would eliminate making unreasonable comparisons such as special education students with students in the regular classroom.

Value added standards must incorporate additional means of assessment. Thus, the teacher may and should use the following as formative assessments along the way to assess if students are achieving state mandated objectives:

1. teacher written test items including multiple choice tests;
2. teacher written essay tests to ascertain how well learners are doing in problem solving;
3. teacher written word problems;

4. teacher assessment of daily work from the basal textbook;
5. teacher evaluation of oral participation in class involving student discussion in using important processes and procedures.

Portfolios are additional approaches to use to document student achievement. A random selection of items from daily work of students may become a part of the portfolio. The following products may then become an inherent part of a portfolio:

1. daily papers completed in a variety of curriculum areas;
2. drawings and diagrams to indicate understandings acquired;
3. snapshots of projects developed in ongoing units of study;
4. self evaluation statements of the learner;
5. teacher written statements pertaining to how the student may achieve more optimally.

Criteria to Use in Teaching

There are definite criteria which teachers should use in teaching. These include:

1. engaging students in interesting activities to achieve objectives;
2. assisting students to perceive reasons or purpose for learning;
3. guiding students to become better listeners to ongoing discussions;
4. having an orderly classroom in which students feel respected and accepted;
5. assisting students, as needed, to become independent learners;
6. helping students to attach meaning and understanding involving relevant concepts and generalisations;
7. teaching students how to work harmoniously in group work;

8. developing positive attitudes toward learning;
9. guiding students to set relevant goals in life;
10. motivating students to achieve vital objectives of instruction.

In Closing

Students do need to achieve as much as possible in a complex world. There is much to learn and students need to acquire, grow, and develop in a positive direction. Persevering and responsible individuals are needed in order to make necessary contributions in society as well as to develop the self.

A rich learning environment needs to be provided so that vital objectives are achieved. The school environment should assist students to accomplish that which is worthwhile and then to build on these learnings in order to be successful individuals in the curriculum of life.

REFERENCES

Cuddeback, Meghan, and Maria A. Ceprano (2002), *"The Use of Accelerated Reader with Emergent Readers,"* Reading Improvement, 39 (2), 89-95.

Ediger, Marlow, and D. Bhaskara Rao (2003), *Improving School Administration*. New Delhi, India: Discovery Publishing House, 141 and 142.

Ediger, Marlow, and D. Bhaskara (2003), *Language Arts Curriculum*. New Delhi, India: Discovery Publishing House, Chapter Thirteen.

Ediger, Marlow (1988), *The Elementary Curriculum*, 2nd Edition. Kirksville, Missouri: Simpson Publishing Company, Chapter Seven.

Epstein, Joyce (1995), *"School/Family/Community Partnerships,"* Phi Delta Kappan, 76: 704.

Friedrich, L.E. (1983), *"The School Budgeting Cycle"*, Winneconne, Wisconsin.

Paris, Scott (2002), *"Centre for Improvement of Early Reading Achievement,"* Reading Teacher, 55 (2), 170.

Richard, Alan (September 4, 2002), *"Florida Sees Surge in Use of Vouchers,"* Education Week, 1, 34.

Risko Virginia J., et. al. (2002), *"Preparing Teachers for Reflective Practice: Interactions, Contradictions, and Possibilities"*, Language Arts, 82 (2), 134-144.

Tyler, Ralph (1949), *Basic Principles of Curriculum Construction*. Chicago: University of Chicago Press.

8

Meeting Student Needs

There are a plethora of needs to meet in order that each student achieves well in school. Highly important is that the student has nutrition needs met. Schools are doing more than ever before in meeting nutrition needs with a breakfast served when students arrive at school, the hot lunch programme served at noon, and a snack served to students involved in after school programmes. There still are gaps here in meeting food needs of students. Not all schools serve breakfast and the noon meal, nor are most children enrolled in after school programmes to receive a snack. The largest gap is on Saturdays and Sundays when no food is served in the public schools. Food pantries and food kitchens operated by churches and other welfare groups have assumed much responsibility in meeting food needs for families on welfare and for the poor in society. But there are still many unmet needs in evidence in a society. Homes for students need to be safe, clean, free from obnoxious insects and animals.

Safety Needs of Students

Safety needs must be met before students can do well in school. Students may not want to attend school because they fear certain individuals. The school bully has been around for a long time. Bullies operate alone or with others to intimate selected individuals. Hallways, along with classrooms, need to be supervised carefully to minimise/avoid bullying. Teachers and school administrators must talk to students on the damages done when bullies operate.

A structurally safe building, also, must be in the offing. Roofs have collapsed on school buildings when the joists become weakened, over time, from rainfall. Cold, drafty buildings make for discomfort, colds, and flu in winter time. A lack of air conditioning makes for uncomfortable learning environments in summer, as well as in late spring and early into the new school year. Steam radiators used for heating are out dated since they heat selected areas excessively and other areas remain too cool/ cold in winter time.

Rest rooms should be kept immaculately clean and properly deodorized. They must be in proper working condition with the facilities contained therein. Classrooms must be kept very clean and free from offensive odors.

Mold and mildew collections have caused illnesses among students and teachers and need to be removed by certified companies.

Clothing Needs of Students

Students need clean, appropriate clothes which harmonise with the different seasons of the year. Clothing worn should fit properly and the comfortable. What is worn should not disturb the learning environment. The educational system should provide necessary learnings to develop the student, individually, and to accomplish appropriate roles as a citizen in society, not to glory or glamorize clothing status.

Clothing should be available for students whose homes cannot afford the necessary attire. The school should have a listing of which charitable organisations assist in providing proper clothes for the needy. In society, there are good, reputable, charitable organisations which provide clothing free for poor people. Families experiencing poverty should have knowledge of these charitable organisations. Neat, proper clothing should facilitate the learning process in the school setting.

Ethical Behaviour in the Classroom

Students can definitely be hindered in goal attainment through negative behaviour from others in the school setting. The following behaviours too frequently are in evidence:

1. rude remarks which hinder in student self development;
2. put downs which momentarily make for feelings of elation by the offender;
3. name calling which is offensive to the receiver of the remarks;
4. harassment from students. This makes for very uncomfortable feelings for the receiver of the harassment;
5. pushing, shoving, and hitting of school mates.

To become a good citizen in school and in society, teachers and school administrators need to stress proper behaviour, presently. The behaviours to be emphasised need to become objectives for students to achieve. There should be time allotted to assessment to determine if objectives for good behaviour are being achieved by learners. Good behaviour is necessary so that each student may achieve optimally. Disruptions in teaching and learning occur when misbehaviour is in evidence. Behaviours such as the following should be stressed:

1. respecting others. Somewhat opposite of respect would pertain to ridiculing others;
2. accepting students as having much worth. Somewhat opposite of acceptance would emphasise shunning;
3. helping each student to develop feelings of belonging to a group and to the class and school. Otherwise, students might well feel as being isolates;
4. recognising the achievements and contributions of peers. Opposite behaviours would stress ignoring or making hostile comments on what others have accomplished;
5. assisting others when needed. Too often students feel ignored when help is needed.

Each student needs to feel he/she is a fully contributing member in school and in society. The student then feel that growth and learning is possible in a positive learning environment.

The Curriculum in the School Setting

The school curriculum needs to provide quality experiences for students. The objectives need to be challenging and achievable. Efforts must be put forth by the student to achieve optimally. The teacher must have high but reasonable expectations of each student. A balanced school day should stress the importance of students developing well academically, socially, emotionally, and physically. Too frequently, academic objectives are stressed largely and these are important for learner achievement. However, the other three areas, namely, social, emotional, and physical development are also salient to stress.

Academic objectives for each curriculum area need to be chosen carefully, using updated criteria. Each objective must be relevant and sequentially arranged for student achievement. The objectives need to be precise so that there is agreement as to what students are to achieve. There need to be objectives which are cognitive or intellectual, affective which stress the feeling dimension in learning, and psychomotor which indicate the use of the gross and the finer muscles.

Learning Experiences for Students

Learning activities selected should assist students to achieve objectives. Each activity needs to capture student attention. Learners need to be fully engaged in the ongoing experience. Students need to perceive the relationship of previous to the new learnings. When feasible, ideas need to be related across the curriculum. Improved retention occurs when relationship of ideas is experienced. Readiness for learning is increased when the student perceives that subject matter is integrated.

Reasons for learning are salient to the student. Thus, purpose may be developed within each learner. The teacher may then state a purpose or learning deductively, or students may be guided to inductively sense purpose for learning. A combination of deductive/inductive approaches may also be implemented to assist students perceive purpose for learning. Learning without perceived purpose may have little value for students.

Each student needs to understand subject matter and skills being taught. Meaning is then being established within a learning situation. Meaningful learning occurs when a student can say in his/her very own words that which was learned. Comprehension of ideas is of utmost importance.

What has been learned must be useful in school and in society. Trivia has little value to the student. Main ideas as well as subordinating subject matter acquired indicates that the student has relevant ideas which may be applied in new situations. With use, ideas are remembered. Recall is an important facet of learning. What is recalled then might be applied in a new situation.

Students need to do something with the ideas acquired. These ideas may be used in critical thinking situations. Thus, separating facts from opinions, fantasy from reality, as well as accurate from inaccurate ideas must be done in order to engage in higher levels of cognition. When subject matter has been analysed it may then be used in problem solving situations. Problem solving is important presently, as well as in the future. Each person has personal and social problems which need solutions. Having an approach to identify problems and procedures involved to solve each problem makes it more probable that the student has solutions to offer. The following steps in problem solving are salient for each person:

1. clarifying a vital problem area;
2. securing data in order to offer possible solutions to a problem;
3. using a variety of reputable information sources;
4. testing the content (hypothesis) directly related to the problem area;
5. modifying the hypothesis if needed.

With the tremendous emphasis being placed upon state mandated objectives, it behooves the teacher to do a quality job of professional instruction. Annual tests are given to students in grades three thorough eight, and in grade ten. Each student needs to pass grade level tests in order to be promoted to the next higher grade level.

Role of Society

Society has a plethora of important roles to play in eleviating/ minimising poverty. Poverty has to do with being unemployed or having a low paying job. With poverty, children tend to fail as students in school. Students tend to feel helpless due to not having privileges as do others from higher income homes and families. Money buys many things such as a decent home in a safe environment, travel experiences to visit and observe important places, music/dance lessons, reading materials in the home setting, among other advantageous opportunities. Then too, safe, comfortable means of transportation are needed. People in society need to feel more compassion and reach out to assist the less fortunate.

REFERENCES

Cuddeback, Meghan, and Maria A. Ceprano (2002), *"The Use of Accelerated Reader with Emergent Readers"*, Reading Improvement, 39 (2), 89-95.

Ediger, Marlow, and D Bhaskara Rao (2003), *Improving School Administration*. New Delhi, India: Discovery Publishing House, 141 and 142.

Ediger, Marlow and D. Bhaskara Rao (2003), *Language Arts Curriculum*. New Delhi, India: Discovery Publishing House, Chapter Thirteen.

Ediger, Marlow (1988), *The Elementary Curriculum*, 2nd Edition, Kirksville, Missouri: Simpson Publishing Company, Chapter Seven.

Epstein, Joyce (1995), *"School/Family/Community Partnerships"*, Phi Delta Kappan, 76: 704.

Friedrich, L.E. (1983), *"The School Budgeting Cycle"*, Winneconne, Wisconsin.

Paris, Scott (2002), *"Centre for Improvement of Early Reading Achievement"*, Reading Teacher, 55 (2), 170.

Richard, Alan (September 4, 2002), Florida Sees Surge in Use of Vouchers", Education Week, 1, 34.

Risko, Virginia J., et. al. (2002), *"Preparing Teachers for Reflective Practice: Intensions, Contradictions, and Possibilities"*, Language Arts, 82 (2), 134-144.

Tyler, Ralph (1949), *Basic Principles of Curriculum Construction*. Chicago: University of Chicago Press.

9

Connecting the Home and the School

To frequently, the home and school are separate entities. Thus, what goes on in the home has no relationship with that of the school. Certainly, this may minimise student achievement. If the two are connected with each other, the student's achievement should be more optimal. Parents and teachers need to attempt more cooperation whereby the student benefits from these cooperative endeavours. One way might well be the traditional homework assignment. Homework has merit if it meets selected criteria such as:

1. possessing purpose or reason for its inclusion;
2. stressing student engagement in what is being assigned;
3. meeting personal needs of the individual student;
4. helping the student to achieve an objective in the curriculum;
5. assisting the learner to achieve sequence in learning.

There should be balance between assigned homework and student initiated learning activities in the home setting. The latter is difficult to implement, but is very important to emphasise.

Relating the School Curriculum to the Home Setting

For student initiated homework to be possible parent/teacher cooperation is necessary. More than parent/teacher conferences once or twice a year are needed. The school and classroom environment for the student need to be stimulating places to be. The bulletin board has a neat displaying pertaining to the present unit being taught. The illustrations and title of the display need to be informative and attractive. Students then have an inward desire to learn from the contents and ideas are discussed with other learners. In the same classroom, there is a place to put student work on the classroom walls. Students have opportunities to share their products enthusiastically with others. Time is provided for questions and answers in the activity. A busy classroom atmosphere is in evidence in which students select what to learn from fascinating centres in the classroom. There is no time for misbehaviour since students intrinsically are choosing and completing products at the diverse centres. Time is given for students to select and read library books in the classroom. An ample supply are available for students to choose the genre and appropriate reading level. Sharing of library book content is definitely possible.

Active involvement of students is observed as students engage in doing science experiments. Commercial and home/ school made equipment is available for doing each experiment. For individual science units of study, there is equipment whereby students may learn by doing. Careful observation is required for each experiment so that students may observe what is transpiring. Hypotheses are developed and tested. Conclusions are recorded in each student's journal.

Mathematics is learned through practical application as well as through quality textbooks, and teacher devised materials of instruction. Thus, students may find the length, width, and volume by experimenting with real materials and actual objects. The mathematics curriculum needs to contain basic learnings such as addition, subtraction, multiplication, division, place value, fractions, decimals, and per cent. These learnings may be obtained by students through an activity centred mathematics curriculum.

Problem solving is emphasised strongly in the social studies. For each social studies unit of study, pupils engage in identifying a problem. They gather information from a variety of reference sources to seek needed answers in developing a tentative hypothesis. They hypothesis is tested in a life like situation and revised if necessary.

An activity centred procedure is used in teaching social studies. The following criteria are being followed in the teaching of social studies:

1. students are actively engaged in learning. They are not passive beings;
2. civic behaviour is stressed when students interact with others;
3. key ideas are being emphasised in the social studies. The key ideas come from history, geography, government (political science) anthropology and sociology, as well as from economics;
4. large group instructions, committee work, and individual study are in evidence;
5. individual differences are being provided for in all learning opportunities presented;
6. essential ingredients emphasised in teaching include student interest, purpose, and meaning theory;
7. student decision making is highly salient;
8. learners possess diverse intelligences and these need to be cultivated (Gardner, 1993);
9. learning styles theory needs ample emphasis (Dunn and Dunn, 1979);
10. student input in the curriculum is a must!

A leaning environment which is conducive to assisting students do well includes the following:

- a mission that teachers, administrators, and students know and support;
- high expectations for all students with a clear definition of the knowledge, skills, and personal attributes students should gain;

- caring and respectful relationships between teachers and students, with every student known well by an adult and engaged in meaningful work;
- qualified teachers who have opportunities to work together and form a professional community;
- a well defined approach to instruction with engaging instructional strategies, such as indepth projects and learning that takes place in the community and the workplace as well as in the classroom;
- active roles for students in all aspects of school life;
- clear connections and pathways to post secondary education, careers, and community participation (Lewis, 2004).

Voluntary Homework

Student enthusiasm in school should filter into the home setting. Motivated students in school tend to indicate their strong interests in doing homework. Students should have ample opportunities to select what they wish to do as homework. Sometimes, student in school enthusiasm alone might well carry over into the home environment. Students may wish to do art projects, health charts and posters, and/or develop games and activities for a quality physical education programme. The homework also may relate directly to the language arts, mathematics, science, and social studies. Thus, for example, in science, students individually may:

1. perform additional science experiments at home with parental involvement;
2. do a research paper on a famous scientist;
3. make a model, such as a dinosaur;
4. solve problem as in how the circulatory system works in a human or in an animal;
5. complete a chart showing the evaluation of plants and/or animals;
6. give an oral report at home and in school on E-coli and listeria deadly bacteria;

7. make dioramas on preventing soil erosion;
8. prepare a project, such as a solar unit, for a science fair;
9. debate the pros and cons pertaining to cloning of human beings;
10. collect news clippings on natural disasters such hail, earthquakes, hurricanes, tornados, volcanic eruptions, among others. Summarise the clippings and share the findings with classmates and parents (Ediger, 1995).

Voluntary homework emphasises the importance of a high degree of interest in students for learning and achievement. Inwardly, students have a desire to become actively engaged in learning. In doing voluntary homework, the student selects what to learn. The teacher or parents may suggest topics and projects. Meeting student interests in learning is vital. Connections between home and school must be made for students individually to achieve more optimally.

A Community of Learners

Each person needs to continue learning throughout his/her life span. Connecting parents more thoroughly with the school is salient. The school, including teachers, supervisors, and administrators, need to provide an inviting atmosphere which encourages parent participation. An informal organisation of interested persons in studying and thinking about an academic discipline and how it should be taught provides a framework for curriculum improvement.

Learning communities have been found to be valuable in education. Why? Within these communities, individuals may achieve a closeness in working on a common interest. This common interest, for example, might be mathematics. By learning together, students might be the ultimate beneficiaries of a quality programme of mathematics instruction. By learning together, quality objectives for students to achieve may be determined cooperatively. The objectives must be chosen carefully and emphasise both the worthwhile and the utilitarian. The learning opportunities to attain the objectives must promote interest, purpose, and provide for individual differences. The learning community can also choose assessments which ascertain learner achievement with validity and reliability. Assessment procedures may be varied to notice a variety of facets of student achievement be it academic, social, attitudinal, psychomotor, and/or ethical. A community of learners in mathematics then can involve those who have a common concern and wish to provide effort to move the mathematics curriculum from where it is presently to where it should be, involving some ideal.

Cooperative endeavours are needed for a community to function and proceed well. Getting along with others and sharing information during a discussion setting is salient. Reference sources need to be available for all participants to use. The reference sources may include video tapes, CD ROMs, films, filmstrips, slides, educational journals, and teacher education books on teaching mathematics to stimulate interest and motivation in improving the mathematics curriculum. Consultant assistance, as needed, should be available to help participants to secure vital information. The ultimate goal is to improve the mathematics curriculum. Providing for each and every student is significant in developing the mathematics curriculum. No student should fail or fall through the cracks. Proposals from the learning community may be presented to the local school board for consideration and/or further study.

Mathematics teachers as a community of learners need to:

1. work together harmoniously studying trends, issues, and current research in teaching mathematics;
2. share information to achieve quality in teaching and learning in mathematics;
3. cooperatively establish objectives for learner achievement;
4. gather information on what other school systems are doing to attain excellence in their mathematics curriculum;
5. do research on testing versus portfolio development to assess learner achievement.

Parents and the mathematics community may study the following:

1. studying research on what works well in the teaching of mathematics;
2. reaching the at risk in mathematics;
3. teaching the culturally different student in mathematics;
4. assisting the gifted in mathematics;
5. helping those with handicaps, such as the mentally retarded.

Students in a community of learners may study:

1. difficulties in motivating students within a classroom whose individual achievement levels differ greatly one from another;
2. problems in providing for students of different socio-economic levels;
3. assisting the potential drop out from failing;
4. involving the slow learner in ongoing lessons and units of study;
5. providing enrichment experiences for those doing well in the mathematics curriculum (Ediger and Rao).

The different groups should compile and summarise information gathered. The findings need to be available to all participants with the intent of implementation of selected ideas. An informed community of learners is necessary for curriculum improvement to take place. Integrating the school, home, and the community is necessary to improve the curriculum.

REFERENCES

Dunn, Rita, and Kenneth Dunn (1979), *Learning Styles/Teaching Styles*, Educational Leadership, 36 (4), 238-244.

Ediger, Marlow (1995), *Philosophy of Teaching Science*," School Science, 33 (3), 1 and 2.

Ediger, Marlow, and D. Bhaskara Rao (2003), *Teaching Mathematics in Elementary Schools*. New Delhi, India: Discovery Publishing House.

Gardner, Howard (1993), *Multiple Intelligence: Theory into Practice.* New York: Basic Books.

Lewis, Anne C. (2004), *"Schools that Engage Children,"* Phi Delta Kappan, 85 (7), 484.

Community Service and the Schools

Much is written about students being engaged in community service, particularly on the high school level. Community service indicates a specific value being held by planners of the secondary school curriculum as well as by those who will participate in the programme. The value of community service consists of doing a s·rvice to benefit others in society. Generally, the community service is to benefit all in society or those who are needy. High school age students are at the age level where they can do much to assist others. The need to be a good citizen is involved in community service ideals. No one is an island unto themselves, but all are members of society and should seek what is good in the societal realm.

Too frequently, the goals of doing community service are slighted with a strong emphasis upon the academic studies in school. To be sure, the academics are important for all. They do provide a broad general education for learners. However, many students will not follow the academic world as adults in the world of work. The world of work requires different talents and abilities. The non-academic world requires brick layers, carpenters, plumbers, electricians, and land scapers, truck drivers, cooks and food workers, and mechanics, among others. Community service opportunities may well provide these students who do not excel in the academics a way of doing other kinds of school work beneficial to the general public.

Values Possessed by Individual Students

Values possessed by students do provide direction in terms of what will be sought in life. It is quite obvious that students individually reveal diversify in values. Values tend to be abstract and provide plans in terms of what is important to the individual. What is of interest does have an attraction component. Thus, inherent interests do provide predictors of possessed values. Aesthetic values are important to many, along with other selected aims. Students who have strong inherent aesthetic values tend to follow through in life with these values. Students, preferring the aesthetic, view the importance of what has beauty. The artist tends to emphasise what has beauty, harmony, and symmetry. He/she loves what is creative behaviour, not conformity. Originality, novelty, and uniqueness are desired in art products and processes.

Theoretical values emphasise those approaches and procedures which make for discoveries of truth possible. Students who possess theoretical values use logic, abstract, and philosophical pursuits. Thinking indepth is very salient for a person possessing theoretical values. Critical thinking and synthesis are also salient skills.

Religious values are strong within selected students. Those pursuing religious values believe in spiritual ideas which may include God, idealism, and/or the deity. Values here pertain to a higher good than the self. These values emphasise doing good works to help others realise more of their optimal self.

Social values are quite important in order to do well in school and in society. The school setting is made up of many individuals and it is necessary to get along well with others. Selected students excel in this area, called human relations in many cases. Individuals with a social values orientation are highly accepting of others. They achieve well when working with others and are very sympathetic toward needy persons. Positive feelings toward others and a desire to assist those who are less fortunate to achieve well are primary goals here.

Economic values are held by those who desire to become wealthy individuals. Motivation here stresses the importance of achieving wealth, and material things. Obtaining more money in salary, dividends, profits, bonuses, interest from investments, and corporate gains are salient in the values domain focusing upon economic interests.

Hedonistic values are those which assist the student to experience pleasure and avoid pain. The pleasure seeking individual needs to observe two dimensions here and that is doing what is enjoyable and at the same time avoiding that which is considered to be harmful. Pleasure versus pain are in opposition to each other. One dimension is good and the other is evil to the beholder.

Political values emphasise seeking power and being highly influential in the societal arenas. Individuals in the field of politics have a strong propensity to govern, rule, and regulate. These are not passive beings but rather attempt to be actively involved in interacting with others to influence and possess power over others, as objectives in mind (as quoted in Rengasamy, 2003).

Community service ideals can embrace many of the above named values, especially the aesthetic (having a beautiful human made environment, the religious (such as being a good Samaritan), and social values (having positive human relations). Community service is an ideal in and of itself in moving from the actual situation to stressing something better.

Objectives in the Community Service Curriculum

Each objective needs to be chosen carefully for students to achieve. The objectives should be challenging, but achievable. In other words, the objectives should not be too difficult to achieve, nor should they be too easy and thus lack high expectations.

One category of objectives for students to attain is knowledge ends. Knowledge is necessary in order to provide background information in achieving objectives. Important facts, concepts and generalisations need to be possessed to attain objectives. More complex ends may be achieved by students through scaffolding. A second category of objectives pertain to students achievi[illegible] vital skills. Skills such as reading, writing, speaking, and listening are salient in any curriculum area and cut across all academic areas. A third category of objectives are attitudes for students to achieve. Positive attitudes are necessary to do well in learning. Quality attitudes to achieve include the following:

1. wanting to do well in community service;
2. cooperating well with others in doing service in the community;
3. desiring to achieve objectives of instruction;
4. wishing to improve in identification and solving of problems;
5. feeling a need to engage in higher cognitive levels of thinking such as analysis, integration of ideas, and assessment of the quality of thinking involved;
6. reflectively thinking about decisions made so that improvement of thought is involved;
7. doing the best work possible in community service;
8. using relevant resources to make plans for community service;
9. respecting the instructor and other learners in the community service curriculum;
10. keeping accurate records of achievements in community service projects (Ediger and Rao, 2003).

The community service programme has essential components which need to be planned for in an effective curriculum. After objectives have been established, then learning opportunities need to be determined. The learning opportunities in community service are concrete and real, not abstract in nature. They stress a learning by doing approach.

Each student is to be actively involved in performing a service for the public. The following activities might well provide this kind of service:

1. assisting at a habitat for humanity setting;
2. working in a food centre for the needy;

3. presenting a programme and visiting with nursing home patients;
4. conversing with the elderly, the bereaved, and the ill;
5. helping the needy, elderly person with a home project such as painting the porch of the house;
6. assisting in a meals on wheels activity;
7. working in the public school setting by listening to young children read aloud and providing assistance in word recognition;
8. assisting in a special school ground or neighbourhood clean up job;
9. helping in play ground supervision in an after school programme;
10. working in a landscape job such as planting trees during Arbor Day or other suitable times.

Community service emphasises those works which are of benefit to the general public. The services given are provided free of charge and are under the supervision of a designated teacher. The teacher must be able to work well with students in a safe, activity centred curriculum. Time on task for community service participants is a must. Students need to achieve valid and reliable objectives of the curriculum. The learning opportunities need to be:

1. purposeful and have reasons for its inclusion in community service;
2. interesting so that motivation for community service participation is encouraged;
3. challenging so that optimal student achievement is possible;
4. individualised to provide for diverse ability levels of students;
5. meaningful so that the student feels the community service activity or project makes sense;
6. designed so that the student perceives the results of his/her work;

7. geared to student self evaluation by using quality criteria;
8. assessment based with the teacher providing feedback to students on how well they are doing;
9. sequential so that past experiences provide background knowledge and skills to achieve the new ends of instruction and experience;
10. broad in scope so that students experience a rich community service curriculum (Ediger and Rao, 2002).

Evaluation is important in any curriculum area with community service being no exception. A comprehensive evaluation system needs to be in the offing. Results from the evaluation provide the teacher as well as students information on how well each is doing. Which techniques might be used to ascertain how well students are doing as well as provide data on determining future sequential learning opportunities? Teacher observation involving quality criteria may be a very good procedure to use in assessing student achievement. The teacher may then notice, for example, which students are achieving and which seem to be mediocre in accomplishments.

Multiple choice tests, well designed with quality validity and reliability may indicate to the teacher what the student has accomplished and what is left to learn.

Essay tests provide opportunities for students to reveal achievement in organising ideas as well as in showing proficiency in the mechanics of writing.

Each student needs to develop a portfolio showing diary entries of what was done as well as snapshots and drawings indicating accomplishments made in community service.

Multiple Intelligences Theory

Multiple intelligences theory emphasised the importance of students possessing a plethora of abilities. There are abilities which are stronger than others. When providing for each learner, the teacher needs to view the strongest intelligence of the student and then teach to strengthen this ability and have the student use this strength. If a student then has strong verbal intelligence, he/she should do much reading and participate in many writing activities as learning opportunities. The question arises, "what about strengthening the other abilities such as the artistic, objective thinking as in science, and/or logical thinking as in mathematics?" A balance might be struck here in that the student may do considerable reading/writing and therein emphasise objective and logical thought. Thus, an integrated curriculum is an end result. However, for objective thinking and logical thought to truly be emphasised, the curriculum areas of science and mathematics, need adequate stress in teaching and learning. To be sure, students may learn much science through reading, but they also need a hands on approach in achieving goals recommended by the National Science Teachers Association. Then too, mathematics is one of two major areas tested in, according to state mandated testing emphasised in all states in the nation. It does require considerable reading and knowledge of mathematical terms. Those educators who advocate a broadly based liberal arts education desire to have students achieve adequately, too, in the social sciences, in art, in physical prowess, and in music. The broadly educated person has always been a prized ingredient in the societal arena. Specialisation may come after the liberal arts component of education has been completed. It is excellent also to integrate general education with community service projects (See Gardner, 1993).

REFERENCES

Ediger, Marlow, and D. Bhaskara Rao (2003), *Improving School Administration*. New Delhi, India: Discovery Publishing House.

Ediger, Marlow, and D. Bhaskara Rao (2002), *Teaching Social Studies Successfully*. New Delhi, India: Discovery Publishing House.

Gardner, Howard (1993), *Multiple Intelligences: Theory into Practice*. New York: Basic Books.

Rengasamy, T. (2003), *A Study of Interest in Social Service, Value Patterns and Personality Needs of Higher Secondary Students in Relation to their Academic Achievement*. Annamalainagar, India: Annamalai University.

The Competent Teacher in the Classroom

Developing competencies is never finished but is ongoing in classroom teaching. The teacher should always grow in achievement from where he/she is presently to some sequential ideal. To achieve sequentially, the teacher needs to participate in a variety of inservice education programmes. These include studying one's own students in the classroom in order to become more familiar with the varieties of student behaviour. Human behaviour in the classroom needs more study so that individual differences are provided for. Growth of the teacher then may come in a plethora of forms including working toward an advanced university degree, workshops attended, as well as professional state and national conventions which emphasise sessions on improving the quality of instruction. What are additional avenues for developing competencies in teaching?

Assisting Students to Achieve

There is much that the teacher can do to assist students to achieve at a more complex level. First, the teacher needs to realise that there are times when a student may excel in an area of knowledge and know more about it than others in the classroom, including the teacher. It become increasingly difficult for a teacher to possess all the knowledge demanded in any classroom. The teacher may then call upon a student who knowingly has richly experienced an answer to a question raised in class. The student's responses need to be respected in the classroom setting. This is one way to handle a difficult question. The teacher may also learn along with students when he/she cannot answer a question raised by a learner. The teacher, as well as students, may look up the need information. The information secured might well provide background information for ensuing learning opportunities. Students and the teacher need to build knowledge and skills based upon past experiences encountered.

Second, students need to be praised for quality work done. The praise needs to be sincere and for definite accomplishment exhibited. Praise for effort put forth encourages further success in learning. With praise given, the need for rebukes or corrections of student behaviour will tend to be limited.

When students ask questions about a specific idea presented in the classroom, the teacher may reply with another question which leads the learner to the correct answer. Not all questions should be answered directly, but students should be guided to think through a situation until it leads to increased correctness. Then too, not all questions raised by students can be answered factually, but require thought, logic, and/or analysis.

Third, when students make specific mistakes, these need to be handled as soon as possible with diagnosis and remediation. This prevents learning which is incorrect and is difficult to change. Incorrect spelling of words, unless invented spelling is emphasised, and incorrect answers to basic arithmetic facts would come in this category.

Fourth, knowledge of results in classroom testing should be provided to the student as soon as possible and immediately when feasible. Students might then remember rather quickly the precise questions on the test and relate the answers provided when knowledge of results is provided. One problem with state mandated tests is that knowledge of results may come seven or more months after the test was taken by students. Remembrance of the testing situation might well be vague indeed! Students should receive practice or have learning opportunities which overcome deficiencies. Drill and practice alone is not the answer, but a variety of rich experiences should be provided learners which overcome the identified deficiencies.

Fifth, students should be engaged actively in learning and not be passive receivers of information. Problem solving might well help students to become more actively involved in learning. The student with teacher guidance in an ongoing units of study identifies a problem. The identified problem requires deliberation and thought for a solution. Information is gathered from a variety of reference sources to develop a tentative hypothesis.

The hypothesis is tested in a life like situation. If upheld through testing, the hypothesis remains as originally established. If the hypothesis is rejected as a result of testing, modification is then necessary. The learner, in problem solving, is actively involved in learning and not a bystander in the learning activity.

Sixth, the teacher needs to use a variety of learning activities. There are a plethora of possible activities and experiences for use in pedagogy. Learning stations may be developed in the classroom. With seven stations set up for a group of 25 students, the learner may choose what to learn with five tasks per station. Each station has five learning activities on task cards which clearly spell out each learning activity. The learner may then select which activities to pursue sequentially. The activities may be individually done or completed within a committee. The learner is the chooser.

Materials used for instruction should be housed at a resource centre in the classroom. Thus, reading materials, AV aids, illustrations, computer technology, among others, may be used readily by the student as needed at a learning station. Quality work needs to be done when evaluating each completed and ongoing task. The learner may then select a variety of learning activities from the different stations and inherent tasks. The student may omit those activities which do not have perceived purpose.

Seventh, the teacher needs to motivate each student in the classroom to achieve as optimally as possible. If students lack motivation, they be rather lethargic in the classroom. Energetic, enthused students need to be in the classroom setting. There are diverse means to motivate students to achieve as much as individual abilities permit. Among others, these include:

- verbal rewards by the teacher for work well done;
- self selection of learning experiences;
- use of preferred style of learning, such as participating in individual versus group tasks;
- use of peer teaching at specific intervals;
- hands on learning experiences;
- use of preferred intelligences in learning;
- use of self evaluation procedures;
- choosing how to reveal or indicate what has been learned.

Eighth, assisting the student to become involved in doing community service. To become a good citizen, the student needs to assist others who are less fortunate. With school supervision and depending upon the maturity of the involved learner, the following individual or group activities are examples when feasible for participation:

- presenting a programme at a nursing home;
- visiting with the elderly, the bereaved, and the sickly;
- sending birthday and holiday greetings to those visited in nursing and assisted living homes;
- do a favour for a known needy person in your neighbourhood. Have a parent go with you;
- paint a porch for an elderly person. This project is designed as a team effort supervised by the high school supervisor;
- do shopping with an elderly person who has mobility problems. A trusted adult should accompany, if necessary.

Ninth, the teacher should assist students, when ready, to become familiar with the community library. Here, the student should learn about the use of computer terminals to locate information. Students also need to learn to use reference books, periodicals, and daily newspapers, among other items.

Tenth, the teacher should realise that the student is the focal point of schooling. All other things are peripheral to the student and should assist the learner to achieve and learn as much as possible. Learning here consists not of subject matter only, but also to become a good citizen. Civility objectives include respecting others and accepting each as having much intrinsic worth.

Assessing the Classroom Teacher

There are a plethora of competencies needed by the classroom teacher. Presentations should be given with clarity of language and on the developmental level of the learner. Subject matter should be presented in an enthusiastic manner. The teacher then is indicating that what is to be learned has value. He/she must share with students what has been read personally. Students then learn that the teacher also reads and not they (the students) only are required to do so.

Voice inflection needs to be emphasised in teaching such as appropriate stress, pitch, and juncture. Questions raised of students should reflect what is salient and useful. Students need to have ample time to think about a possible response. Questions raised of students should be valid and cover what they have had a chance to learn. Higher levels of cognition should be involved in answering a question such as analytical thinking, synthesising, and evaluation. The teacher needs to relate knowledge such as building upon what a student has said.

The teacher must be able to work with diverse personalities in the classroom. Students differ from each other in a plethora of ways such as being:

- aggressive as compared to being more reserved;
- academically inclined as compared to desiring a hands on approach in learning;
- a very quiet classroom as compared to those liking a business like environment with an acceptable noise level or recorded music in the background;
- studying together with others as compared to working by the self;

- highly sociable as compared to being more of an introvert.

The teacher needs to use tenets of the principles of learning from educational psychology. The principles of learning provide guidelines for effective teaching of students. Thus, the teacher needs to secure learner interest so each becomes fully engaged in learning. Wholehearted involvement is important. With inherent interest, the student achieves from within rather than sources from without. Intrinsic motivation then is preferable to extrinsic motivation of students. As a result, the learner pursues and achieves on his/her own based on personal interests in ongoing lessons and units of study.

The teacher must use developmental psychology in teaching. He/she observes students carefully in determining the complexity level of what is to be taught. Also, the teacher takes careful note of using concrete (objects and items), semi-concrete (DVDs, video disks, video tapes, slides, filmstrips, films, illustrations, among other visuals), and abstract (textbooks, library books, reference books, internet) learning activities when thinking of assisting each to do well. The kinds of instructional materials selected might then be used in teaching and learning experiences to provide for diverse levels of student abilities. Each student needs to interact with those kinds of materials which are beneficial in optimal achievement.

Meaning theory must be inherent in all learning experiences. Thus, what is learned must make sense and is useful. Too frequently what is taught has not been understood by the student. If content is not understood, it cannot be used. Meaning needs to be present in all learning so that what has been learned may serve as building blocks for the new subject matter to be mastered. So often if students do not understand subject matter presented, they tend to memorise it for testing purposes. But this has little value to the student. What is meaningful can be transferred to new situations in life.

Reasons for learning must be accepted by students. The chances are that what is not purposeful will be rejected for study by the learner. The teacher may very briefly explain why selected items are important to learn within an ongoing lesson or unit of study. Or the teacher might assist students to inductively develop reasons for achieving selected objectives. Establishing purpose for student learning need not take long and yet the benefits there from may be quite great!

Sequential learnings need to be provided for students. With quality sequence, students do achieve more optimally as compared to non-sequential materials of instruction. Previously acquired information is then used to understand new content presented. Good sequence makes it so that what was presently learned may now be used as background information for the new ideas to be encountered.

Assessment procedures used by the teacher provide feedback on the quality of instruction provided as well as on student achievement. A variety of procedures, valid and reliable, need to be developed and used to ascertain progress in teaching and learning. These include:

- true false test items whereby the incorrect part is crossed out of a false statement by the student and then corrected with the correction written above each item;
- multiple choice test items in which each of the four distractors is plausible;
- completion test items in which there is enough information provided in each item so that students know what is wanted, but not too much so that clues are given as to which is correct as a response;
- matching tests whereby one column has more responses than the other so that the process of elimination may not be used excessively toward the end of taking this test;
- essay test items which require higher cognitive levels of thinking;
- observation methods which may be used rather continuously to diagnose and appraise as well as assist students to make continuous progress;
- results from state mandated tests to indicate which areas of knowledge and skill need more emphasis.

REFERENCES

Ediger, Marlow (2003), *"Challenge in Children's Literature,"* Journal of Research in Education, 2 (2), 9-13.

Ediger, Marlow (2002), *"Assessing Student Progress in Science"*, School Science, 39 (1), 61-66.

Malini, J. Sujatha (2002), *Competencies Required for Primary School Teachers to Handle Learning Difficulties in Children*. Karaiku, India: Alagappa University.

Mayer, R.E. and V.K. Sims (1994), *"For Whom is a Picture Worth a Thousand Words?* Extensions of a Dual Coding Multi Media Theory of Learning", Journal of Educational Psychology, 86, 389-401.

Mohanty, Jagannath, *"Education in Transition"*, Edutracks, 3 (3), 16-21.

National Science Teachers Association (2001), Classroom Assessment and the National Education Standards, Washington, DC: The Association, NSTA.

Searson, Robert, and Rita Dunn (2001), *"The Learning Styles Teaching Model"*, Science and Children, 38 (5), 22-36.

Assisting the New Teacher to do Well

The new teacher in school faces a plethora of challenges, especially a beginning teacher. There is a much that principals and experienced teachers may do to guide the new teacher toward excellence in teaching. A friendly accepting atmosphere needs to be in the offing. The new teacher must feel welcome to become a part of the faculty. He/she realised this is a new endeavour and needs to relate well toward other professionals as well as toward children in the school and classroom setting. What might be done to make for a positive beginning for the newcomer?

Accepting the New Teacher

The new teacher may feel acceptance in numerous ways. A reception should be held in the receiving school to introduce the new teacher to others in the school setting. A pleasant atmosphere can do much to initiate the new teacher to his/her role as a teacher. Name tags for each are a must. Individual teachers and the principal should each introduce themselves and converse briefly with the new teacher.

New teachers should also be introduced to where the school supplies are and how they are obtained, if there is a formal procedure. Prior to this time, the new teacher has seen the lunchroom and noticed how students are served here in terms of time schedule and rules of conduct. Proper manners of students, eating habits, and use of the environment to facilitate oral language skills of learners through conversation are salient to observe. The school is a teaching and learning institution and the lunchroom has its role to fulfil here. Misbehaviour needs to be channelled so that students are respectful and encouraging beings. An environment of excellence needs to pervade the lunchroom to include students achieving from where they are presently to a more ideal situation.

A mentor whose personality harmonises with the new teacher may become the person to assist in initiating the new teacher to achieve optimally (Ediger and Rao).

The Classroom Setting

The classroom setting is where the new teacher has many important responsibilities. The mentor teacher needs to assist the new teacher with the school's discipline code as well as implementation of the standards for appropriate behaviour. Quality means of motivation for learning will cut back on discipline problems. The new teacher needs to know how to motivate students to achieve. Motivated students do better in class as compared to the non-motivated. Diverse strategies to motivate and encourage learning need to be in the offing. Each student is important and should not be left behind. Rich learning opportunities need to be chosen so that there is something worthwhile for each learner to do and to achieve. Bulletin boards need to show student work. Interest centres need to possess fascinating things for students to look at and learn from items for these centres may come from children, from the school and from the teacher. Sometimes, local libraries have selected items to loan to schools for teaching and learning situations.

Directly outside the classroom door, displays of students' work may be poasted on the wall pertaining to an ongoing unit of study. Library books in the classroom need to be on diverse genres and different reading levels. They need to be readily accessible. The central library needs to have schedules in which learners may browse and check out desired reading materials. Library books should relate to units presently being studied, as well as for sustained silent reading, and for individualised reading.

Different ways of grouping students for instruction need to be discussed with the new teacher. The mentor teacher might then discuss teaching the class as a whole, small group instruction, individual work, homogeneous as well as heterogeneous grouping of students for instruction (Ediger, 1995).

Schedules need to be drawn up in terms of the allotted time for reading, mathematics, social studies, science, art, music, and physical education. Thus, there may be an integrated curriculum of science and mathematics. Other curriculum areas might also be taught in relationship to each other such as language, arts and social studies. The block of time, use of learning stations, peer learning and teaching, as well as other innovative instructional ideas will enter in to the way students are grouped for instruction. Scheduling for lunch, recess time, and special instruction in reading need adequate consideration. The role of the teacher in developing Individually Prescribed Plans (IEPs) for mainstreamed or full inclusion students need to follow federal and state guidelines. If, for example, a handicapped autistic child is assigned to a regular classroom, the teacher needs to have been involved in developing and then following the IEP criteria. Evidence needs to be shown if a student has achieved what is required in the IEP. The regular teacher, hopefully, will have an aide who can truly work with the handicapped student.

Planning Instruction

The mentor teacher may assist the new teacher in planning units of study and lesson plans. The objectives of instruction need careful selection. Each objective needs careful assessment. The objectives indicate what students are to learn as a result of instruction. Subject matter objectives need to be well sequenced and meaningful to students. Here, the new teacher may have problems in bringing down to the learner's understanding level the facts, concepts, and generalisations to be emphasised in ongoing lessons and units of study. Ideas expressed in highly complex terminology in university classrooms now need to be made meaningful in terms of subject matter to be taught to students. Skills objectives taught need to be properly sequenced and placed in order that each student might achieve these as optimally as possible. From the subject matter and skills learnings, the new teacher might also have students attain desirable attitudes as a result. What is learned must be applicable to new situations. The level of application is important. Each student needs to be assisted to use subject matter and skills acquired in salient, ensuing experiences.

By emphasising the psychology of learning, the new teacher helps each student to become engaged in ongoing activities to achieve objectives of instruction. Activities should be varied and include the concrete (objects, items, and excursions), the semi-concrete (illustrations, videos, CD ROMs, DVDs, films, filmstrips, slides, the interent, among others, to provide for individual differences), and the abstract (reading, writing, listening, and oral communication) experiences.

The interests of students need to be aroused which assist students in developing indepth learnings. The student and the curriculum then become one and not separate entities. Then too, purpose needs to be stressed in teaching and learning situations. With perceived purpose, students accept reasons for active involvement in learning. Passive recipients in learning then no longer are in the classroom (Ediger, 1996).

Assisting the New Teacher in Assessing Learner Progress

Much Stress is placed upon assessing student achievement. State mandated assessments have become a major hurdle for beginning teachers to plan for and to assist learners to do the best possible. These required tests are given in grades three through eight in reading and mathematics only, at this point. Students individually must pass the test to be promoted to the next higher grade level. Special tutoring may be necessary to help students do well on test day. If a school does not meet requirements two years in row, known as average yearly progress (ayp), students may then transfer to a passing school which might include a parochial school. Tuition costs are paid for by the sending school district. The failing school or school system has two years to eliminate weaknesses. If improvements are not adequate, the state may take over a school or complete district. There is pressure put onto school district to assist students to make adequate yearly progress. In grade ten exit tests are given to ascertain if students are to receive a high school diploma.

Report card data from each school pertaining to results on the state mandated test are to be printed in the local media to inform parents and others how well each school is doing in assisting student achievement.

States may vote to not give the state mandated test. But then they do not receive the allotted federal moneys. Punishment is there to motivate schools to do the best possible to help each student achieve as well as possible. High expectations are to be stressed in student achievement.

Since the state mandated tests are given yearly in selected grade levels, it behooves each classroom teacher to devise tests to periodically measure if students are achieving the state mandated objectives. These objectives are available to all teachers. The state mandated objectives provide some assistance to the teacher as to what will be tested upon in the mandated tests.

The mentor teacher needs to assist new teachers to devise tests to measure classroom achievement. Multiple choice test items generally will be written since this kind of test item appears on the state mandated test. Appropriate standards must be used to write multiple choice test items. The test must be valid and thus cover what has been taught. Clearly written multiple choice test items will tend to improve reliability or consistency in each student's test results.

Quality multiple choice test items have four responses, one of which is correct unless otherwise announced. Each of the four responses should be of similar length so as not to give away to the test taker which is the correct one. If a stem is used in a multiple choice test item, the stem and each response should make for a grammatically correct answer.

Should true/false test items be written by the teacher to measure student achievement, then students hold draw a line through the false part and correct it to make the item true. Students then do not guess if the item is false, but they need to show what is correct when the false part is crossed out.

There are a plethora of other procedures to use in the evaluative process:

1. use discussions to ascertain how much students have learned;
2. do teacher observation to notice on task behaviour;
3. keep diary and log entries on each student's achievement;
4. diagnose and remediate student errors and weaknesses in ongoing lessons;
5. model critical and creative thinking, as well as problem solving for students;
6. have students meet in small groups for specific purposes and assess their achievement needs therein;
7. conduct conferences with individual students as well as with small groups to obtain feed back from learner achievement.

Assisting the Beginning Teacher With Multiple Intelligences

Students in school possess multiple intelligences. Thus, a student may be strong in reading and writing, in particular. Another student may prefer art work to show achievement and progress. Individuals then are different from each other. There are different interests, purposes and goals which students have in mind and reveal to others. The following are examples of multiple intelligences:

- verbal intelligences. These individuals tend to excel in reading and writing endeavours;
- logical intelligence as in logic and reasoning emphasised in mathematics;
- musical/rhythmical as in writing lyrics and putting the words to music;
- interpersonal intelligence whereby the individual excels in working by the self;
- intrapersonal intelligence in which learning and the results of learning are best revealed through committee or small group work;

- bodily/kinesthetic intelligence whereby the learner learns best through and reveals what has been learned through manual dexterity;
- objective thinking as in ongoing sciences units of study (Gardner, 1993).

By studying each of the above named intelligences, the new teacher may notice that students certainly do differ from each other in many ways and these differences need to be taken into consideration in teaching and learning situations.

REFERENCES

Ediger, Marlow (1995), *Philosophy in Curriculum Development*. Kirksville, Missouri: Simpson Publishing Company.

Ediger, Marlow (1996), *Curriculum Improvement*. Kirksville, Missouri: Simpson Publishing Company.

Ediger, Marlow, and D. Bhaskara Rao (2003), *Elementary Curriculum Improvement*. New Delhi, India: Discovery Publishing House.

Gardner, Howard (1993), *Multiple Intelligence:* Theory into Practice. New York: Basic Books.

13

Teacher Education At Its Best

Universities need to update their objectives frequently. These knowledge, skills, and attitudinal ends need to be highlighted in the instructional arena. They must be carefully selected, from among alternatives. Committees within the university need to be chosen carefully since these members must deliberate indepth in selecting the objectives of instruction. Emphasis needs to be placed upon what university students need to learn during the twenty first century. Faculty members across the different schools within a university need to be actively involved in determining the kind of student to develop and promote.

Students who are able to identify and solve problems are needed. Higher levels of cognition need to be in the offing. Students then must be able to think analytically and creatively. Factual knowledge is to be used as building blocks to support main ideas and major generalisations. What is learned by students must be meaningful so that it can be applied in diverse situations. Learnings obtained must be related to the objectives of instruction.

The Role of the School of Education

The school of education within the university must turn out teachers who can stimulate pupil achievement. With state mandated objectives of instruction in the public schools, teachers have a major responsibility in assisting learners to:

1. perceive interest in learning. Engaged pupils are motivated to realise high expectations;
2. perceive purpose or reasons for achievement;
3. perceive the need to provide for individual differences among pupils;
4. perceive the need to assist pupils to accept each other in an atmosphere of respect;
5. perceive the need to work for home/school cooperation and harmony.

Schools of education need to strengthen the subject matter component of teaching. Working together with committees from the different academic divisions, faculty members from the school of education may assist students to integrate methods of instruction with subject matter, in the curriculum. This is a task which is well worth the involved effort. Teachers in the public schools need to be well versed in subject matter taught to pupils. A solid grounding in the academic discipline(s) taught as well as methods of public school instruction need to be well developed by students on the university level. A series of well planned meetings then need to accrue in working toward subject matter and methods of teaching strengths among preservice teachers. University accountability for strengthening both areas is necessary. Students on the university level need to be challenged to achieve high expectations and yet be successful in learning. Students are to become self motivated in learning in the academics as well as in the art/science of teaching. Higher levels of cognition must be stressed by the university professor in classes attended by students. Thus future teachers have a role model in emphasising critical and creative thinking, as well as problem solving in the public schools.

The self concept of students is important when working toward a university teaching degree. Friendly relations between students and faculty must be in the offing. Good human relations experienced by the university student provide a quality model for later experiences as he/she becomes a regular teacher in the public school classroom. University faculty members should be available when students have questions about teaching and learning situations, as well as about subject matter content. Problems and questions which students may have include:

1. how to keep public school pupils on task;
2. how to develop and implement lesson plans which stress pupils working on committees;
3. how to get reticent pupils involved in ongoing learning opportunities;
4. how to use, effectively, diverse kinds of computer programmes in teaching such as tutorial, drill and practice, simulation, and games. High standards in word processor use must be achieved by all pupils. State of the art technology must be in the offing and needs to be available so that each pupils may become skilled in gathering, organising, and using information;
5. how to assist pupils in multimedia approaches of instruction.

Students selected for teachers education preservice programmes need to be chosen carefully. They should come from the upper fiftieth percentile in academic achievement from their high school graduating class and be committed to teaching as a profession. Student scores from the SAT or ACT should be on the fiftieth percentile or higher. Teachers need to be able to make many choices and decisions in a school day and possessing mental acumen is salient. Preferably, portfolio of the senior year in high school accomplishments should provide the basis for an interview between a university faculty member from the school of education and the student. Prospective teachers should be of good moral character. They need to be able to work effectively with others. Positive human relations is of utmost importance. Continuing education for any teacher must be emphasised to develop knowledge and skills of the latest trends in teaching and learning.

For self development and good citizenship, public school pupils need the best education possible. The good citizen:

1. works for the good of the community;
2. cares for the welfare of others;

3. assists in promoting quality education for all;
4. assumes responsibility for actions taken;
5. works well with others in taking care of community responsibilities;
6. keeps up with local, state, and national news;
7. shows willingness to take on community positions and offices when asked to do so;
8. supports community efforts in improving society;
9. helps to achieve societal goals;
10. indicates a desire to serve others.

The School of Education

Within the school of education, instructors of teacher education classes need to have a broad base of general education as well as be highly qualified to teach pedagogy. Quality instruction for students presents a model to emulate in later public school teaching and learning situations. Methods of teaching need to stress, inductive and deductive procedures, problem solving, inquiry approaches, probing, application of learnings, and brain storming, among others. It is important for students to understand the purposes of different means of grouping pupils for instruction. These include team teaching, the non-graded school, heterogeneous and homogeneous grouping, learning centres, enrichment stations, small group instruction, and individual endeavours.

In teaching reading, students need to learn about and implement diverse strategies in word recognition including use of phonics, syllabication, context clues, and picture clues. Pupils need to achieve well in analytical thinking, synthesising, and indepth questioning skills.

Relevant theories of learning need to be acquired and practiced. These include stimulus response, reinforcement theory, hands on approaches, and gestalt psychology. Classroom climate and styles of learning are salient to consider when planning for instruction. The noise level, temperature reading, interpersonal versus intrapersonal activities, as well as:

1. emotional elements such as conformity versus non-conformity. Preferences in terms of what to learn needs consideration;
2. collegial relations versus structure in the curriculum;
3. seated in rows and columns versus flexible ways of grouping for instruction;
4. psychological factors in being analytic learners who focuses on step by step instruction as compared to global learners who desire to relate what is learned to the self and then study the related facts;
5. a teacher determined curriculum versus units of study involving pupil/teacher planning (See Searson and Dunn).

Multiple intelligences theory needs to be presented and demonstrated in the university classroom as well as by professors within student teaching experiences. Multiple intelligences emphasises that a single IQ score does not exist, but that within a group, pupils possess numerous kinds of intelligence. These include:

1. verbal as in reading and writing;
2. logical as in reasoning. Mathematics provides a god model for the use of reasoning skills;
3. musical/rhythmical as in writing lyrics and putting them to music;
4. intrapersonal as in pupils revealing optimal achievement in working by the self;
5. interpersonal whereby a pupil reveals intelligence in group or committee situations;
6. bodily/kinesthetic as in optimal skills shown in manual dexterity learnings;
7. scientific intelligences as in objective thinking in science and other academic learnings (See Gardner).

The teacher then needs to be aware that pupils in any classroom show strengths in learning in different ways. Pupils differ from each other in a plethora of ways and this includes what each can do best. It is good to use the strengths of individual pupils in teaching and learning situations. For any inservice teacher, there are numerous variables to consider when planning for instruction. One variable is to know each pupil well in terms of what he/she shows ability in. Thus, careful observation of each pupil's behaviour will be in evidence. Recorded behaviours should be made. Meticulous observations of each student in terms of strengths possessed should be recorded and dated. It is easier to make careful observations if sequence is in evidence. Review of written observations must be made to refute or corroborate previously recorded information. In time, the teacher should make quality observations which assist in identifying individual talents of pupils. Units of study in any academic area may be strengthened by using pupils abilities. Talents not used hinder a pupil's development and achievement.

In committee endeavours, pupils may identify and use learner abilities in developing and completing a project. Pupils should never be minimised for trying but rather encouraged to attain, grow, and accomplish.

The school of education also has a major responsibility in faculty members using proper standards for evaluating the progress of university teacher education students. There are six worthwhile goals in assessment from the National Research Council (NRC) and include the following:

- articulate a research based rationale for helping teachers improve classroom assessment;
- clarify the concept of effective classroom assessment;
- provide illustrations and guides to the development and selection of assessment processes and tools;
- assist teacher educators and staff developers who will include assessment in their work with prospective and practising teachers;
- address issues that school and district decision makers face in their efforts to improve classroom instruction.

Valid and reliable tests and assessment need to be used to appraise learner progress. Formal and informal procedures need to be used. Formative evaluation points to a way of improving instruction within a time frame whereas summative evaluation indicates an end of unit or end of term evaluation. Passing state mandated tests has become an object of concern for pupils. Schools of education in their course offerings need to emphasise the importance of quality instruction to meet these mandates.

REFERENCES

Aiken, Adel G., and Lisa Bayer (2002), *"They Love Words"*, The Reading Teacher, 56 (1), 68-75.

Astleitner, Herman (2002), *"Teaching Critical Thinking Online,"* Journal of Instructional Psychology, 29 (2), 53-76.

Chappuis, Stephen, and Richard J. Stiggins (2002), *"Classroom Assessment for Learning"*, Educational Leadership, 60 (1), 40-41.

Ediger, Marlow, and D. Bhaskara Rao (2000), *Teaching Reading Successfully.* New Delhi, India: Discovery Publishing House, Chapter Eight.

Ediger, Marlow (2002), *"Developing a Reading Community"*, Edutracks, 1 (4), 16-19.

Ediger, Marlow (2002), *"Social Studies and the Guidance Counsellor"*, Experiments in Education, 30 (9), 176-181.

Ediger, Marlow (2002), *"Improving Spelling"*, Reading Improvement, 39 (2), 69-70.

Gardner, Howard (1983), *Frames of Mind: The Theory of Multiple Intelligences.* New York: Basic Books.

Maslow, A.H. (1954), *Motivation and Personality.* New York: Harper and Row.

Meyer, Richard J. (2002), *"Captives of the Script: Killing Us Softly with Phonics"*, The Reading Teacher, 79 (6), 452-461.

National Science Teachers Association (2001), *Classroom Assessment and the National Education Standards.* Washington, DC: the Association, NSTA.

Searson, Robert, and Rita Dunn (2001), *"The Learning Styles Teaching Model"*, Science and Children, 38 (5), 22-36.

Teaching Vocabulary Development

There are a plethora of approaches which teachers may use to teach vocabulary. Each procedure needs to be assessed in terms of how it assists students to use words more accurately and qualitatively. There are rather exact terms to use in speaking and writing which are quantitative. Others are used more effectively if a qualitative emphasis is in the offing. Sometimes, a metaphor or smile might then say things more thoroughly. How should vocabulary development be taught?

Memorisation of Vocabulary Terms

When being a senior in a small rural high school during the 1945-46 school year, a plan was developed by the faculty whereby each student was to keep a vocabulary notebook with ten new words chosen and their respective definitions entered therein each week. The notebooks were collected on Friday, evaluated, and returned on the following Monday. A few students did a short cut by merely listing ten words contained in a dictionary and writing their related meanings. These students placed very little effort into writing the vocabulary terms. Other students did put forth effort in developing a new list of functional words. There were very few directions given by the faculty for selecting new vocabulary terms to be entered into the vocabulary notebook. Was there any value in doing this kind of an activity and requirement? The author still remembers a few words he entered in his vocabulary notebook. It seems as if some learning accrued here in vocabulary development and remembered in time. The notebooks were evaluated each week by an instructor and specific comments made. Might better ways have been used to teach and learn vocabulary (Ediger and Rao).

Contextual Vocabulary Development

There are numerous ways in which vocabulary development may accrue within a context. Thus, new words may be located, and studied in context. A good example here is to assist students to use contextual clues. If a student does not recognise a word in reading, the surrounding words might provide the word and its meaning. This does leave leeway for other words to fit into context in addition to the correct word. However, even then, vocabulary development is taking place in word play and in a thinking situation. With context clues, New words and their respective meaning(s) are being studied where relationships are being stressed. When students perceive relationships, they will have a tool to use in identifying correct meanings in vocabulary development.

An unknown word may also be recognised and understood through the use of syllabication. If the student takes away either the prefix/suffix of an unknown word, the word might then be knowable. There are very common prefixes and suffixes which the student may recognise. Thus, with stripping a prefix/suffix, the word which was unknown and is now identifiable. These affixes also have a meaning which assists students in vocabulary development. Thus, the following have a morphemic meaning: un, ex, and ir beginnings and er, ly, and dy endings.

Vocabulary Development Across the Curriculum

Many educators are emphasising the across the curriculum psychology of learning be it in vocabulary, writing, speaking, reading, and listening. There are vocabulary terms common to all curriculum areas as well as those related to a specific academic discipline such as meridians, parallels, degrees, longitude, and latitude in geography. It is wise for teachers to stress vocabulary in all academic disciplines since there is a transfer of learning to all curriculum areas.

There are viable terms which need identification, not trivia, which should aid students to become better readers, writers, speakers, and listeners. There are valuable goals in school and in the societal arenas. Which criteria should teachers then use to choose integrated vocabulary terms of worth?

1. they should possess challenging, frequency of use possibilities;
2. they should have intrinsic student purposes and yet challenge students to reach out, achieve, and accomplish new objectives;
3. they should be interesting for student use;
4. they should be meaningful to learners;
5. they should assist students to apply that which has been learned.

Multiple intelligences theory emphasises that each student has one or more intelligence (Gardner). These talents of students may be revealed in different ways such as in the following:

1. verbal intelligences as in reading and writing;
2. logical reasoning to secure information and to show what was learned;
3. musical/rhythmical such as in writing lyrics and then setting them to music;
4. intrapersonal intelligence whereby the learner indicates best what has been learned through individual endeavours;
5. interpersonal intelligence in which a learner may show much talent to achieve well within a group;
6. bodily/kinesthetic in which a student shows much ability in physical prowess and use of the gross/smaller muscles;
7. scientific intelligence which is the heart of the science curriculum. Objective thinking can be stressed much in abilities possessed within all curriculum areas.

The teacher needs to establish high goals which are achievable in vocabulary. A wide variety of learning opportunities must be used in vocabulary development. They are necessary in order that the student becomes increasingly interested in broadening horizons to communicate more effectively. Each listed intelligence has opportunities for indepth, vocabulary achievement. Thus, in a science unit on "The Changing Surface of the Earth," the student in a meaningful context might well attach understanding to the following: earthquakes, floods, tornados, hurricanes, mudslides, erosion, hail, and rock slides. A rich learning environment with varied experiences may help a student to attach meaning to any identified vocabulary term. Quality assessment methods should be used to ascertain achievement.

Computer Use and Vocabulary Development

There are a plethora of computer programmes in vocabulary. In addition to commercially written programmes, proficient teachers, individually and/or cooperatively, have developed programmes to assist students in this area. These programmes may stress:

1. a gaming approach whereby students individually or in a committee work on competing in a game. There may be wholesome competitive sides involved in playing the vocabulary game. The game should focus on words and their meanings within a rich learning environment;
2. a diagnostic and remediation programme assists students to learn techniques and procedures in attaching meaning to newly encountered words. These kinds of programmes extend student learnings as well as encourage, not discourage, interest in learning;
3. tutorial programmes assist students to attain sequentially new vocabulary terms. Programmed items focus upon a logical order which helps students to acquire needed skills in word, term recognition as well as attain a meaningful vocabulary in ongoing lessons and units of study;

4. simulation programmes assist students to achieve and learn within a life like situation. The simulation attempts to breathe life into what students are learning (See Coiro).

Carefully, written programmes help learners to enjoy and accomplish in the ongoing vocabulary development curriculum. The programme might stress vocabulary achievement in a specific academic discipline or across the curriculum. Computerised programmes are another avenue to place high priority in guiding students to increase skills in oral, written, reading, and listening abilities. Appropriate programmes adapted to learner needs must be found. These programmes need to capture student attention and be engaging. They need to sustain learner attention to optimise achievement. Working by the self or with others might well be fascinating to learners.

Learning Styles Theory

Learning styes theory has much to offer in assisting students to achieve vital objectives. It emphasises conditions under which more optimal learner achievement is possible. The teacher needs to study the learning environment and make conjectures on what it is which will help students to learn, grow and achieve. Learning styles theory looks at opposite ends of the continuum as to the kinds of environments students might best learn under. Thus, the teacher needs to study and gather information on each student in the following, among other, areas of a learning environment:

1. does the student do better on individual or group endeavours?
2. does the student achieve more optimally with a structure programme or student centred curriculum?
3. does the student prefer a relatively quiet environment for learning or does a busy classroom, with positive sounds indicating students are engaged in learning, assist in more optimal achievement;
4. does the student prefer conformity as compared to positive open ended class work in the school setting?

5. does the student prefer being seated in rows and columns or should there be flexible seating arrangements?
6. does the student prefer an abstract subject centred curriculum as compared to a hands on approach in ongoing lessons and activities (See Searson and Dunn)?

Differences such as those listed above come in degrees of preference between opposite ends of the continuum. For example, a student might prefer individual endeavours some of the time and committee work at other times. Or, a hands on approach in learning periodically, and then reading experiences at other times.

Conclusions

Vocabulary development may be emphasised throughout the teaching and learning day. It is essential that learners develop a rich vocabulary to communicate more effectively with others. Listening, speaking, reading, and writing vocabulary proficiencies need to be planned for as well as implemented spontaneously in the language arts. Teachers need to share ideas on enriching learning opportunities for students in vocabulary use. Application of what has been learned may accrue in diverse methods and procedures in the curriculum.

REFERENCES

Coiro, Julle (2003), *"Exploring Literacy on the Internet"*, The Reading Teacher, 56 (5), 458-464.

Ediger, Marlow, and D. Bhaskara Rao (2003), *Language Arts Curriculum*. New Delhi, India: Discovery Publishing House.

Searson, Robert and Dunn, Rita (2001). *"The Learning Styles Teaching Model"*, Science and Children, 38 (5), 22-36.

Gardner, Howard (1993), *Multiple Intelligence; Theory into Practice*. New York: Basic Books.

Speaking, Listening, and Writing

The Forgotten Language Arts Areas

With much emphasis being placed upon reading and mathematics in state mandated testing, it behooves school personnel to not forget speaking, listening, and writing in the curriculum. Testing tends to stress what are deemed essentials for student mastery. However in the daily operations of the classroom, much emphasis is placed upon speaking, listening, and writing, even in the case of drill on the fundamentals in preparation for statewide testing. These three language arts areas are used heavily in school and in society. They are salient across the curriculum.

Speaking Activities in the Curriculum

Students need to develop proficiency to communicate orally. There are diverse kinds of experiences which require oral communication. These include classroom discussions, oral reports, debates, making introductions, reading aloud, committee work, and cooperative endeavours such as in doing construction/art activities. There are ongoing objectives which students need to achieve in oral communication. These include:

1. speaking so all can hear clearly what is said;
2. using pitch, juncture, and stress appropriately within sentences;

3. facing the ones spoken to in face to face interaction;
4. emphasising politeness in the communicative act;
5. stressing facial expressions and other non-verbal means which facilitate communication;
6. giving everyone a chance to participate in informal conversation;
7. being positive in interacting with others;
8. using good sequence of ideas when speaking;
9. observing facial expressions of listeners to notice if the methods of presentation are conducive to good listening;
10. show by example the kinds of behaviours desired of students.

Oral communication experiences should be pleasant to the speaker as well as to the listener. Eagerness to communicate with others indicates an interest to use oral means of communication. If rudeness or impoliteness exist in difficult interactions, then confidence in the self and others may go downhill. It is much better to encourage an I/thou feeling whereby both the speaker and the listener are important. This feeling facilitates communication among those involved. If students are habituated to use put downs, intimidation, and haughty remarks, then goals need to be set to stress behaviour conducive to ideas circulating between and among persons involved in oral communication. Frequent assessment needs to be in the offing to notice if progress is being made toward achieving these goals.

Listening Across the Curriculum

An excellent way of learning may well be to become a good listener in the school and community. Students realise many times that they have missed out on salient ideas because of poor listening in an ongoing classroom discussion. Or, they wished that more careful listening had been involved in conversing with a friend. It would then not have been necessary to ask to have so many statements repeated. Good listening habits can be developed through effort. Much work goes into becoming a good listener, it may not come easy, but it is certainly important to be attentive.

Which are selected criteria to follow in learning to listen well?

1. consider it a personal goal to work in the direction of becoming a good listener. This is an ongoing objective;
2. have a relevant purpose in mind for listening, such as wanting to learn more about agriculture in the Middle East in a social studies unit;
3. attempt to focus on the spoken content only. Do not pay attention to distractions;
4. notice points of emphasis being made in oral communication. The presenter of ideas is stressing certain points more than others;
5. organise ideas being listened to in terms of major and subordinate content;
6. secure background information, if possible, before listening to ideas being presented;
7. rehearse ideas after a listening activity has been completed;
8. reflect upon acquired ideas through critical and creative thinking;
9. an intrinsic want to become a better listener;
10. develop an attitude of feeling the importance of quality listening.

It is important to develop good attitudes within students for improved listening. If students do not feel that purpose is involved in listening, the chances are listening will fall by the wayside. An attitude of wanting to and feeling purpose in listening are musts! Then too, students and the teacher need to work on securing student interest in the subject matter to be listened to. Interest is a powerful factor in listening and learning.

Writing Across the Curriculum

What is spoken and what is listened to can be put into writing. Thus, listening, speaking, and writing are integrated language arts areas. However, there are specifics which apply to the area of writing. Writing, perhaps, is the most difficult of the three language arts areas. Why? It consists of abstract symbols (graphemes) which need to relate to the graphemes (sounds) of a language. Perceiving grapheme/phoneme relationships are essential in order to write effectively and this comes with practice. A variety of rich learning activities need to be in the offing to provide for sequential achievement. Developmentally appropriate experiences must be provided for students individually as well as collectively. Individual differences need to be provided for in the classroom. What are additional criteria to implement in teaching writing?

Writing must be an engaging experience. Students must be thoroughly involved in each writing activity. Essential, achievable goals need to be emphasised. Each student must perceive the need for writing. A needs based writing curriculum should then be emphasised. The student perceives needs as well as the teacher observing carefully what individual students need. Then too, each writing opportunity needs to make sense to the student. Nonsense activities, rarely if ever, make for optimum learning, or even any learning at all. Meaning theory is of utmost importance to stress in writing. Thus, there needs to be student input in an ongoing experience. The teacher is a guide and motivates student learning. He/she possesses knowledge of writing which, hopefully, students will also master. The teacher should model what quality writing is so students may emulate the model. Writing activities should emphasise that which is achievable and then gradually more complex experiences need to be in the offing. Doing much reading benefits students much in learning increasingly more complex vocabulary terms as well as word recognition techniques. The teacher needs to read aloud interesting literature to whet appetites for students reading to the self. The oral reading activity stresses student listening and the ideas read may be discussed orally. A transfer of learning may then take place to written work. It takes a plethora of interesting ideas to do writing. The student must be something to write about. Many of the choices in topics for written work should be selected by students. Students tend to write more effectively when self selection of ideas is in the offing.

A beginning writing activity may stress a student dictating content to the teacher who in turn writes the ideas on a sheet of paper. If the group dictates the ideas, then these may be printed, also, in neat manuscript style on the chalkboard. The student(s) may read the ideas together as the teacher points to the words read aloud. Students may copy the contents from the paper or chalkboard, resulting in a meaningful, understood writing experience. The contents for an experience chart should become increasingly more complex. Many times, motivated young students will practice writing ideas on their own. Soon, students will have developed a basic writing vocabulary which will grow with increased emphasis being placed upon written work. It is good to have a reading/writing connection since reading does provide many suggestions for written work. With the modelling or writing in experience charts, students will notice how words can record oral communication. Students need to notice the values of writing. The experience chart concept or individual student writing may be used in many forms of written work such as in the following:

1. writing announcements such as for an upcoming Parent Teacher Association meeting;
2. writing invitations for a birthday party which include the four w's of *what* will occur, *when* it will occur, *where* it will occur, and *why* it will occur;
3. writing a poem involving subject matter of one's own choosing;
4. writing a narrative or an expository selection;
5. writing a description of objects on an interest centre;
6. writing a joke or humorous incident;
7. writing for pleasure;
8. writing a summary or conclusion;
9. writing to show sequence in completing a task;
10. writing an introduction to a story.

There are a plethora of purposes in writing which may be dictated to the teacher who will be doing the writing. A peer who writes might also copy the dictated words. The student needs to engage in doing the written work as soon as necessary skills are in their domain. Generally, children are eager to begin actively participating in written work when readiness is in evidence. The dictation phase of written work leads to active participation in writing. Encouragement of learners is salient in order for the student to develop feelings of efficacy, independence, and motivation. What might the teacher do to stimulate a classroom atmosphere of motivated writing?

1. display student written work on a bulletin board in the adjacent hallway of the classroom;
2. show and discuss written work of the student to the parent in parent/teacher conferences;
3. write articles to the local newspaper informing the community of what students are doing in written work in the classroom;
4. discuss with students the importance of being good writers such as the need to communicate in everyday situations including the writing of business and friendly letters;
5. show students what you, the teacher, have written recently. This can be a model for children;
6. read children's writings aloud from magazines written for public school pupils;
7. assist students to submit a writing for publication in an appropriate journal;
8. develop a writer's club in school which has a definite time and place for meeting;
9. invite parents to assist their offspring in writing for a variety of purposes;
10. send home written work of the student to parents and ask for comments. The school and the home need to work cooperatively for the good of the child.

There are indeed an abundance of writing opportunities for students. Each student needs to develop port folio of written work completed in school. A random sampling of written products should be inherent in the port folio. The port folio might well stress accountability of the teacher for student achievement. Many educators are recommending students keep a port folio to show achievement. Port folio entries may be selected at different intervals of time. Standardised tests are given once a year, at the most, but port folio results are ongoing and continuous in evaluating learner achievement and progress.

Student use of the word processor should be encouraged as readiness permits. Most find the word processor an interesting and facilitating device to use. Errors made in writing may be corrected rather readily on a word processor with no typing paper involved. Thus on the monitor, students may notice errors of sentence structure, spelling, as well as punctuation marks. These may readily be corrected without starting over again in the written content. The student must always remember that:

1. words misspelled need to be close enough to the correct spelling so that spell checkers may provide the correct spelling. Being a good speller is as important as ever. At the same time, spell checkers can indeed provide the student with much assistance in the mechanics of writing;
2. much knowledge of correct punctuation is still as necessary as ever, but the marks may be inserted in the written work shown on the monitor;
3. sentence structure may be modified or corrected on the monitor. Starting completely anew in using the key board is not necessary when the word processor is used;
4. a satisfactory writing may be seen on the monitor before a final copy is printed with the use of the attached printer.

Factors in Learning

There are selected factors which need emphasising in speaking, listening, and writing activities. These factors are contained in the following methods of teaching which assist students to achieve well:

1. securing the attention of students with engaging experiences;
2. stressing meaning in whatever students pursue in the curriculum;

3. emphasising reasons or intrinsic purpose for pursuing learning activities;
4. pursuing creative endeavours whereby uniqueness and originality of subject matter is ongoing;
5. having students engaged in assessing the self.

REFERENCES

Brown, Kathleen J. (2003), *"What Do I Say When They Get Stuck On A Word? Aligning Teacher Prompts With Student's Development"*, The Reading Teacher, 56 (8), 720-733.

Dewey, John (1916), *Democracy and Education*. New York: The MacMillan Company.

Douillard, Kim (2002), *"Going Past Done: Creating Time for Reflection in the Classroom"*, The Language Arts, 80 (2), 92-99.

Ediger, Marlow (1997), *Teaching Reading and the Language Arts*. Kirksville, Missouri: Simpson Publishing Company, Chapter Five.

——(2002), *"Measurement Theory Versus Constructivism"*, Journal of Research in Education, 1(1), 7-10.

——(1998), *Teaching Reading Successfully in the Elementary School*. Kirksville, Missouri: Simpson Publishing Company, Chapter Eight.

Ediger, Marlow, and D. Bhaskara Rao (2003). *Elementary Curriculum*. New Delhi, India: Discovery Publishing House, Chapter Eight.

Hoff, David (September 3, 2003), *"Large Scale Study Finds Poor Math, Science Instruction"*, Education Week, 23(1) 3.

Gardner, Howard (1993), *Multiple Intelligence: Theory into Practice*. New York: Basic Books.

Searson, Robert, and Dunn, Rita (2001), *"The Learning Styles Teaching Model"*, Science and Children, 38 (5), 22-26.

Slavin, R. L., and N.I. Karweit (1984), *"Mastery Learning and Student Teams: A Factorial Experiment in Urban General Mathematics Classes"*, American Educational Research Journal, 21: 725-736.

Symonds, W.C. (2000, September 25), *"A Technology Revolution is About to Sweep America's Classrooms"*, Business Week, 116-128.

Listening in the Language Arts Curriculum

Listening is the first skill experienced by the individual. Much is involved in listening to that which is meaningful. Comprehension of content is the major goal in listening. To do this a plethora of subskills need development. The individual needs to be aware of specific sounds such as phonemes. Each phoneme comes in a selected order or sequence. Understanding the meaning of each sound, or combination thereof, is important to the listener. Sounds are made up of phonemes or phonetic elements, as well as morphemes which make up the smallest unit of meaning. To assist in comprehending, the units of sound are made up of consonants, vowels, diphthongs, and digraphs.

Meaning in Listening

The listener must arrive at some order of the individual and collective sounds made in oral communication. This order must become automatic to the student in order to achieve the major goal of listening and that being communication. Parts of speech assist in providing order. Nouns indicate what is being spoken about and in traditional grammar names a person, place, or thing. Verbs indicate an action or a state of being pertaining to the noun, or in this case the subject of the sentence. Verbs may indicate a present, past, or participle tense or time. Adjectives add meaning to nouns. In other words, adjectives modify nouns. Adjectives may be single words, phrases, or clauses. Adverbs also modify and thus indicate the change of meaning of a verb, adjective, or other adverb. These four parts of speech are called form words. They do provide structure to a sentence.

Function words include prepositions which show a relationship, for example, between two things or a person and an object, e.g. The man sat in the chair. The preposition "in" indicates a relationship between "man" and "chair". Prepositions are few in number, basically. These include the following: on, in front of behind, beside, into, from. A second function word, conjunction, joins together that which is of equal value. The word "and" is a very common conjunction and may join two nouns, verbs, adjectives, phrases, or pronouns. Pronouns represent a third function word and they substitute for nouns. There are few pronouns in number, including he, she, it, we, you, they, them. The fourth function word, namely interjections, are single words or a phrase, which emphasise strong feeling, e.g. "Oh!"

Parts of speech are learned sequentially as students mature in language use. Some may never or seldom use, orally, the words "part(s) or speech," but they do provide building blocks in oral and written communication. Writers tend to be very much aware of these parts of speech. Communicating ideas involves listening, speaking, reading, and writing. These four language arts areas permeate the different curriculum areas. Thus, it is important to emphasise the four vocabularies of the language arts in literature, science, mathematics, social studies, art, music, and physical education.

Listening, the first skill encountered by an infant, emphasises sequential achievement. This involves:

1. building blocks for accumulating knowledge;
2. vocabulary concepts to use across the curriculum;
3. ideas to use in critical and creative thinking;
4. diverse purposes such as securing directions, and background information for an activity;
5. identification of a problem, development of a tentative hypothesis, and of testing the hypothesis;

6. ability to interact with others in a discussion;
7. locating main and subordinate ideas;
8. the separation of relevant from non-relevant information;
9. intonation and pauses within subject matter listened to;
10. review of previously acquired subject matter.

There are a multiplicity of listening activities available in the classroom setting. Teachers then need to stress listening in all curriculum areas. Purposes needed to be established for any activity involving listening. Thus within a lesson involving textbook subject matter, the teacher may notice the quality of listening on the part of students. Criteria to emphasise include all participating and no one dominating the discussion. Respect for the thinking of others is important. Ideas should circulate within the discussion group. Teacher directed as well as peer lead discussions should be in the offing. Adequate time needs to be given for thought when ideas are being presented. Interrupting others should not be permitted. Rules of conduct for discussions may be developed and posted in the classroom. Periodically, students with teacher guidance need to assess how well the recommended criteria for the discussion are being achieved.

When project methods are used in teaching, the teacher needs to motivate students in thinking about the kinds of projects to develop. Worthwhile projects have instructional values and assist students to attach indepth meaning to what is being studied. There are definite objectives for students to attain in developing a project. Students with teacher guidance need to keep the objectives in mind when pursuing the project. Planning must be done so that quality is in evidence in the project. Ultimately, there needs to be evaluation of the finished project. Standards need development in order to assess the worth of the project. Listening, speaking, reading and writing are important while projects are worked on toward completion. Developmental projects which might be emphasised include the following:

1. a model farm scene showing modern practices in farming. Here, learnings are revealed by students in a social studies unit of study;

2. a mural indicating changes in the earth's surface as in volcanic eruptions, erosion, mudslides, folding, and faulting. Students indicate what was accomplished in a science unit.

Construction activities stress the importance not only of what has been constructed, but also growth in achievement in the four language arts areas of listening, speaking, reading and writing. Construction activities might well involve constructing a solar unit in science, geometric figures (squares, rectangles, triangles, trapezoids and parallelograms) in mathematics, and a bedouin village when studying the Middle East in social studies. The construction activity should stress "what is worth doing, is worth doing well". Quality standards need to be kept in mind when constructing that which relates directly to an ongoing unit of study. Neatness and effort should come forth when construction activities are in the offing.

Journaling should be experienced by all learners. With the keeping of a journal, the student records what has been learned in an ongoing unit of study. Major ideas and specific facts acquired may be discussed in a committee setting before being recorded. Or, the recorded ideas may be shared with others in a group setting. With the journal as a reference source, the student may review major generalisations achieved. Not only may students review what has been learned, but they also have a use for these ideas and that being to apply in writing what is salient.

A classroom newspaper may be written and developed to tell what students are studying in the different curriculum areas. The articles for each academic area need to be discussed by designated committees. Sharing of ideas and assessing the content for each curriculum area are significant. Each participant needs to have his/her ideas heard in an atmosphere of respect. Committee work should be a pleasant experience whereby satisfied learners are an end result. When committee work is enjoyed, participants perceive the values of cooperative learning.

There should also be ample opportunities for students to work individually. There are a plethora of good learning activities for individual study. Thus, a student may discuss with the teacher in doing a set of illustrations relating to what was achieved from reading the basal. These carefully planned and completed illustrations indicate what the student has learned, for example, in;

1. a unit on the Middle Ages in a social studies unit. The illustrations may show workers in a guild in being a beginner, a journey man, and then a master in making a tea set;
2. illustrating a rock collection in a unit on Rocks and Minerals, in science;
3. showing the digestive system in health education study.

These illustrations may be shown and discussed with peers in a small group or whole class session. Careful listening is important during the discussion.

There are good ways to assess listening quality among students in the classroom. Informally, the teacher may notice which students are attentive in responding to questions. Those who are more reserved in responding may indicate learnings acquired in testing situations. However, the reserved student should also be encouraged to participate fully in discussions. Rewarding the shy student for participating is a must! Success in learning makes for more success. The self concept of the reserved learner needs attention so that he/she feels well about the self. These students should never be ridiculed, put down, or minimised. Rather the student needs to feel good about the self intrinsically. Confidence in the self to achieve, develop, and grow is highly salient. This is true of listening as well as in all facets of life and living.

Methods of Teaching

There are many excellent methods of teaching which might well enhance good listening habits. The teacher needs to use interesting methods of instruction. These methods tend to engage the student in learning. The teacher may observe which students are and which are not actively involved in learning as a result of the activity being emphasised. If a few students are not engaged in learning, the teacher needs to think of and implement that which captures learner interest.

The teacher needs to make certain that students understand what is being presented in a lesson. Meaningful learning is important for good listening to occur. Many times, student have turned off in listening due to not understanding the inherent subject matter content being discussed. When students take part in a discussion, it is good for them to show understanding by putting the content into their very own words. By doing this, students indicate they understand what has been read.

Salient purposes need to be in the offing for a listening activity. There are times when students might wish to discuss selected questions during a discussion. At other times, the teacher may state purposes for discussing. Students do need to perceive purpose for a discussion. These purposes become rational reasons for a specific learning opportunity.

A variety of learning opportunities need to be provided students so that boredom does not set in and interest is renewed. Personal needs of students may be met with change, as needed, in learning activities. From a reading experience, of adequate duration, to a writing activity emphasises providing for individual differences when developmental tasks are in the offing. There are a plethora of activities available for students including the concrete (objects, items, realia) semi-concrete (video tapes, filmstrips, slides, and illustrations) as well as abstract tasks (listening, speaking, reading and writing as well as computer use). All students should sequentially develop mastery in word processor applications.

Each student should experience high expectations in doing quality work. The high expectations should include student success in learning. The self concept is developed more fully with students feeling that they can succeed in life. Students should also develop feelings that they belong to the group and classroom setting and that esteem needs can be met. With esteem needs being met, students can be recognised for doing well. There are many needs which students possess. To achieve optimally in listening and the language arts, students need to have physiological needs met such as appropriate food, clothing, water and clean/safe shelter. They need to feel wanted and accepted in the home/school setting. Students need to develop feelings of worth and purpose in the societal realm.

Conclusion

Quality objectives, learning activities to achieve the stated ends, and a good, valid and reliable, assessment programme need to be in the offing for each student. Meeting needs of students is important if optimal achievement is to be in evidence!

REFERENCES

Cuddeback, Meghan, and Maria A. Ceprano (2002), *"The Use of Accelerated Reader with Emergent Readers"*, Reading Improvement, 39 (2), 89-95.

Ediger, Marlow, and D. Bhaskara Rao (2003), *Improving School Administration*. New Delhi, India: Discovery Publishing House, 141 and 142.

Ediger, Marlow, and D. Bhaskara Rao (2003), *Language Arts Curriculum*. New Delhi, India: Discovery Publishing House, Chapter Thirteen.

Ediger, Marlow (1988), *The Elementary Curriculum*, 2nd Edition. Kirksville, Missouri: Simpson Publishing Company, Chapter Seven.

Epstein, Joyce (1995), *"School/Family/Community* Partnerships", Phi Delta Kappan, 76: 704.

Friedrich, L.E. (1983), *"The Second Budgeting Cycle,"* Winneconne, Wisconsin.

Paris, Scott (2002), *"Centre for Improvement of Early Reading Achievement"*, Reading Teacher, 55 (2), 170.

Richard, Alan (September 4, 2002), Florida Sees Surge in Use of Vouchers", Education Week, 1, 34.

Risko, Virginia, J. et. al. (2002), *"Preparing Teachers for Reflective Practice: Intentions, Contradictions and Possibilities"*, Language Arts, 82 (2), 134-144.

Tyler, Ralph (1949), *Basic Principles of Curriculum Construction*. Chicago: University of Chicago Press.

Identification of New Words in Reading

There are a Plethora of Methods to Use in Assisting Students to Identify Unknown Words in Reading. Each has its advantages in assisting the learner to comprehend and attach meaning to what is being read. The ultimate goal in teaching word recognition techniques to students is to guide optimal reading comprehension. Identifying words correctly helps the student to understand narrative, expository, and creative content. Which procedures may be used by the teacher to guide students in correct word recognition?

Providing for Individual Students

To identify an unknown word, the teacher may immediately pronounce the word correctly to the student. When the student is reading silently and raises his/her hand for assistance in recognising an unknown word, the teacher or a peer might provide immediate help. There are advantages in using this procedure.

1. The student might then read on with little loss of sequential ideas.
2. The student is not frustrated by waiting for help in that there is a designated person to give aid shortly.
3. The student may emphasise ordered ideas in reading comprehension.

Many reading specialists will criticise this methodology in that a student is not taught needed skills to decode a word. The unknown word then does/might not become a sight word in the reading vocabulary. The student receives immediate assistance in identifying unknown words, but there is no app·oach in guiding the student to become an independent reader. The writer when in grade school experienced the immediate pronunciation of a word that caused a problem for students in recognition. Very frequently, he was asked to pronounce words to students who raised their hands when reading silently. There are better procedures available to be sure, but each student received assistance when needed and could then proceed with the reading task at hand. Then too, the author did retain selected of these immediately pronounced words as sight words.

Use of Context Clues

Many reading specialists advocate the use of context clues to identify an unknown word. The learner then is asked to provide a word for the unknown which fits in meaningfully with the rest of the words in the sentence or paragraph. The student is helped in making the correct selection when also looking at the initial consonant of the needed word as compared to the one chosen by the student. The latter is a check for the student in producing the correct contextual word or to receive increased information on which word to select initially. This may take considerable time for the student and he/she may lose out on understanding, sequentially, the subject matter read.

Using context clues may well assist the student to become an independent reader and this certainly is a major objective in the teaching of reading. Perhaps, there are times when an unknown word needs to be pronounced immediately as well as in assisting a student to use context clues during the ongoing reading activity. Thus, a student may need to know the word, correctly identified, at once to proceed in a needed project.

Using Phonics in Word Recognition

Phonics taught as needed or taught systematically has always had its advocates in educational history. Phonics taught as needed may be stressed when introducing new words for a reading lesson. These new words are printed in neat manuscript letters on the chalk board. From these five or six new words, student attention is drawn to likenesses and differences in initial, median, and final sounds. Students, too, are to focus careful attention to consistencies and inconsistencies between symbol and sound within a word.

Phonics as needed might also be emphasised when an individual student needs assistance while reading silently or orally. The teacher may then point out to the learner where there is consistency or a lack thereof within a word. Inductively, the learner may also be assisted to develop phonic generalisations. Clues may then be given by the teacher to help the student identify a word correctly.

Phonograms may also fit into the pattern of phonics instructions. Common phonograms which students may learn to identify and which follow a pattern include the following:

ack, ail, ake, ate, an, ask, at, ate, aw, eat, ell, est, ice, ick, ide, ight, ill, in, ine, ink, ip, it, ock, op, oke, op, ore, ot, (See Margaret Taylor Stewart (2004), Early Literacy Instruction in the Climate of No Child Left Behind, The Reading Teacher, 57 (8), 732-743). Thus, for example, the first phonogram listed above, "ack," has a plethora of patterns by adding a different initial consonant resulting in the following rhyming words: back, hack, lack, jack, pack, rack, sack, tack. Pupils need to be instructed to seek a familiar phonogram in order to identify an unknown word.

Systematic phonics emphasises a scope and sequence of its very own. There are definite objectives for students to achieve in phonics in a basal text or a teacher designed programme of instruction. The objectives are arranged in ascending order of complexity. Learning activities in phonics need to be aligned with the objectives. Evaluation to notice student achievement provides information on students having achieved the desired ends. The teacher may stress application of phonics learnings in the ongoing reading programme in order to show the usefulness of phonics to the learner. If the scope and sequence of systematic phonics instruction emphasises a core of learnings, then at a later point in instruction, students, hopefully, will use what has been learned. This tends to separate meaning acquired in learning subject matter and content from the specific phonics learning stressed in a systematic approach. Best it is to integrate phonics instruction as closely as possible with the narrative expository, or creative ideas expressed in the reading curriculum.

The Big Book Approach

A promising procedure in initial reading instruction is a big book procedure. Here, all students being taught need to be able to see clearly the print and the illustrations in the literary device used. The contents be it narrative, expository, or creative should have accompanying illustrations. The teacher needs to have students notice the illustrations carefully and predict what the story will be about. This is followed by the teacher reading aloud the subject matter in the book and pointing to words and phrases being read aloud. It is important to notice if each learner is following the print carefully. The content is then read aloud, together, with students as the ensuing words are being followed. Rereading may be done as often as needed and desired. Sometimes, students wish to read aloud the contents several times. With the big book approach, students learn:

1. ideas presented in print;
2. observe each word as it is being read loud;
3. develop a sight vocabulary of words necessary for independent reading;
4. word recognition in context;
5. review words for instant recognition as frequently as needed;
6. specific phonics brought in within a contextual situation, but not isolated from the reading of ideas;
7. enjoyment of literature;
8. success in achievement in that if a word is not known, others assist in the group process to identify the unknown;
9. holism in reading content with gestalt psychology in evidence;
10. meaning in reading content.

Individualised Reading

Individualised reading may assist many students to identify words due to the high interest factor in what was chosen to be read. Individualised reading may consist of an entire programme of instruction based on sequential library books selected by the individual. Following the reading of a library book, the student may have a conference with the teacher to check comprehension and fluent oral reading progress.

Individualised reading might also be stressed in Silent Sustained Reading (SSR) in which a student has a selected library book to read, when within a designated time all in the classroom read a book, including the teacher. The teacher as well as all learners in a classroom provide models for reading. Adults, too, should provide that model! There are a few schools where everybody in a building reads at specific time, including custodians and maintenance personnel. This model may be extremely difficult to implement, but the idea therein has merit in that children might see everyone read a library book at a given time. As a student continues to read, he/she encounters new words in a self selected, interesting library book. Interest is a powerful factor in learning to identify unknown words. Then too, the self selected library book will generally be on the comprehension level of the reader. Basically, the student will then recognise 95 per cent of the running words read as well as comprehend 75 per cent of the ideas encountered. This leaves room for five per cent of the running words to be learned through instruction in word recognition as well as 25 per cent increase in comprehension. The achievement level may be increased through teacher/peer assistance in scaffolding, direct instruction, and discovery learning. Familiarity and interest of subject matter read does assist the student to hurdle numerous difficulties in the total act of reading.

Use of Basal Readers

When basal readers are used in teaching and learning situations, the teacher may use the accompanying manual which lists possible new words for students to learn to identify. In addition to these words, the teacher also needs to choose other words from the new reading lesson which may give problems to students in word identification. These words need to be printed in neat manuscript letters on the chalkboard. Each of these words needs correct identification and pronunciation so that students will identify them correctly while reading. Thus, readiness is being developed for reading. Included in the readiness experiences are the following:

1. students need to attach meaning for a definition and/or contextual use of the new word;
2. students need to use the new word correctly in a sentence;
3. the students need to possess adequate background experiences to understand story content;
4. the students need to develop questions for which answers will be found through reading the story content;
5. the students will indicate achievement from the reading activity through discussions, related art and construction projects, committee work, and enrichment experiences.

Keeping Track of Mastered Words in Reading

There is much merit in having students keep a record of new words mastered in identification. Each sequential word mastered may be printed in neat manuscript letters and numbered on a special sheet of paper. This should be a motivator to the student in that the increase in word mastery may readily be noticed. A star might be printed or stamped for every five new mastered. Periodically, the student needs to review the list for retention purposes. Extrinsic motivation may periodically be used such as a printed or stamped star. The author generally favours intrinsic motivation for learning whereby the student inwardly has a desire to learn to read and does much reading. There are selected factors in the psychology of learning which do assist in motivating student learning. These include the following in which learning opportunities need to:

1. engage students in reading. Active involvement is preferred to be passive recipients of what was presented;

2. assist students to perceive interest in reading;
3. help students to establish reasons for reading;
4. guide students to perceive meaning and understanding in subject matter read;
5. help students to summarise, review, and apply what has been learned.

Students need encouragement to do much reading continuously. In this way students are meeting up with new words in reading as well as reviewing those previously recognised.

REFERENCES

Adams, M.J. (1990), *Beginning to Read: Thinking and Learning About Print.* Cambridge, Massachusetts: MITT Press.

Cambourne, Brian (1995), *Toward an Educationally Relevant Theory of Literacy Learning*. The Reading Teacher, 46 182-190.

Ediger, Marlow, and D. Bhaskara Rao (2000), *Teaching Reading Successfully.* New Delhi, India: Discovery Publishing House. Chapter Seven.

Ediger, Marlow and D. Bhaskara Rao (2003), *Language Arts Curriculum*. New Delhi, India: Discovery Publishing House, Chapter Eleven.

Ediger, Marlow and D. Bhaskara Rao (2003), *Elementary Curriculum,* New Delhi, India: Discovery Publishing House, Chapter Fifteen.

Hibbing, Anne Nielsen, and Jean L. Rankin—Erickson (2003), *"A Picture is Worth A Thousand Words: Using Visual Images to Improve Comprehension for Middle School Struggling Readers"*, The Reading Teacher, 56 (8), 758-769.

Stanovich, K.E. (1986), *"Matthew Effects in Reading: Some Considerations of Individual Differences in Acquisition of Literacy"*, Reading Research Quarterly, 21, 360-406.

Analysing the Goals of the National Reading Panel

The National Reading Panel (NRP) of USA stated five goals for teachers to use in teaching students. These goals are to assist young learners to become good readers. The panel was selected to study research results on what makes for good reading practices. The five elements which the NRP came up with are phonemics, phonics, vocabulary, fluency in reading, and comprehension. Each of these five elements will be discussed separately in this paper.

Phonemics in Reading

The first element emphasised by the NRP was phonemics. Phonemic awareness stresses the importance of students hearing specific sounds in English. Words are made up of separate sounds. The word "had" has three separate sounds h/a/d. Each can be clearly enunciated. There are a plethora of words in which each letter in a word makes a consistent sound. The *man* family of words is an example in which several words pattern when changing the initial consonant. – ban, can, dan, fan, nan, pan, ran, tan, van. The word *hen* is spelled consistently between grapheme/phoneme, but few words pattern— den, men, pen. Then there are words spelled inconsistently such as cough, bough, dough, thought, through. Each of these words has an "ough" spelling, but the resulting sounds made are quite different. With a phonemic emphasis in beginning reading instruction, several issues arrive:

1. will students learn isolated sounds, unrelated to reading? Any word can be segmented to specific sounds— m/a/t/ch, th/ink, b/a/ll;
2. will each isolated sound be related to its corresponding grapheme?
3. will pictures be used in teaching phonemics? Thus, a picture of a bat, with its naming word, will be shown and students point to each letter as its corresponding sound is pronounced;
4. will chants with isolated phonemes be used to develop proficiency in reading readiness?
5. will students tend to separate sounds to the point that difficulty results in blending letters (sounds) to make words?

Phonics in Reading Instruction

Phonics has been taught over the centuries to help students in word recognition. Some teachers have used a systemic approach in teaching phonics. Here, there is a definite sequence in instruction with a basal phonics text used in teaching students. The thinking has been that each student needs to be able to associate sound with symbol for independent reading to take place. Independence in word recognition, according to advocates, may then take place with heavy reliance upon phonics. Phonics instruction certainly has its strong points in having students learn to recognise words in reading which are spelled consistently between grapheme and phoneme. However, there are words which lack this consistency and might well need to be learned by sight. Questions which may be raised about phonics instruction in the reading curriculum are the following:

1. will students minimise comprehension by paying an excessive amount of time in sounding out words?
2. will reading emphasise sounding out words and thus minimise fluency of content read?

3. will phonics instruction crowd out reading for meaning?
4. will student interest in reading be minimised when heavy emphasis in placed upon phonics instruction?
5. will strong stress placed upon phonics truly make for better readers?

Fluency in Reading

As a third ingredient in a quality reading programme, students need to become fluent readers. Good teaching and much practice is involved when students become proficient readers. Reading experiences need to be challenging and satisfying. Interesting materials need to be in the offing for student reading. Growth and achievement in reading is ongoing and never reaches a terminal point. There is always room for a student to increase proficiency in reading. Thus, fluency in reading is an ever present objective of reading instruction.

Fluency in reading may be hindered when a student is unable identify words in context. Struggling to identify words hinders understanding of content. Failure to read in thought units also is a hindrance to attaching meaning to what is being read. Generally, a lack of fluent reading indicates the subject matter read is too complex for the involved student. Appropriate reading materials may be located for these students by using an informal reading inventory (IRI) in determining individual reading levels. Selected teachers may prefer, instead to use a standardised oral reading test to ascertain a student's reading level. In general, a student, while reading, should be able to identify 95 per cent of the running, words correctly and be able to answer 75 per cent of the questions covering subject matter read. A lack of fluency in reading is noticed when a student substitutes words, omits or adds words, disregards punctuation marks, and repeats, words read correctly. Teachers need to diagnose a student's reading to notice the kinds of errors made which hinder fluent reading. Teaching needed reading skills then becomes a necessity if fluency is to become a reality!

Vocabulary Development

A fourth ingredient in a good reading programme, according to NRP, is student vocabulary development. This is essential. Many times, students have not done well in reading due to limited vocabulary. Reading comprehension does emphasise having a vocabulary whereby meaning is attached to what has been read. A rich set of learning opportunities which permeate each school day are necessary to assist students to develop their listening, speaking, reading, and writing vocabularies. When students do much reading to themselves with the use of library books, their vocabularies are being enriched and extended. The teacher needs to supplement these experiences by reading quality literature aloud to students. Special times may be set aside for Drop Everything and Read (DEAR) sessions whereby each student selects a library book to read to the self. As the student reads to the self, he/she increases strengths in vocabulary development. Each book read needs to be developmentally appropriate. The learner then understands content read. Meaning is being attached to acquired ideas.

When basal texts are being used in instruction, the teacher may introduce the daily, new vocabulary terms by printing each in neat manuscript letters on the chalkboard, student are then guided to identify each word correctly as well as go over the meaning of these words. It is best to go over the new vocabulary terms contextually within a sentence. Words are a part of a sentence, a paragraph, and a sequence of paragraphs. The related illustrations in the basal, used by the teacher in teaching and the student in learning, might well provide a sense of meaning for each new vocabulary term. Students need to use the vocabulary terms in oral communication as well as in written work. Vocabulary terms acquired could also be recorded in a notebook for student review.

The Glossary in a basal as well as a grade level dictionary may provide necessary assistance to a learner in securing meanings of selected words in ongoing language arts areas. Vocabulary development must be emphasised in all academic areas as well as on all grade levels. When students attach meaning to the listening, speaking, reading, and writing vocabulary, they are well on their way to an enriched life style.

Comprehension in Reading

The ultimate goal in reading is comprehension. Individuals read to comprehend content. Comprehension may be on different levels of achievement. Thus, a student may comprehend on a literal level. He/she might then say in his/her own words that which has been read. If a student uses words directly from a textbook selection read, the learner may not understand what has been read. A higher level than literal comprehension is for the student to analyse what has been read. Here, facts are separated from opinions, accurate from inaccurate statements, as well as fantasy from reality. Creative reading is also important. Here, the student comes up with a unique interpretation of what has been read. He/she is able to develop unique and novel ideas pertaining to subject matter read. Originality of interpretation is salient. The student, too, needs to assess the worth of content read. This is the evaluation level of comprehension. Definite criteria may be developed to note the worth of content read.

When comprehending subject matter, it is noteworthy to be able to apply subject matter to new situations. Many uses can and must be made of acquired subject matter. With problem solving, the content may be used as a solution to an identified problem area. Thus within a unit of study, students with teacher guidance may identify a problem. The problem is a dilemma with multiple facets of possible solutions. A variety of data sources may be used to secure needed information. An hypothesis which is tentative results. The tentative hypothesis needs to be tested through additional study. The answer to the problem is then modified, accepted, or reputed. Problems chosen need to be on the developmental level of the learner. They should attract learner attention and provide motivation to persevere toward a solution.

Comprehension of content may also involve understanding printed directions, reading to secure a main idea as well as subordinate ideas and reading to obtain vital factual information. Comprehension is the ultimate goal of reading. Within the framework of comprehension are a plethora of skills, including using that which has been read. To use information obtained through reading, the content needs to be critically appraised.

Attitudes Toward Reading

To achieve well in reading, appropriate attitudes need to become a part of the self. They might well be the driving force in becoming a good reader. Attitudes result from ongoing reading and other experiences in the total environment of the learner. Success in reading is basic in becoming good reader. The reading teacher needs to start any student in reading where he/she is achieving. To go beyond this level may frustrate the learner and make for failure in reading. To limit the learner in reading challenging materials may well make for boredom and a lack of engagement in learning. From that baseline of where the student is presently achieving, the teacher needs to provide sequential learning opportunities which assist the learner to experience continuous optimal progress. The ideal of maximum achievement in reading cannot be overemphasised for each student.

REFERENCES

Aiken, Adel G., and Lisa Bayer (2002), *"They Love Words"*, The Reading Teacher, 56 (1), 68-75.

Astleitner, Herman (2002), *"Teaching Critical Thinking Online"*, Journal of Instructional Psychology, 29 (2), 53-76.

Chappuis, Stephen, and Richard J. Stiggins (2002), *"Classroom Assessment for Learning"*, Educational Leadership, 60 (1), 40-41.

Ediger, Marlow, and D. Bhaskara Rao (2000), *Teaching Reading Successfully*. New Delhi, India: Discovery Publishing House, Chapter Eight.

Ediger, Marlow (2002), *"Developing a Reading Community"*, Edutracks, 1 (4), 16-19.

Ediger, Marlow (2002), *"Social Studies and the Guidance Counselor"*, Experiments in Education, 30 (9), 176-181.

Ediger, Marlow (2002), *"Improving Spelling"*, Reading Improvement, 39 (2), 69-70.

Gardner, Howard (1983), *Frames of Mind: The Theory of Multiple Intelligence*. New York: Basic Books.

Maslow, A.H. (1954), *Motivation and Personality*. New York: Harper and Row.

Meyer, Richard J. (2002), *"Captives of the Script: Killing Us Softly With Phonics"*, The Reading Teacher, 79 (6), 452-461.

National Science Teachers Association (2001), *Classroom Assessment and the National Education Standards*. Washington, DC: The Association, NSTA.

Searson, Robert, and Rita Dunn (2001), *"The Learning Styles Teaching Model"*, *Science and Children*, 38 (5), 22-36.

19

How Often Should Students Be Tested in Reading?

Students in the public schools are required to take annual tests in grades three through eight to notice achievement and if students should be promoted to the next higher grade level. They also are required to take and pass a test in grade ten. The latter test is to evaluate if a student should receive a high school diploma. These are state mandated tests in reading and mathematics. Passing the single test indicates a student has mastered the basics. State mandated tests are *summative* in that this is the end result of testing at a given time, such as toward the closing of a school year.

Teachers along the way, also need to assess students to see if the stated objectives for the state mandated tests are being achieved. *Formative* tests are then written by the teacher. Many teachers are pressured to drill students in reading and mathematics in order that satisfactory state mandated test scores result. There are punishments for schools and school systems if adequate yearly progress (ayp) is not achieved, such as students being able to transfer from a school which failed to meet the ayp standard. These students may then transfer to a school with satisfactory test results.

Which Additional Tests Are Given in Reading?

There are a plethora of other tests which may also be administered to students in the reading curriculum. The

Qualitative Reading Inventory (See Leslie and Caldwell, 1988) may be administered to find the reading level of a student. This informal test consists of narrative and expository content. The student is first asked selected questions, by the teacher, to familiarise the test taker with the ensuing topic. After reading content on the test, the student is asked to retell what was read. He/she may also choose to answer comprehension questions. The purpose in giving the test is to determine the student's instructional level of reading. The test results analyse the student's ability to identify words correctly as well as understand/comprehend what was read.

A teacher may also ascertain a student's reading level by having him/her read aloud, without previous practice, from the beginning of the basal text. This is known as an informal reading inventory (IRI). The text is assumed to be on the instructional level if the student identifies 95 per cent of the running words correctly as well as answers three out of four questions correctly to assess comprehension. Below those approximate per cents, the student is reading on the frustrational level. The instructional level of reading makes it possible for a learner to succeed in that there is room for positive growth in word recognition and in comprehension skills.

In addition to reading inventory tests, as well as state mandated tests, there are school districts who administer their own achievement tests. These tests are developed on the district level and generally measure achievement in the following four curriculum areas— reading, mathematics, science and social studies. Selected schools, too, have devised these tests to provide feedback from test results to teachers on what is left for students to learn. A problem of these tests is possessing adequate validity and reliability.

A major purpose of state mandated testing is to document what students have achieved and make results available to parents and other interested, responsible persons. However, testing as a means to assess student achievement can be carried to an extreme. Teacher observation with the use of quality criteria may also be used successfully. With careful observation, the teacher may notice how well students are learning and how much progress is being made. Why might testing be carried to an extreme?

1. it is very costly to write mandated tests;
2. pilot studies need to be made of each test to determine and secure adequate validity and reliability;
3. computer time needs to be paid for and at the same time there may be glitches in providing student test results;
4. it takes time away from regular instruction to test students and to drill them in preparation for test taking;
5. it limits students as to what is significant to learn since reading and mathematics are the two curriculum areas generally being emphasised on state mandated tests (Ediger and Rao, 2003).

A fourth kind of test given to students is standardised tests published by a leading publishing company. There are states which have substituted these standardised tests for their state mandated test. Standardised tests, as defined here, tend to have no accompanying objectives for teachers to use as guidelines in teaching. Standardised tests have everything objectified with precision in their writing and administration in that:

1. time limits for test taking are the same for all students. No allowances are made for handicapped students;
2. subject matter content is the same for all test takers, regardless of ability and achievement levels. Sameness is to be contrasted with allowing for differences among students taking the test. For example, South Dakota experimented with adaptive testing. Thus, if a student continuously responded incorrectly to sequential test items, the programmer determined the present level of the student's achievement and adapted the programmed items. The adaptation for the learner was made in terms of the present achievement of the student. He/she then had developmental test items adjusted to the present individual achievement level. It measures nothing if a student can only provide incorrect or guessed responses:
3. the same key is used in scoring all tests;
4. norms are provided students for each test taken;

5. numerical results are provided to show a student's progress.

Standardised tests follow the same format, basically, as do many state mandated tests. The latter have been developed on the state level whereas the former are developed under the auspices of leading publishing companies. State mandated tests can also be designed by a commercial company which meets the standards of a state. The lines have been blurred increasingly so, between state mandated and standardised tests.

Miscue Analysis Reading Test

Selected teachers give miscue analysis tests to students to ascertain specific kinds of errors students make in reading. A miscue analysis test attempts to identify specific kinds of errors made by students in reading. Selections from the test are read aloud while the teacher marks/checks the precise errors made by the student. Reading aloud is then required during the assessment. The kinds of identified errors made, as indicated on a miscue analysis test, may well be the following:

1. mispronouncing words;
2. incorrectly identifying words;
3. substituting of words;
4. omitting words while reading;
5. hesitating while reading a word, but still identifying the word(s) correctly. The hesitation is counted if it is at least two seconds in length;
6. repeating words and phrases read correctly;
7. adding of words to a sentence;
8. rereading a sentence, even if it was read correctly;
9. words pronounced by the test giver, if a student hesitates for five seconds in attempting to identify a word (See Y. Goodman and Marek, 1996).

The miscue analysis test is given to determine which kinds and types of hindrances prevent a student from reading fluently. It also provides the teacher with information on which goals to stress in reading instruction. If words are mispronounced (problem one above), the inherent difficulties in mispronunciation may be noticed such as in making phoneme/grapheme associations. Problems #2 above, the student may not be using context clues for word identification. Problems #3, the student is not paying careful attention to the words being read. In problem four, the student is not attempting to make sense of what is being read. Meaning needs to be attached to ongoing content being read. Number 5, the subject matter may be too difficult and not on the developmental level of the student, if there are too many hesitations. Number 6, the student may feel uncertainties about reading, if originally the content was read correctly. Number seven, the student, again, is not paying careful attention to the words in context. Number eight, the student is getting ready to identify words in the next sentence to be read, so he/she repeats the sentence just read correctly.

There are selected inherent problems in viewing the results of a miscue analysis test. These include the following:

1. words may be mispronounced, but are clear in meaning to the learner;
2. words identified incorrectly might be synonyms to the correct word and thus not change the meaning of a sentence. The same may be true of substituting words;
3. words omitted may not matter when looking at the meaning of the sentence;
4. hesitating while reading may mean the text used for reading is too difficult for the learner. This would be true if there are continuous hesitations. There also need to be other kinds of errors made in making decisions about a student being shifted to less complex reading materials;
5. there may be some repeating of sentences, even thought read correctly, if a student is thinking about or rehearsing meaning to previously read sentences;
6. adding of words to a sentence may be an attempt by the student to read that which is meaningful and makes sense;
7. rereading a sentence read correctly, previously, may be done by the learner to think about its contents.

However, if a student mispronounces too many words; identifies words, consistently, incorrectly; omits words and hesitates on too many words being encountered; among other kinds of errors made while reading, the chances are that many objectives need to be stressed in reading and a less complex set of reading materials need to be in the offing. Decisions need to be made by the professional teacher on objectives, learning opportunities, and evaluation techniques in reading. A miscue analysis test in reading may provide necessary assistance to the reading teacher. The Retrospective Miscue Analysis (RMA) is an example of this type of test which analyses student errors in reading fluently.

There are additional kinds of tests which may be administered to students. They include individual/group IQ tests. These kinds of tests are not as important as they were two decades ago and longer. To indicate the importance of IQ tests, the Detroit, Michigan Schools, in 1920, emphasised the xyz plan whereby students were grouped homogeneously using IQ test results only. It took only a year to notice that IQ was not a good basis for homogeneous grouping in that there are a plethora of other variables which might be used in the grouping process. Presently, it is difficult to define what is inherent in an IQ score. More attention is paid to multiple intelligences. Students possess diverse intelligences such as verbal, logical, musical/rhythmical, intrapersonal, interpersonal, bodily/kinesthetic, and scientific (See Gardner).

Personality tests may also be given to students. Presently, it is frowned upon in schools, for a teacher to administer a personality test due to confidential information contained therein. Then too, personality tests posses a relatively high standard error of measurement meaning that any score may fluctuate much depending upon what has transpired within the life of the student at the time of test taking. The writer has used the California Test of Personality in research conducted. Guidance counsellors and school psychologists may give diverse tests to individuals and small groups, depending upon the purpose involved. Thus, a high school counsellor may give a vocational preference test to a student, as an example.

Guidelines for Administering Tests

There needs to be a definite purpose in giving tests to students. Presently, much testing is done in the public schools. Too much testing robs a student of instructional time. Then too, an excessive amount of time may be given to drill and review for a future high stakes test. Tensions might be elevated due to the stress and strain of actual testing and the anticipation of negative results therefrom. Certainly, there needs to be a clear reason for giving a test. It is not a frivolous event. Results from quality test administered need to provide feedback for improving instruction.

REFERENCES

Ediger, Marlow, and D. Bhaskara Rao (2003), *Language Arts Curriculum*. New Delhi, India: Discovery Publishing House.

Gardner, Howard (1993), *Multiple Intelligences: Theory into Practice*. New York: Basic Books.

Goodman, Y., and A. Marek (1996), *Retrospective Miscue Analysis: Revaluing Readers and Reading*. Katonah, New York: Richard C. Owen.

Leslie L., and J. Caldwell, Editors (1998). *Qualitative Reading Inventory*. New York: Harper and Collins.

Reading and the Internet

The internet has become very useful in gathering information to answer questions for students in the classroom setting. The questions should be salient to students and relate directly to ongoing lessons and units of study. The rapidity with which information can be forthcoming from the interent is truly astounding. Students may be left out of obtaining viable content in the information age unless interent skills are developed and used. Each student then needs to develop relevant abilities in internet use. These skills are valuable to secure necessary subject matter.

Reading is a major problem to hurdle for many students. The subject matter is not sequential in difficulty as is true of many of the graded materials used in the classroom. Thus, assistance in reading the needed subject matter must be provided as needed.

Reading Problems and the Internet

Which reading problems might learners experience when using the interest in information gathering? Word recognition may well be one major hurdle for selected students. Some of these unrecognised words will be identified contextually. Thus, the unknown word will be surrounded by its relationship in fitting together with the other surrounding words. This is a first word attack skill which should be used. An unknown word then needs to make sense in context.

To provide additional clues in word recognition, the student may need to sound out a word. Phonics then may be helpful when the letters possess consistency between symbol (grapheme) and sound (phoneme). This will work if the letter(s) correspond to consistent sounds. A little bit of assistance with phonics may well guide the student to correct word identification. There are words which do not correspond with consistent grapheme/phoneme relationships. These need to be learned by sight and when using the internet, they can be pronounced quickly by the teacher or another student. Gathering information from the interent should not become a course in reading instruction, but rather help is provided as is necessary for the student to use context clues, phonics, and syllabication. Syllabication skills may be the last needed skill to identify unknown words. Thus, if a student does not know a word on the internet, it becomes familiar by subtracting a prefix or suffix. Thus the word becomes knowable.

Being able to recognise and identify words is a tool to increase reading skills. Fluent reading is the major goal to stress in reading. With fluent reading, comprehension increases. With internet reading, students are to comprehend subject matter read. Indepth learning is an ideal for learner achievement. To achieve indepth knowledge of subject matter, students need to develop diverse thinking abilities (Ediger and Rao, 2000).

Indepth Reading of Subject Matter

The teacher needs to assist each student to read proficiently using internet subject matter. Thus, students need to acquire *vital* facts. These are important and serve as building blocks for higher levels of cognition. Reading to achieve relevant concepts emphasises a more complex level of achievement. Concepts are broader in subject matter coverage as compared to facts. Thus, there may be a plethora of facts in single concept. Concepts are single words or phrases. By themselves, they have rather limited use unless they become a part of a generalisation. A generalisation is a complete sentence made up of two or more concepts. Generalisations are useful in that they:

1. are broad statements of related inherent ideas;
2. are more likely to be remembered than a multiplicity of isolated facts and unrelated concepts;
3. are helpful in retaining facts since the broader generalisation brings to mind the specifics located therein;
4. are recalled more readily as compared to many smaller units of information;
5. are related ideas and perceiving these relationships assists in making for enduring subject matter.

Reading for main ideas is broader in scope as compared to reading to form a generalisation. In other words, there are several generalisations in one main idea. To assess student ability and growth in reading for a main idea, the teacher may have students tell in one sentence what has been read from an internet selection consisting of several paragraphs. This can become an interesting game since students may challenge each other if a stated main idea does/does not hold water. The main idea must give an overview of an entire set of paragraphs. No part should be omitted in the main idea provided by a student. Wholesome discussions in which learners respect each other makes for higher levels of thinking (See Templeton).

Additional Considerations

Students do need prerequisites taught in internet use. They will be at different levels of achievement in these mechanics and other facets of being proficient in using the interent. Key board skills will vary from student to student in versatility and effectiveness. These need to be practiced for locating information, for summary writing, and for diverse purposes in doing written work. Taking care of grammatical mistakes and spelling errors is a must. Spell check solves many, but not all problems in correct spelling of words. Proper paragraphs, sequence of ideas, indentation, capitalisation, and punctuation marks need continuous diagnosis and remediation, as well as achievement in general. Having adequate paper for the computer and knowing what to do when the feeder does not work properly is salient. An evaluation chart may be developed whereby each student's progress may be monitored for needed assistance in computer work (Ediger and Rao, 2003).

The locating of needed information is the heart of computer and internet use. If, for example, students are studying the Middle East as a unit of study or in current events, they may need to secure information to the following questions and problems:

1. How did the Balfour Declaration affect the present day situation for Arabs and Jews?
2. Which boundary lines were in effect between opposing sides after the first Arab/Israeli War of 1948?
3. How were these boundary lines changed during the 1967 six day war?
4. What attempts did Egypt and Syria make in 1973 when attempting to retrieve the Sinai peninsula which Egypt lost and the Golan Heights which Syria lost, during the 1967 six-day war?
5. What kind of peace treaty did Egypt and Israel work out in 1978 so that the former received the Sinai peninsula which was lost to Israel during the 1967 six-day war;
6. What will Israel/the Palestinian Arabs work out with the Gaza strip which the former captured from Egypt in 1967.

The above are the kinds of questions/problems which students may secure necessary information from internet use. When using the internet, students do run across additional unit related or enrichment information. Thus, they might well perceive vital information on the prized, walled city of Jerusalem. Students then may well notice things such as the following:

1. The Wall around Jerusalem is two and one half miles in distance.
2. The preset wall was built in 1542 by the Ottoman Turkish Empire.

3. There are seven gates or entrances into Jerusalem. The eighth, the Golden Gate, is closed until the Messiahs returns to earth.
4. There are three places, in particular, which are holy to devout Muslims, Jews and Christians.
5. For devout Muslims, the Dome of the Rock, an octagonal Mosque built in 691 AD, is the place where Mohammed ascended into heaven and came back to earth again. For devout Jews, the Western Wall is a remnant of the ancient temple of King Solomon, built 960 BC, approximately. For devout Christians, the Church of the Holy Sepulcher is the place of entombment and resurrection of Christ. This structure was built in 1142 AD (Ediger, 1999).

The internet then can be a viable source of information for the user. Subject matter secured must always be assessed in terms of accuracy, usability, and relevancy. The internet has sources of information which may well interest and fascinate learners. Along with other reference materials, it can truly involve students in problem solving and higher levels of cognition. With the possible involvement of the interest factor, the attitudinal dimension of students might also improve. With good attitudes, there tends to be an inward desire to learn and achieve.

In Closing

There are selected things which teachers need to stress when students engage in internet use:

1. students need assistance at specific times in the mechanics of internet use;
2. students need to pinpoint the precise problem(s) they wish to pursue as a requirement or as a voluntary extra credit project in an ongoing unit of study. Vagueness in topics being pursued lacks in being goal centred;
3. students need to be responsible learners;
4. students may work on an individual activity or within a committee;
5. students should feel free to ask for assistance as needed, without being labelled negatively;

6. students need to develop wholesome attitudes toward internet use so that optimal progress may come about;
7. students need to develop an inward desire to learn more about the internet and its uses;
8. students need to share information secured with other learners;
9. students need to meet reasonable deadlines in completing project/activities work on the internet;
10. students need to develop feelings of curiosity when obtaining knowledge and information (See Carico and Logan, 2004).

REFERENCES

Carico, Kathleen, and Donna Logan (2004), "*A Generation in Cyberspace: Engaging Readers Through Online Discussions*", The Language Arts, 81 (4), 293-302.

Ediger, Marlow (1999), *The Holy Land*. Kirksville, Missouri: Simpson Publishing House.

Ediger, Marlow and D. Bhaskara Rao (2000), *Teaching Reading Successfully*. New Delhi, India: Discovery Publishing House.

—— (2003), *Language Arts Curriculum*. New Delhi, India: Discovery Publishing House.

Templeton, Shane (1997), *Teaching the Integrated Language Arts*. Boston: Houghton Mifflin Company.

Writing in the Mathematics Curriculum

Students do need to become proficient writers. Writing should be emphasised across the curriculum. Mathematics, as one curriculum area, can and does make a plethora of contributions toward writing proficiency. The teachers needs to observe the kinds of errors students make in written work. These may be recorded on a check sheet so that the teacher knows which goals need to be stressed in ongoing mathematics lessons.

Lessons should not stress drill in written work, but rather contextually, as needed, students should be assisted to write well. To start out with suggestions for writing in mathematics, students need to form each numeral legibly. If a numeral is written in reverse form by a young learner, for example, then assistance must be given to write each correctly. This may be done by having students write how many are pictured on a series of cards, such as in each set of cats. With diagnosing student daily work, the teacher needs to assist where reversals are made or a lack of clarity is involved. Help given needs to be specific be it in students not knowing the basic facts or not understanding borrowing/carrying in performing a mathematical operation.

Criteria to Use in Mathematics Writing

Learning need to be meaningful. The student then needs to make sense out of what is being learned. He/she needs to think of when they personally, for example, counted something real, such as a set of coins, a place setting for visitors at a dinner table, pet fish in a bowl, and new born kittens. Journal writing is important here, in that a student may record what was learned and what is left to learn. Needed assistance in writing might be provided by the teacher or peer. Journal writing assists students to reflect upon what was learned. It may provide necessary insight in what was not understood so that the student is increasingly successful in future learnings. Thinking about mathematical experiences helps students to analyse, synthesise, and evaluate what has transpired in order to grow in mathematics achievement.

Interest is a powerful factor in learning. The mathematics teacher needs to provide for the interests of learners. Student choice in activities may well promote interest in learning. An enrichment centre in the classroom can provide those choices. Each task at the interest centre needs to stimulate students in mathematics achievement. A hands on approach should also be stressed at the interest centre. For example, students may measure, weigh, and find the volume of different containers and *record* their findings. Thus, students may ascertain how many pints in a quart by actually using these containers to find out. Hands on experiences meet the personal styles of many students to achieve well in mathematics. Thus, concrete experiences may become a part, as well as within numerous other learning activities for all in the classroom. Concrete activities assist in making learnings meaningful for students.

Students should perceive purpose in written experiences in mathematics. Writing then should not be done for the sake of doing so, but rather to achieve a definite goal. Thus to increase experiences in doing and understanding word problems, students may be challenged to write these kinds of story problems which might well challenge other learners to complete. Numerical values used and the type of problem written may well relate to what is currently being studied or has been studied recently. The mechanics of writing such as correct spelling of words, proper sentence structure, and meaningful punctuation must prevail as end products. Peers may assist each other in the mechanics of writing. The heart of the story problem should truly stress the solving of a problem. Learners need to think clearly and carefully when pursuing a problem. Dilemma situations take time in coming up with solutions to mathematics problems. Developmentally appropriate problems must be written. Students should feel challenge and yet be able to be successful in achievement. Experiencing failure makes for negative feelings in and toward mathematics. The feeling dimension is salient to stress as objectives in the mathematics curriculum. Positive feelings through successful achievement should assist students in wanting to do more work as well as enjoy mathematics.

Students should work individually as well as collectively in ongoing learning experiences. A preferred learning style for some is to work by the self in assignments to complete as well as in doing voluntary work at an interest centre. Others like to work together with others in order to achieve objectives. In *society*, people work at things individually as well as within a group setting. Students should have opportunities to follow personal preferences in the style of preferred learning. Maximum learning from a student may accrue from using the style of learning preferred.

The total learning environment should be conducive to maximum student productivity. Thus, the noise level should not be excessive so that students may concentrate on the tasks at hand. A busy classroom environment will produce some noise, but unnecessary noises need to be kept to a minimum. Teacher developed standards of conduct should be printed on a chart for all in the classroom to see clearly. These criteria should be referred to when students violate a standard. Each standard needs to be written as precisely as possible so that agreement exists when a standard has been violated. Rules need to be in the offing what the punishment should be for rule violation. There, are teachers who have been successful with rules developed cooperatively with students in the classroom. The feeling is that students then own the standards they have helped to develop and prefer to abide by them. The goal here is to develop a classroom environment which assists optimal achievement in mathematics.

The mathematics teacher also needs to use methods of instruction which harmonise with student preferences.The following are some of the preferences which students possess:

1. direct approaches versus more open ended procedures of instruction;
2. student selection of peers to work on a committee versus teacher determination of members;
3. the mathematics textbook being a major source of learning activities as compared to using a variety of sources;
4. learners seated in rows and columns versus flexible patterns of sitting arrangements;
5. a logical versus a psychological sequence in ordering learning opportunities.

Organising the Mathematics Curriculum

There are selected approaches available in organising learning opportunities. A separate subject curriculum may be in the offing whereby arithmetic becomes the heart of the curriculum. The basic operations, for example, of addition, subtraction, multiplication, and division are stressed in ascending order of complexity. Geometry may be added as an integrated component. Here, students perceive relationships between arithmetic and geometry. For increased integration, algebra may be incorporated, as well as tenets of statistics.

When thinking of the integrated mathematics curriculum, one can incorporate history such as historical data pertaining the Roman system of numeration when this system is being studied. All numerals have an attached history such as during the Middle Ages, the concept of one-half could not be visualised by most, since taking a whole and breaking it up into halves, such as a circle, made for two parts. Students with teacher guidance may select a topic to write on dealing with the history of number. When ready, the student should use the word processor. Editing becomes more enjoyable with word processor use. Spell checkers is a good aid to check for spelling errors. Revisions may readily be made with the word processor by using the delete key, cut and paste from the Edit icon, as well as insertions made conveniently as needed.

Programmed mathematics has made for excitement and variety in mathematical learning experiences. Drill and practice programmes assist learners to reinforce previous learnings.

Simulation programmes provide opportunities for students to simulate mathematical activities as they actually occur in the real world. Tutorial programmes emphasise new learnings for students in sequence from the easier to those gradually more complex. Games stress individuals or teams challenging each other in a competitive game, involving mathematics.

A teacher at Boston Academy used a computer programme called the *Geometer's Sketchboard* to stimulate high school students in inquiry procedures (Wiske, 2004):

Her students constructed geometric figures and then analysed such data as angles, side lengths, and ratios, among other different measures. They developed and tested their own conjectures for measuring, dragging, reshaping, and comparing geometric objects. The software, which records and displays the mathematical relationships of objects, allowed students to examine a similar set of cases, observe patterns, and make generalisations. The accuracy and speed of the computer programme freed students from the tedium of construction with traditional tools yet enabled them to experience the process of arranging and analysing shapes.

New technologies help students understand concepts, methods of reasoning, and effective ways of presenting their ideas in many subject areas. Graphing calculators that instantly relate the graphic and the symbolic representations of mathematical expressions can help students appreciate the nature of variables and functions. Computer based simulations enable students to see and manipulate abstract concepts—such as density—and to model complex ideas such as predator/prey relationships.

Computer programmes in mathematics may well provide new experiences for many students. The excitement of challenge and high expectations may indeed stimulate students to achieve at higher levels in mathematics. It might well assist students to perceive the relationship of subject matter. Interest factors are powerful to consider in teaching. The fascination which many students have with computers may encourage increased levels of learning. Quality programmes need to be selected which guide the student to become increasingly independent in learning mathematics.

Inservice Growth of Teachers

Teachers need to be open in listening to the methods and ideas on teaching mathematics from peers. Peers need to share means of assisting students to attain more optimally. Thus, mathematics teachers need to meet together periodically to share ideas in developing a quality mathematics curriculum, including the writing component. It is good for mathematics teachers to discuss with peers what is being done on the next as well as the preceding grade levels of teaching. This will assist teachers to improve sequence in learning. New objectives for student attainment should be built upon the previously achieved objective(s).

Workshops may be devoted to helping teachers reach more students such as minority individuals, English language Learners (ELL), learners with handicaps, as well as those where English is the Second Language (ESL). With heterogeneously grouped students in a classroom, the mathematics teacher has a demanding job in providing for individual differences.

Faculty meetings may involve discussions on such items as guiding students in mathematical writing experiences, scaffolding learnings for students, innovative materials of instruction, new ideas in grouping for instruction, and learning environments conductive for student achievement. There needs to be an assessment of how effective each plan of inservice education is. Has inservice education programmes for mathematics teachers helped student achievement? Quality assessment programmes should help to answer this vital question.

Research projects conducted by a committee of mathematics teachers may focus on developing the integrated curriculum whereby the language arts areas of writing, reading, listening, and speaking permeate the mathematics curriculum. A variety of reference sources need to be used such as educational journals, university teacher education textbooks, the internet, resource personnel, among others. A comprehensive study should provide detailed information pertaining to a good integrated mathematics curriculum.

Observing excellent teachers teach provides models in innovation. A teacher may be able to refine methods of student inquiry learning by observing model situations of instruction. A carefully written observation report may then be shared with other mathematics teachers.

Mathematics teachers need to use the best objectives, methods of instruction, and assessment procedures possible in teaching and learning situations. Hopefully, students will achieve well under these plans. With state mandated testing, it behooves the teacher, in particular, to aid students to achieve optimally.

REFERENCES

Ediger, Marlow, and D. Bhaskara Rao (2000), *Teaching Mathematics Successfully*. New Delhi, India: Discovery Publishing House, Chapter One.

Ediger, Marlow (1995), "*Current Concepts in Teaching Mathematics*", Philippine Education Quarterly, 7-10.

Ediger, Marlow (1989), "*Psychology in Teaching Mathematics*", Delta K, Vol. 27, No. 4, 20-23.

Maslow, Abraham (1954), *Motivation and Personality*. New York: Harper and Row.

National Council Teachers of Mathematics (1989), *Curriculum and Evaluation Standards for School Mathematics*. Reston, Virginia: NCTM.

New, Rebecca S. (2003), "*Reggio Emilia; New Ways to Think About Schooling*", Educational Leadership. 60 (7), 34-39.

Peressini, Dominic (1997), "*Parental Reform of Mathematics Education*", The Mathematics Teacher, 90 (6), 423-427.

Wiske, Stone (September, 2004), "*Use Technology to Dig for Meaning*", Educational Leadership, 62 (1), 47-48.

Writing in the Science Curriculum

Students engaging in writing assists many areas of science instruction. This includes reading carefully what has been written as well as making subject matter meaningful. It does assist a student to clarify and make ideas understandable in science. Writing should also be stressed across the curriculum. It is a complex skill to develop since there are many component parts including correct spelling of words, sentence structure, and punctuation. Writing may include the young student dictating science content for the teacher to record as well as the student being independent in writing.

Writing in Science

There are a plethora of learning opportunities in which writing may be stressed in ongoing units of study in science. Each needs to motivate students to achieve and accomplish. Good attitudes toward science should also be an end result. Quality attitudes assist students to develop favourable feelings toward science subject matter.

For young students and selected older learners who are weak in writing, the teacher may record what has been learned and stated orally. If students have been studying dinosaurs in a unit on "Prehistoric Life", they may see talk written down by dictating ideas such as the following:

There are many kinds of dinosaurs. The T-Rex has serrated teeth and very short front limbs. He/she has a huge appetite and is a meat eater. The T-Rex was feared by many other dinosaurs.

The length of what is dictated for the teacher to write depends upon what students have to say. Individual as well as committee work may be recorded by the teacher. When seeing talk written down, the student attaches meaning at a young age to words and sentences. An inward desire to write generally accompanies seeing talk written down. The goal here is for the teacher to assist students to become independent and proficient writers.

Experimentation should be at the heart of the science curriculum. Each experiment must have a problem, a tentative hypothesis, a testing or evaluating of the hypothesis, and a conclusion. The hands on learning activity may be recorded by students with teacher guidance. An appraisal of the write-up should include emphasising clearly what is involved in conducting a scientific experience.

Reading from the science textbook provides a plethora of opportunities for student writing. Adequate readiness needs to be in offing prior to students engaging in the reading activity. Thus, students needs to possess background knowledge, be able to identify new words in context, and have a purpose for reading. This assists students to engage in meaningful learning, necessary for doing written work. Students may then be encouraged and challenged to summarise what has been read. Writing main ideas, sub divisions, and details need adequate attention in writing. The mechanics of writing may be stressed as needed. Writing content helps learners to analyse and do depth thinking of subject matter read.

Internet sources may well provide much needed subject matter for students, such as in problem solving. Here, students need to clearly develop and delimit a problem area within the science unit being taught. An hypothesis, tentative in nature, must be achieved as a possible solution to the problem. A variety of reference sources must be used in gathering information to test the hypothesis. The internet may be a valuable source of information. From the acquired information the hypothesis is may be accepted, rejected or modified.

Teacher written guides may be used by students in ongoing science units of study. The guide lists questions for which students need to secure answers. Resources should be listed and used to locate information. For each question, students need to write a possible answer. The questions and answers assist students to secure information in an organised way. If there are questions pertaining to erosion, the student might then respond to diverse kinds of erosion in categories such as wind, water, sheet, and gully erosion.

As another writing activity, students may do outlining from handouts provided by the science teacher. Learners then sequence the content in outline form. The subject matter for the outline may be divided into major ideas with indicated Roman numerals, sequential related subtopics with capital letters, and the specifics under each subtopics. In this way students elaborate on the content as the outline is being developed. Then too, they perceive improved order of content being studied.

Poetry, as a writing activity, may be written pertaining to the present science unit being studied. The student should choose which kind of poem to write be it free verse, a couplet, triplet, quatrain, limerick, haiku, or tanka. The poem should contain science subject matter, chosen by the student, and presented in a creative way. Subject matter selected for the poem may be emphasised in an open ended way, reflecting novelty and originality in ideas used. The poem should have a title and be filed in a classroom booklet, electronically or as done traditionally.

When studying a unit on "Biographies of Famous Scientists", students may write a dramatic presentation. Personnel in the written drama should have clearly indicated speaking parts, using direct quotation. Play parts need careful proof reading and refining. Time needs to be given to practising the play and then presenting it to others. The play parts need not be memorised. This will not be a polished performance, but one which has educational values. As a variation, students may write parts for a reader's theater experience. Here, students read aloud their individual, respective parts. The background information for the setting of the play requires a separate reader. Students may be seated in a circle as is true of reader's theater presentations. No props or background scenery is necessary.

Oral reading activities may also be stressed from a basal science textbook. Reading with enthusiasm and with voice inflection is important. Fluent reading must be emphasised. Selected students will need help with word recognition. If the basal used in science instruction is too complex for selected learners, a text on an easier reading level may be located containing the same science units of study. This is done to provide for optimal achievement on the part of the learner. A student needs to benefit from the reading activity and not feel continuous frustration. Oral reading experiences reveal to the teacher the kinds of assistance needed in reading silently, such as reading in thought units or assistance in phonics instruction. What has been read may be used to write a conclusion, a specific purpose in writing.

When readiness is in evidence, students individually or in a committee setting, might multiple choice test items covering content read. Relevant subject matter, not trivia, needs to be chosen for each test item. Proper standards in writing multiple choice test items should be used, such as:

1. each distractor of the four should be of equivalent length so as to not provide clues as to which answer is correct or incorrect;
2. the stem should be grammatically correct with each of the four distractors;
3. each distractor should be rational and not ridiculous.

Teaching of Writing Methodology

The science teacher needs to follow appropriate criteria when having students engaged in written work. Thus, students need to perceive purpose or reasons for writing. Written work is not done for the sake of doing so but rather to achieve a goal of instruction. The teacher should briefly state the reason for writing in a clear manner.

The interests of students need to be cultivated in writing. As much as possible, students need to choose the subject matter to write about such as in poetry writing. Here, the student may select subject matter to incorporate in a poem.

Authentic learning opportunities provide students with life like situations to write about. A park area or nature centre attached to the school provide opportunities to observe and engage in descriptive writing. The changing of leaf colours of trees can make for excellent observations in describing that which was observed. These are concrete learning activities.

Semi concrete experiences involving AV aids provide for variation in learning activities. These may provide students with valuable learning opportunities in ongoing science units of study. Journal writing from a variety of learning activities may include feelings about the science curriculum as well as of subject matter learned and that which is left to learn.

REFERENCES

Astin, P. and C. Buxton (2000) *Science as Inquiry,* Boblinks, 10 (2), 10-15.

Blough, Glenn O., and Julius Schwartz (1984), *Elementary School Science and How to Teach It*. New York: CBS College Publishing.

Condrey, Jean Friend (1996), *"Focus on Science Concepts"*, The Science Teacher, 63 (4).

Dewey, John (1916), *Democracy and Education*. New York: The MacMillan Company.

Ediger, Marlow (1999), *Teaching Science in the Elementary School*. Kirksville, Missouri: Simpson Publishing Company, Chapter Seven.

——(1995), *"Designing Science Units of Study,"* School Science, 33 (1), 14-15.

Melber, Leah M. (2003). *"True Tales of Science"*, Science and Children 41 (2), 24-32.

National Research Council (1996), *National Science Educational Standards,* Washington DC: National Academy Press.

Ward, Kathleen, et. al. (1996), *"Constructing Scientific Knowledge"*, The Science Teacher, 63 (9).

Wolf, Kenneth (1996), *"Developing An Effective Teaching Portfolio"*, Educational Leadership, 53; 34.

23

Writing in the Social Studies

Writing assists students to clarify ideas in the social studies. Meaning is increased when students write for a variety of purposes. When writing subject matter, students need to do depth thinking since sequential content must be forthcoming when expressing ideas in writing. Traditional longhand or the word processor may be used as the tool for written expression. What is important is that students have a plethora of opportunities to write across the curriculum. In this paper, the social studies will be discussed in helping students to achieve in writing.

Writing Experiences and the Social Studies

The social studies basal may be used in instruction as a spring board for writing. There are diverse purposes to be stressed here. Thus, students may be guided to perceive purpose in writing a summary. Readiness needs to be in evidence for all writing experiences. After students have completed reading a selection, they may notice essential elements in summarising subject matter. In writing a summary, the social studies teacher may model aloud how this is to be done. He/she may ask students which are highlights of the selection. These are called major ideas. The major ideas should be written on the chalkboard. In a discussion, students may analyse which are key ideas and which are not. The agreed upon major ideas then become the summary of the selection read.

Ideas from the selection read which support the major ideas can be sorted out as being subordinate.

Authentic experiences are important for students. These kinds of activities represent reality or realia in society. Excursions may be taken directly related to what is being studied in an ongoing unit. The excursion might be right on the school grounds to observe soil erosion and grass seeded nearby to avoid/minimise an eroded area. If an excursion is taken to a museum, located further away from the local school, artifacts may be studied by students, for example, pertaining to an early native American culture. To increase retention, students may take notes over observations made and these can be further discussed in the classroom. Note taking is a valuable writing activity since students will take notes when attending college courses or when attending an important event in society.

Letter writing or E-mail messages sent might well be a salient activity, presently as well as in the future. Students may order free and inexpensive things, relevant to the unit being studied. Not only do students receive practical experiences here, but there also is a purpose in sending these messages. Correct form needs to be used in writing a business letter with legible handwriting. Correct, spelling is definitely possible with word processor use. However, the student needs to be close enough to the correct spelling of a word for spell checkers to be effective. Word processor use and sending, E-mail messages are salient for all students to learn to use skillfully.

Multiple choice test items may be written by students when readiness is in evidence. The test items should follow proper form such as:

1. each of the four distractors should be of similar length so that clues are not given as to which is the correct response;
2. the stem together with each distractor should be grammatically correct;
3. each distractor should be rational and not ridiculous.

Test items, as is true of all written work, need to be proof read carefully.

Journal writing may assist students what has been learned since this is recorded. The feelings and emotions may also be entered in pertaining to selected learnings obtained in the ongoing social studies unit of study. Students should show improvement in writing when viewing previous versus later attempts in doing written work. As a variation of journal writing, students may keep a diary on a day to day basis. The diary entries need to indicate major learnings obtained. To avoid "sameness" in writing experiences by a student, committees may be formed in writing the diary entries. These entries may be open for all in the classroom to see and thus better retain subject matter and skills acquired. Logs can be written to summarise the diary entries. By using the information gleaned from the diary entries, students are making application of previous learnings obtained.

A project method of learning provides a plethora of opportunities for doing written work. In doing a project, such as making a committee based model farm scene, students need to make accurate plans, put the plans into operation, and then evaluate the project in terms of clearly written criteria. Much discussion goes into decisions made when making and completing a project. Sequential plans need to be in the offing.

Doing a mural requires the committee to decide upon who does what with definite objectives to achieve. A city block or several blocks may be shown in the mural. Art media, design, and application are salient factors to consider in mural making. Mural quality may be assessed in terms of accuracy, neatness, thoroughness, and effort put forth by committee members. By planning and applying, students learn subject matter increasingly in depth.

Portfolios may also be developed by students with teacher guidance. Each student needs to plan what goes into his/her portfolio. The portfolio needs to have a title, table of contents, as well as carefully sorted and arranged products, including:

1. written products involving a variety of purposes;
2. snapshots/digital illustrations of projects too large to place into a portfolio;
3. art work pertaining to products of diverse social studies units;
4. self appraisal sheets involving personal achievement;
5. an introduction indicating what the student's purpose was for portfolio development. Thus, the student is to answer the question of which objectives were achieved and which are left to achieve.

A library book relating to the social studies unit being taught may be selected by a committee. The content of the library book, in this case, should be suitable for developing a reader's theater presentation. Parts need to be written for each committee member to present in a reader's theater. Practice in reading the parts fluently and well is important when making a presentation to others. Voice inflection and intonation need much emphasis in reader's theater. Reading and writing connections are always salient to stress.

For young readers and those who read in a halting manner may benefit much from experience chart development. Here, for example, students may observe objects or pictures dealing with a social studies unit and then provide subject matter orally for the teacher to record. Students then see talk written on the chalkboard. Together, students with teacher guidance read aloud what has been written. In this way, students notice what is said can be recorded using letters of the alphabet. Sight words are learned by students for future reading. Rereading may occur as often as desired. When ready, students should do their own writing for an experience chart.

When studying a unit on elections, students may do persuasive writing in attempting to persuade classmates to vote for a candidate. Campaign posters may also be made. Pointers should be discussed by the teacher in elements which are involved in attempting to persuade others.

A variety of purposes must be emphasised when writing is being emphasised in ongoing social studies units of study. These purposes or reasons should be clear to the learner. If purposes are clear, then students will put forth increasing effort in the written product.

Methods of Instruction

Methods of instruction used should harmonise with the psychology of learning. First, students need to be fully engaged in the ongoing learning activity. If students feel that the written activity is not important, the chances are minimal effort will be forthcoming. Generally, cultivating the interests of students make for student effort in learning. As much as possible, student choice of content is important to emphasise, such as in writing a poem relating to the ongoing unit of study. The learner may select not only the content to write about but also the type of poem to write be it free verse, couplets, triplets, quatrains, haiku, tanka or limericks conditions do students learn best. There are students who learn best in small group activities whereas others learn best on an individual basis. Opportunities need to be given to have students work under those conditions which foster more optimal achievement.

Seating arrangements in a classroom need to foster student progress in learning. Flexible seating arrangements are more suitable for some as compared to others. Thus, students may be seated within committees in which membership changes depending upon what is being emphasised. A few may be working, individually, at study carols. Some may prefer the more traditional seating arrangements such as being seated in rows and columns. Teachers should discuss with students what preferences they have in seating arrangements for more optimal achievement.

Student preferences in the psychology of learning may vary much from each other. Acceptable noise levels, temperature reading, as well as formal as compared to informal procedures of instruction, will vary from individual to individual. Also, conformity versus non-conformity behaviours will vary as to what is preferred. Style of learning, too, will have preferences among learners. Visual, auditory, and tactual learning preferences need as much teacher attention as possible when making provisions for teaching and learning situations.

Analytic versus global learners as preferences need adequate attention by the social studies teacher. The analytical learner prefers moving from parts to the whole or a generalisation, whereas globally orientated individuals prefer wholeness to begin with and then move on to the parts of specifics of subject matter content (Searson and Dunn).

Conclusion

To emphasise quality writing experiences in the social studies, the teacher needs to stress carefully chosen objectives of instruction, and learning opportunities which assist students to achieve the desired objectives. Assessment approaches used need to ascertain if the objectives of instruction have been achieved by students. If students are to become proficient writers, the teacher needs to plan for written experiences in each social studies unit as well as across the curriculum. Good writers are needed in school and in society.

REFERENCES

Anderson, T.H., and B.B. Armbruster (1984), Studying. In Pearson, Barr, Kamil, and Mosenthal (Eds.), *Handbook of Reading Research* (pp. 657-659). New York: Longman.

Ediger, Marlow, and D. Bhaskara Rao (2000), *Teaching Reading Successfully*. New Delhi, India: Discovery Publishing House, Chapter Eight.

Ediger, Marlow (1997), *Teaching Reading and the Language Arts in the Elementary School*, Chapter Twelve.

Ediger, Marlow (1998), *The Holy Land*. Kirksville, Missouri: Simpson Publishing Company, 53-59.

Ediger, Marlow and D. Bhaskara Rao (2001), *Teaching Social Studies Successfully*. New Delhi, India: Discovery Publishing House, 114-115.

Gardner, Howard (1993), *Frames of Mind: The Theory of Multiple Intelligences*. New York: Basic Books, Inc.

Gerke, P. (1996), *Multicultural Plays for Children*. Lyme, New Hamesphire: Smith and Kraus.

Gunning, Thomas G. (2000), *Creating Literacy Instruction for all Children*, Third Edition. Boston: Allyn and Bacon, 366-372.

Murray, D.M. (1989), *Expecting the Unexpected:* Teaching Myself—and others—to Read and Write. Portsmouth, New Hampesphire: Boynton/Cook.

Searson, Robert, and Rita Dunn (2001), "*The Learning Styles Teaching Model,*" *Science and Children*, 38 (5), 22-36.

Tiedt, Iris M. (1983), *The Language Arts Handbook*. Prentice-Hall, Inc., Chapter Thirteen.

Reading, Writing and Relevancy in Mathematics

Integrating reading and writing into the mathematics curriculum assists the student to perceive the relationship of knowledge and skills. A curriculum area then does not specify separate academic disciplines but stresses the wholeness of student experiences in learning. State mandated testing emphasises students being tested in grades three through eight, as well as in grade ten. Each student's achievement is then monitored for promotion to the next grade level. Passing the state mandated test for the tested grade level indicates progress and achievement. Social promotion is not to be stressed, but rather promotion is based upon demonstrated achievement via test results. Two major academic disciplines are to be tested upon—reading and mathematics initially.

What might the teacher and school do to integrate subject matter from mathematics and reading, both of which do emphasise much written work?

Reading in Mathematics

Readiness for a new lesson may be provided with relating the activities to students' personal experiences. If students can relate their own lives to what will be covered in a new lesson, meaning involving the content should be in evidence. This includes the vocabulary to be used as well as the unique use of terminology in the ongoing lesson.

When reading a mathematics assignment from the basal textbook, students together with the teacher may read aloud the involved word problems. Each student needs to follow along in the read aloud from the test. As the read aloud continues, students may observe each word read so that misunderstandings do not occur due to word recognition problems. After the read aloud, definitions for attached meanings not understood may be clarified. The read aloud assists students to attach meaning to subject matter in mathematics.

If the students are talented, a discussion of the possible new words to be encountered may be clarified without the cooperative read aloud.

What is important is that students in mathematics:

1. read words and symbols with understanding;
2. increase vocabulary development;
3. use what has been learned in new situations;
4. become proficient in problem solving;
5. engage in critical and creative thinking;
6. become increasing proficient in writing;
7. do much discussing so that oral use of language is in vogue and proficiency is developed therein;
8. engage in reflective thinking whereby rehearsal and diagnosis is involved;
9. appraise the self in making progress toward achieving objectives of instruction;
10. have an inward desire to learn (Ediger, 1998).

Students who read in a deficient manner might need assistance in word recognition techniques, such as phonics, in order to associate graphemes with phonemes; syllabication skills to recognise common syllables/root words and thus identify unknown words; and context clues such as relating the unknown word to the rest of the words in the sentence. Reading instruction is then inherent in the mathematics curriculum.

When students engage in written work in solving word problems, the writing needs to be:

1. legible and neat;
2. meaningful and possess clarity;
3. readily interpreted.

When students write word problems, they need to follow the above three criteria, but also increasingly:

1. follow rules of grammar such as having a subject and a predicate within a sentence;
2. have modifiers such as adjectives and adverbs in the proper modifiable position;
3. use conjunctions which do connect clauses of equal value and also those being of subordinate value;
4. emphasise diverse kinds of sentences such as simple, complex, compound, and compound/complex;
5. place punctuation marks appropriately such as periods, commas, semi-colons, colons, quotation marks, question marks, and exclamation points.

Whatever is taught must be developmentally appropriate. The subject matter taught should not be too complex whereby failure to achieve is in evidence. Neither should it be too easy where student boredom and low achievement may be in the offing. Mathematical content needs to be assessed in terms of being useful and not based upon tradition. At national teacher education conventions, the author has listened to mathematicians debate the value of the application of the following having use in society:

1. the area and perimeter of a circle;
2. the volume of a cylinder, a cone, a sphere, and a pyramid;
3. the hypothenuse of a right triangle (See Ediger and Rao, 2000).

Sometimes the uses for determining the values of the above are difficult to assess. To be sure, the author has always prided himself in being able to ascertain the answers to each problem from basal textbooks involving the above. This has been true even if very minimal applications are involved. However, there are values in perceiving the relationships of:

1. of a square (radius squared) times pi (3 1/7). Thus, there are three and one seventh squares in a circle when using the above named formula;
2. once the area of a circle has been found, then this amount is taken times the height. This makes good sense to the student in finding the volume of a cylinder;
3. then, to find the volume of a cone, meaningful learning again is possible. One third the height of the cylinder is equal to the volume of the cone. The student may even experiment with the cone being filled with water three times to fill a cylinder with both having the same base size.

An eighth student of the writer, during the 1955-56 school year asked the following questio: "Why not just put the picnic fork into the carrying case to see if it would fit?" This was asked in relation to a word problem which gave the length and width of the carrying case and the length of the picnic fork. The word problem asked if the picnic fork would fit into the carrying case with the dimensions given. The purpose was to have students determine the answer by finding the hypotenuse of a right triangle. To be sure, the student was right by saying, put the picnic fork into the case and see if it fits without using the formula to determine the hypothenuse".

It is difficult to know which mathematics learnings will be needed by students in society beyond basic addition, subtraction, multiplication, and division as well as decimals, fractions, and per cent. However, those going into specialised fields and professions such as different branches of engineering need to go much beyond these basics. The writer when writing his doctoral dissertation made much use of levels of statistical significance, standard error of measurement, standard error of the mean, standard deviation, and T and F tests. He also considered for his study the use of stanines, multiple regression analysis, as well as multiple and partial correlation.

Perhaps, by finding the hypotenuse, students will be able to determine the answers meaningfully to other mathematical problems faced in society. When being in the seventh and eighth grades, the mathematics textbook used by the writer (1940-1942 school years in particular) contained many problems pertaining to agriculture such as the number of pounds of wheat (60), corn (56), or oats (32) in a bushel; the number of square rods in an acre (a rod is equal to five and one-half yards); the number of acres in a section (640 acres in a section or square mile). These learnings are commonly used and known by farmers presently.

There was a time in educational history where practicality alone was emphasised in textbooks (1920-1930). Problems such as the following appeared, "If a family, burned five and one-half tons of coal for each of five months during winter, how many tons were burned in five years? At $2. 76 per ton, what was the total cost of coal used for the five years during the winter months? Even though the problem is dated in time, there are similarities between that problem and one of today pertaining to the cost and use of propane in home heating. Thus, there are learnings in mathematics which definitely do transfer to other problems in time and space.

When the author was a teacher and relief worker on the West Bank of the Jordan, 1952-1954 school years. A carpenter in the Mennonite Central Committee carpentry school in Jericho was making beautiful, decorative boxes of olive wood. He held up a meter stick for measuring the length of a piece of olive wood. The author then asked the carpenter if that was a yard-stick. The carpenter was puzzled with what was a yard-stick and a yard in measurement. Mind you, he was a carpenter! Well, the author had no knowledge of what a metre was and the carpenter had zero knowledge of what a yard was. The author learned much about the metric system hurriedly including buying raw vegetables by the kilo, not by the pound.

Perhaps, selected philosophers and philosophies may shed light on what is salient for students to learn in mathematics. The present day emphasis upon state mandated testing stresses the importance of a body of knowledge which all students need to master and develop proficiency in. These basics have a long history in education. William Chandler (Bagley (1874-1946) was an essentialist in philosophical beliefs. Bagley believed in common learnings for all students in that a core of knowledge is out there which all students need to master. Thus, for each grade level, educators need to identify what is important for students to learn in mathematics. Major reasons given for students to achieve competency in the basics, according to Bagley were the following:

1. this eliminates teaching trivia;
2. teachers focus on what is vital for students to learn;
3. the basics are useful now and later when students are adults in society.

All students then need to master those identified mathematical learnings which are the basics. These learnings are essential now as well as in the adult world. Mathematics, as well as all academic disciplines, should keep their separate identities (Wahlquist, 1942).

John Dewey (1859-1952) believed that school and society should be integrated, not separate entities. His thinking followed the experimentalist philosophy of education. Dewey had a Laboratory School at the University of Chicago from 1897 to 1907 whereby he put into action his educational thinking. Students with teacher guidance identified problematic situations. These problems identified contextually aided students to clearly identify a problem. Clarity was important in problem identification. Next, students gathered information from a variety of reference sources in answer to the identified problem. The adopted tentative answer became an hypothesis to be evaluated in a life like situation. If the hypotheses was upheld, the solution to the problem was there. If not, the hypothesis was refuted and a new one developed or a completely different problem was chosen. Dewey believed in having students working on what is useful in society, not textbook problems. What is necessary to learn then in mathematics depends upon the problems identified by learners. This would truly emphasise the integrated curriculum since mathematics, reading and writing are stressed as needed to solve identified problems. What is relevant to learn is contained in the process of problem solving (Dewey, 1916).

There have always been advocates of using quality adopted textbooks in the mathematics curriculum. The textbooks have been graded so each grade level has its own appropriate text. Advocates of this approach believed that specialists in mathematics needed to develop a curriculum which has problems and computations for each grade level of students. These specialists then have taken care of much work for teachers in planning and sequencing the mathematics curriculum. It is the teacher's role to implement the curriculum with appropriate oral content and explanations, diagrams, drawings and concrete/semi-concrete teaching materials. The teacher may revise what he/she deems to be necessary to improve mathematics teaching and learning. The textbook plan of teaching mathematics has its critics in that it can become too formal with the same material (the textbook) used in each day of instruction. Individual differences among students may not be adequately provided for when a single text drives instruction. It is true that the teacher might implement the integrated curriculum with students reading content from the text, as well as working problems and computations on paper or with the use of the word processor (Ediger and Rao, 2001).

Final Comments and Questions

It is certainly possible to integrate reading, writing, and mathematics in a relevant curriculum. What is truly salient in teaching mathematics is to develop:

1. student interest in mathematics;
2. reasons for learning;
3. meaning within students in what is being taught and learned;
4. sequential learnings within students;
5. assist students to reflect upon what was learned.

In considering a reading programme, educators should ask several key questions:

- is there scientific evidence that the programme is effective?
- was the programme or its methodology reviewed by the National Reading Panel?
- in reading instruction, are phonemic awareness and phonics taught systematically?
- how are students taught to approach an unfamiliar word? Do they feel empowered to try to analyse and sound out unfamiliar word parts first rather than guess the word from the pictures or context?
- does the programme also include plenty of opportunities for students to practice reading, develop fluency, build vocabulary, develop reading comprehension strategies, write and listen to discuss stories (Shaywitz, 2003).

Updating the Curriculum

An increased number of schools have provided laptop computers for each student such as the middle school level. Homework may then be completed on the laptop. Technology is used increasingly more and more for students to do, not only homework, but also complete in class activities. Handwritten experiences are then on the decline with less paper being used in ongoing learning in opportunities. Topics are searched on internet for research and learning accrues through the latest in technology. Subject matter content and summaries of the research are typed into the laptop. Classroom lessons are experienced online and interactive software used for student questions. Even test may be taken online. This may include taking state mandated tests online.

Technology is costly with the purchase of laptops and personal computers. Add to these costs the updating of the new technology, repair costs and software. Increased technology use is the wave of the future.

REFERENCES

Dewey, John (1916), *Democracy and Education*, New York; The Macmillan Company.

Ediger, Marlow (1998), *Teaching Mathematics in the Elementary School*. Kirksville, Missouri: Simpson Publishing Company.

Ediger, Marlow, and D. Bhaskara Rao (2001), *Philosophy and Curriculum*. New Delhi, India: Discovery Publishing House.

Ediger, Marlow and D. Bhaskara Rao (2000), *Teaching Mathematics Successfully*. New Delhi, India: Discovery Publishing House.

Shaywitz, S. (2003), *Overcoming Dyslexia: A New and Complete Science Based Programme for Reading Problems At Any Level*. New York: Knopf.

Wahlquist, John (1942), *Philosophy of American Education*, New York: The Ronald Press Company.

25

Developing Enthusiasm for Mathematics

Students need to develop feelings of enthusiasm in each lesson and unit of study in mathematics. A higher energy level for learning will then be in the offing. The enthusiastic learner puts forth effort for mathematics achievement. A zest for achievement should then be an end result. Instead of being a passive student, the learner becomes actively involved in achieving objectives of instruction. There are selected psychological avenues which teachers need to consider when assisting students to achieve, grow, and develop. Enthusiasm for learning might well be one of the ends of instruction.

Number One, The Interest Factor

Student interest in mathematics needs to be fostered. Methods of instruction should emphasise interest in learning. Too frequently, students are turned off on in ongoing lessons/units of study. Rather, interest in mathematics needs to be stressed. Interest may be developed through:

1. varying activities such as the use concrete, semiconcrete, and abstract materials of instruction;
2. stressing active student involvement such as using a project approach in learning;
3. emphasising student/teacher planning where feasible;

4. observing off task behaviour and bringing these students into the instructional sequence in an interesting manner;
5. provide adequate background information prior to students working on a specific activity.

Developing student interest in learning mathematics is paramount to their attaining quality attitudes toward learning.

Number Two, the Purpose Factor

Student purpose for learning is salient. If purpose is lacking, there are a lack of reasons for achieving. Clearly stated purposes are essential for students to accept in working on a given lesson. It may take just a few minutes at the most to say why a given lesson is important for students to complete. This is time well spent. Students then perceive reasons for learning and achieving. Motivation accrues when student purpose is involved in learning. Purposes given by the mathematics teacher may include the following based on stated objectives:

1. we need to work more on borrowing in subtraction since several missed answers of yesterday's assignment;
2. we need to do more work on understanding why we carry in addition, since this was evident in completed work handed in;
3. we need to show the formula again for finding the area of a right triangle to indicate why the ideas work.

There are students who possess much purpose for learning in mathematics. They get to work right away after having been given an assignment. These students tend to pursue a task until it is completed. Others need more assistance in understanding reasons for doing an assignment. Purpose in school work and in all of life is vital for students to increase knowledge, skills, and attitudes in mathematics. Mathematics is precise and useful.

Number Three, the Meaning Factor

Meaning theory is very important to stress in teaching mathematics. If students do not understand a new process, more time needs to be spent thereon or reteaching needs to be in the offing. Understanding subject matter indepth is necessary. Why? If students fail to understand subject matter being taught, the new learnings which follow will not make sense. Each objective achieved provides background information for the next sequential goal. It would indeed be difficult for a student to be enthusiastic about mathematics if he/she did not understand what is taught. This lack of undemanding tends to build up as the ensuing grade levels are followed the public school years. Social promotion has been frowned upon by educators and the lay public. That is a major reason that state mandated objectives have been developed whereby students are to be tested in grades three through eight for promotion purposes, as well as in grade ten for the exit test to receive a high school diploma. An opposite point of view pertains to how degrading it must feel to fail on any grade level and be held back, while peers and friends move on to the next grade level. Social promotion might then be desired. The question is, "Might academic achievement and social promotion both be emphasised? It can never be over estimated how important it is for students to attach meaning to the different topics and processes being pursued in mathematics.

Number Four, the Sequence Factor

Students may not do well in mathematics due to having problems in thinking sequentially. Thus, when doing multi-step story problems, the learner must be able to emphasise sequential thinking in coming up with a correct solution. Enjoyment of mathematics includes being able to make sense in thinking sequentially within problematic situations. The following need to make sense but do not require sequential thinking in and of themselves:

1. the commutative property of addition and multiplication;
2. the associative property of addition and multiplication;
3. the distributive property of multiplication over addition.

However, meaning still must be attached as to why the order factor is not important in the above three enumerated items Meaning theory, patterns, and sequence in thinking need to harmonise in ongoing mathematical learnings. Much teaching and practice must be given in order for students to order learnings properly. Selected students will not be able to develop necessary learnings unless they receive direct instruction. This is needed so that enthusiasm for mathematics remains high since its inception.

Number Five, the Individual Differences Factor

Students differ from each other in a plethora of ways. Multiple intelligences theory states that students possess unique strengths in the curriculum. Hopefully, mathematics will be represented in these intelligences possessed. The chances are students will reveal strengths and weaknesses in abilities and talents possessed. Those who are strong in mathematics with its logical thinking emphasis need the best curriculum possible. So do those who may not reveal their intelligence as being strong in mathematics. The latter need a curriculum which also motivates optimal achievement (Gardner, 1993). Society emphasises strongly that individuals be able to take care of their own financial management and economic affairs. How might the mathematics curriculum be implemented so that each student learns as much as possible?

1. stress learning activities whereby students may enrich learnings beyond basal textbook use. Thus, one or more learning stations, in the classroom, with appropriate tasks may be in the offing for students to make voluntary or extra credit choices in learning opportunities. Busy learners in worthwhile tasks should assist in the enjoyment and enthusiasm for mathematics;
2. emphasise that some time be given to cooperative learning. Here, students may receive assistance from peers, as needed. A peer may benefit from this arrangement in that teaching a process makes for indepth learning. There needs to be balance among individual endeavours and cooperative learning. In society, it is important for individual to be able to do important things individually as well as with others in social settings. Enthusiasm may be developed within students for both methods of instruction;

3. use materials of instruction which harmonise with the developmental level of students. Selected students then need more of concrete materials with a hands on approach in learning whereas others can deal more with the abstract phase of achievement;

4. implement facets of learning styles theory which attempts to provide for optimal necessary conditions under which a student learns and achieves. Enthusiasm for achieving may then be emphasised through either an activity centred procedure of learning or a more formalised teacher directed approach; learning by the self versus working within a committee setting; and an activity centred approach versus a basal textbook procedure, in teaching and learning situations (Searson and Dunn, 2001);

5. vary the grouping patterns of students such as using homogeneous and heterogeneous patterns.

Number Six, the Reading Factor

To develop and maintain enthusiasm for mathematics, students need to be proficient in reading subject matter. Being proficient may mean receiving assistance in word and symbol recognition as the need arises. Proactive procedures may involve the following:

1. printing in neat manuscript style new words which might present problems in recognition for selected students, prior to students reading the ensuring content;
2. reading the subject matter aloud with chosen students from the basal as each student follows along;
3. having students say aloud in their own words how a problem is to be worked, after its initial reading.

It is good to have students become as independent in learning as possible. For these learners, independence may promote the necessary ingredient of enthusiasm for and in mathematical reading. Independence may be fostered through:

1. a student proceeding with a task at hand with minimal or a completely unaided procedure;

2. a student assisting those who need help to stay occupied in mathematics;
3. peer teaching being in the offing to students who may benefit from this procedure;
4. materials of instruction being of a developmental level in order that all may develop feelings of success and enthusiasm for mathematics;
5. establish a mathematics club for all levels of achievement with the goals of the club being to foster enthusiasm for mathematics.

Factor # Seven, The Problem Solving Factor

Enthusiasm for problem solving generally is a motivator from its inception to the end. Problem solving skills are salient in school and in society. Society expects individuals to be able to identify and solve relevant personal and social problems. It almost appears that life consists of doing problem solving. There are endless problems to solve in the societal realm. The curriculum area of mathematics is ideal to stress this skill. Students need assistance to identify relevant mathematical problems. These need to be concisely stated so that appropriate solutions may be found. Next, vital information needs to be located in answer to the problem. The answer is tentative and subject to scrutiny. It is important to deal with life like situations but simulated experiences also may be considered as being worthwhile by students. Which mathematical problems might be solved by students:

1. textbook problems may be taught realistically by the teacher;
2. personal problems involving numeracy might well be quite challenging to students;
3. simulated experiences may be made life like and real to students;
4. student written problems involving mathematics might foster enthusiasm;
5. computerised experiences involving problem solving activities.

With problem solving experiences, there are inherent dilemma situations in which students need to think, analyse, synthesise, and assess information. Rote learning and memorisation are greatly minimised in problem solving, but application is made of what has been learned previously. Rearrangement of ideas and subject matter acquired previously, and then a part of seeking a solution to a problematic situation. Problem solving involves complexity in coming up with a possible and probable solution to a unique setting involving creativity in its application. Many times, old solutions to problems do not work and a different approach needs to be found (NCTM, 1989).

Additional Factors Which Need Consideration

Enthusiasm for learning emphasises that challenge be a vital factor in learning. The challenges, however, need to be realistic and not overwhelming. Thus, new objectives need achievement for student growth and achievement to take place. But, with effort the new learnings are attainable. Scaffolding may well need to be in the offing. With scaffolding, the student is able to hurdle the new mathematical learnings through appropriate learning opportunities. A purpose of scaffolding then is to assist students to overcome hurdles at a given time in order to proceed with sequential learning. Not providing the appropriate scaffold hinders the learner from achieving objectives of instruction.

Success is an important point in teaching and learning situations. Failure to achieve indicates:

1. the subject matter is too complex with improved instruction needed;
2. the subject matter may need to be adaptive to the present developmental level of the student;
3. diagnosis and remediation need to be in the offing so that each student may acquire what has not been learned so that continuous progress may be in the offing;
4. encouragement is needed to keep the student on track for sequential achievement;
5. peer learning may assist students to help each other cooperatively and thus achieve more optimally.

Being goal centred helps students to achieve and to attain enthusiasm for learning. The mathematics teacher then should briefly discuss goals to achieve with students so that the latter focusses upon instructional processes. Goals for students need to be clear and acceptable. The teacher may clarify the goals and assist students to perceive the worth of each. Worth can be emphasised with the use which might be made of mathematical knowledge stressed in class. Learnings achievement in class need to be linked with what is important in society. School and society then become integrated, not separate entities.

Motivation always is an important factor in learning. The motivated learner in mathematics will learn more, all things being equal, as compared to the non-motivated. There is an old debate between intrinsic versus extrinsic motivation. The former stresses the importance of students having a higher energy level for learning which comes from within the individual. Extrinsic motivation emphasises a reward system which encourages learning. When teaching graduate students in a curriculum courses, the author elaborated on the topics of intrinsic versus extrinsic motivation. One teacher mentioned she preferred not implementing extrinsic motivation due to the bother involved therein. Another graduate student stated that there are too many who do not achieve in class because there are no physical awards. The discussion was lively and interesting. Both sides felt they had logical arguments for stressing either intrinsic versus extrinsic rewards in mathematics learning. Much depends upon needs of students and the philosophy of the teacher. A teacher believing more in stimulus/response psychology would tend to believe in extrinsic rewards. Humanism, as a psychology of learning, stresses that learning is self motivated and does not require prizes for its forthcoming.

REFERENCES

Gardner, Howard (1993), *Multiple Intelligences: Theory into Practice*. New York: Basic Books.

NCTM (1989), *Curriculum and Evaluation Standards for School Mathematics*. Reston, Virginia: NCTM.

Searson, Robert, and Rita Dunn (2001), *"The Learning Styles Teaching Model"*, Science and Children, 38 (5), 22-36.

26

Learning Opportunities in Science

Students need to experience diverse learning opportunities in science. Each student differs from others in interests, purposes, and needs. It behooves the teacher then to provide for students who differ in a plethora of ways. Diverse activities are available and, also, may be devised to assist students to optimise achievement. The science teacher needs to be on the lookout for promising approaches to use in teaching and learning situations. Which learning opportunities might then be used in the instructional arena?

Assisting Students to Achieve in Science

Learning opportunities need to be challenging to students. Each needs to be actively involved in learning. Basal science textbooks are still being used in teaching science. A good science teacher can do much to make the use of the basal interesting to students. How might a teacher use the science textbook, single or multiple series, to develop optimal achievement within learners? Before reading from the basal, students need to see the new words to be encountered on the chalkboard. These need to be printed neatly in manuscript style. Students need to be actively involved in determining their meanings. The meanings need to correspond to how they are used in the basal. Students need to also develop background information as they discuss the meaning of each new word as well as when viewing the illustrations that relate contextually to the text content to be read.

A hands on approach in learning is salient in the science curriculum. Thus, an experiment may be devised and used to assist students to understand the new words and for achieving background information. For example, if students are to read about the Changing Surface of the Earth, they may show "folding" from different flat layers of horizontally, placed coloured clay, and then gently pushing in from each end of the layers of clay which will cause folding to occur. The science textbook will also show the concept of "folding" as illustrated in the basal. Whenever feasible, a hands on approach should be used involving experimentation before, during, and after the reading of salient subject matter.

Science should make its contributions to the language arts, including reading. If a student can not recognise a word, the science teacher might assist in the following ways:

1. help students in associating phonetic sounds with symbols (graphemes). The relationship shown between sound and symbol must be consistently spelled. Inconsistently spelled words need to be learned mostly by sight, e.g. "through, thought, threw, phone," among others;
2. assist students to use context clues. Thus, if a word is not identified, the reader must use in its place a meaningful word which makes sense. The injected word must be meaningful in relationship to the other words in the sentence or paragraph;
3. guide students to look for a meaningful syllable or word within an unknown word;
4. divide the unknown word into a prefix/suffix and base or root word. The student might then recognise parts to make for a whole word;
5. use onset and rime to identify an unknown word.

New words may be made meaningful for retention if related models are made. A model showing *erosion* as an unknown word may involve a hands on approach to learning. A wooden box may then be taken with soil therein. The box might be at a certain angle of slope. Water poured onto the box will show erosion, especially with no cover crop and a high level of slope. The runoff may be caught in a glass container at the end of the sloped box to show the amount of erosion.

Comprehension of subject matter read is a second dimension of reading, in addition to word identification. The author recommends the following kinds and types of comprehension depending upon the developmental level of the reader:

1. reading for cause and effect. Thus, earthquakes have their causes. Students with teacher guidance may make drawings of faults to indicate causes of earthquakes. Many references sources containing illustrations of a fault may also be used to increase understanding. A model volcano might be made from plaster of paris. Tempera paint should be used to make the sides of the model volcano appear realistic;
2. reading critically. Here, students may separate factual information from opinions to understand faults. Then too, the student must separate the salient from the lesser important ideas on *faults;*
3. reading creatively. This involves developing unique ideas from subject matter read. Novel ideas might be quite salient to achieve when writing poetry pertaining to volcanic eruptions such as of Mount Vesuvius, Mount Etna, ancient Pompei, and Mount St. Helens. Unique ideas too are necessary in problem solving activities such as, "What causes volcanic eruptions?"
4. reading for vital factors. There are important facts to read and remember, pertaining to volcanic eruptions, including lava, heat, pressure, cinder, ashes, smoke, fissures, and eruption;
5. reading for a sequence of ideas. There is a specific order of events which transpire to understand scientific phenomenon. Thus, when students are studying rock formation, they may read about, look at, and handle igneous, metamorphic, and sedimentary rocks;

6. reading to develop inferences. Not everything which is read is direct information such as facts. Data may be read which require the reader to supply an inference. For example, if data is presented in table form pertaining to the dates and places of volcanic eruptions, students may be asked to furnish a conclusion. Thus, from the information presented in tabular form, the learner needs to generalise on what was observed.

Students need guidance to develop each of the above named reading comprehension skills in science. The No Child Left Behind (NCLB) federal law requires students to pass state mandated tests for promotion purposes in grades three through eight, as well as pass an exit test in grade ten. There is no reason that the science teacher cannot assist students to do well on reading. Reading is a salient way of learning in science. Then too, reading may guide students, also, to do well in hands on experiences. Hands on learning with science experiments should be the heart of the curriculum. Objectives, learning activities, and assessment procedures need to reflect the major goals of science education. Learning opportunities need to meet the following criteria for instruction:

1. They need to actively engage students. The interests of students need to be secured for optimal learner achievement to take place.
2. They need to make sense to the learner. If meaning is not attached to what is being learned, the chances are students will be turned off on learning. Understanding key facts, concepts, and generalisations, as well as salient skills being emphasised does help students to feel that science is an enjoyable curriculum area.
3. They need to perceive purpose for learning. Purpose for learning invigorates and challenges the student to achieve objectives. The teacher or student may state reasons for learning in a given lesson, deductively. Or, students may be challenged to state inductively a purpose involved for achieving an objective.

4. They need to meet the learning styles of individuals. A student might learn best by the self. Others might achieve more optimally with committee/group endeavours. Perhaps, a combination of the two should be in the offing since society stresses that people be able to use time wisely individually as well as be able to work harmoniously with others in a group setting.

5. They need to feel motivated to learn. A variety of types of learning opportunities should then be in the offing. Concrete (experiments and demonstrations in science), semiconcrete (CDs, DVDs, internet, video tapes, charts, graphs, and study prints), and abstract (print sources), activities. Motivated students tend to achieve more optimally than otherwise would be the case.

Assessment Procedures

The success of any learning opportunity depends upon how well students achieve objectives. State mandated testing is common is most states in the nation. Science achievement, presently is not being tested in most states, but will be starting in 2007. Thus, those academic disciplines not being tested may receive short schrift. What is taught tends to be tested in the school curriculum. Schools are under considerate pressure to have students pass sequential tests to be promoted in grades three through eight and grade ten.

In selected states where science content is inherent in state mandated tests, teachers are provided with a statement of objectives. These objectives provide guidance as to what to teach. By having students achieve the objectives, they should do well on the state mandated tests providing that:

1. the objectives are clearly stated and are meaningful to the teacher;

2. the test items are professionally written;

3. each test item possesses high validity and reliability.

State mandated tests are *summative* in nature. They emphasise what has been accomplished at the end of a grade level. It is still necessary to evaluate along the way, before yearly summative testing. Thus, formative evaluations need to be in the offing.

Formative evaluations might well be in evidence to notice sequential student achievement:

1. teacher observation, using quality criteria in the assessment process;
2. emphasising diagnostic and remediation approaches;
3. writing teacher written test items such as essay, true/false, matching, multiple choice, completion, and short answer;
4. stressing peer assessment or cooperative learner assessment of a project or activity. Standards for the assessment may be developed by students with teacher guidance.

Recommended Student Behaviour to Increase Achievement

Civility and good citizenship need to be empahsised to increase student classroom achievement in science. Rude behaviour toward others in ongoing learning opportunities distracts from student achievement. Intimidation, bullying, and being hostile are further negative behaviours. A good citizen accepts and respects others when working within a committee or the class as a whole. Students need to assist others when help is needed to make sequential progress in science. The student who fears bullies deemphasises learning and achievement. This is true of personal or web site bullying. Hate groups are already too active in society. Tolerance and positive behaviour is necessary. Achievement occurs when there is assistance in aiding students to belong. Shunning and cliquish behaviour ostracizes individuals. Acknowledging the presence of others indicates a willingness to work together.

Belonging to a group and being accepted therein has another ingredient to stress and that is recognising achievement of each positive contribution made. Thus, esteem needs must be met! The student needs to like the self as well as others. Success makes for positive feelings in life. No student desires to be a failure. Failing is unpleasant. There are times when each will feel as if he/she, in degrees, is a failure in life, but success should be the dominant experience. Reasonable objectives to achieve, learning activities in science which bring in the interests of students, and assessment procedures designed to ascertain achievement are wanted.

Within committee work, each student:

1. needs to participate actively and fully;
2. must be given a fair chance to succeed, but not dominate group endeavours;
3. encourages ideas to circulate within the group;
4. must respect the thinking and contributions of others;
5. desires all to be successful in committee tasks.

REFERENCES

Astin, P, and C. Buxton (2000) *Science As Inquiry*, Boblinks, 10 (2), 10-15.

Blough, Glenn O., and Julius Schwartz (1984), *Elementary School Science and How To Teach It*. New York: CBS College Publishing.

Condrey, Jean Friend (1996), "*Focus on Science Concepts*", The Science Teacher, 63 (4).

Dewey, John (1916), *Democracy and Education*. New York: The MacMillan Company.

Ediger, Marlow (1999), *Teaching Science in the Elementary School*, Kirksville, Missouri: Simpson Publishing Company, Chapter Seven.

—— (1995), "*Designing Science Units of Study*", School Science, 33 (1), 14-15.

Melber, Leah M. (2003), "*True Tales of Science*", Science and Children 41 (2), 24-32.

National Research Council (1996), "*National Science Education Standards*, Washington, DC: National Academy Press.

Ward, Kathleen, et. al. (1996), "*Constructing Scientific Knowledge*", The Science Teacher, 63 (9).

Wolf, Kenneth (1996), "*Developing An Effective Teaching Portfolio*", Educational Leadership, 53; 34.

Current Events in Science

The current events curriculum emphasises what is happening presently. Causes for these happenings may be determined through problem solving. Newscasts may be observed with teacher guidance. The classroom library needs to have up to date magazines with current happenings in science. There are a plethora of happenings which deal with the world of science. Thus, mother nature has many positive as well as negative affects on the planet earth.

Soil Erosion

Much damage is done to soil each year due to heavy rains. Generally, a heavy rain of two inches in 24 hours will cause much erosion to land which does not contain a grass covering or a covering of crops such as corn, wheat, and oats. With bare land, that same rain may cause considerable erosion damage. The amount of damage will be affected, too, by the amount of rainfall from the pervious day. Rainfall, of course, is needed to grow farm crops to produce food and fiber. Express rain then causes soil erosion. Gully erosion cuts a gorge in the soil whereas sheet erosion takes a top layer of soil away. Even light rains causes a small amount of erosion if there is no covering of the cropland such as grass and cereal grains.

The minimise soil erosion, many farmers seed hilly land to grass. Trees also may be planted to prevent soil erosion. Grass can be grazed by cattle, but trees may have few economic values. High quality walnut trees do produce income, but they may have to grow twenty years, from planting time, in order to mature for harvesting and selling.

Students do need to study the causes of soil erosion and learn about methods of conservation of natural resources. Resources personnel specialising in soil protection, CDs, DVDs, farm magazines, video tapes, flims, filmstrips, textbook content and newspaper articles, among others, may well be used as learning activities to secure needed information.

Floods

Flood waters occur when there is too much rain for the soil to absorb and creeks, rivers, water sheds, and lakes over flow. Floods can be very damaging to the top soil; cities may not have adequate storm sewer drainage for flood protection. The flood waters then may be deep enough to heavily damage houses, cars, highways, and washout bridges, depending upon the severity of the heavy rainfall. Houses built on slopes of hills and mountains have been toppled due to heavy rainfall resulting in erosion of soil, which provided a supporting foundation. Houses, cars, highways and washed out bridges can be a complete loss. Additional cleanup expenses accrue. Students need to study and learn indepth causes for natural phenomenon.

Tornados And Their Aftermath

Tornados occur more frequently in Kansas, the Oklahoma Panhandle, Nebraska, Missouri, and Iowa than at other places geographically, but they can strike almost anywhere. Tornados, depending upon the strength of the resulting winds can cause extreme damage to a well built, new house. Trees may be completely rooted out. Cars and trucks may be lifted off the ground and left in a destroyed condition. Tornados may be followed by heavy rains and flood waters. A solidly built new school building was completely demolished at Udall, Kansas, in a tornado with 200 mile per hour wind in the early 1970s! While watching a television programme on natural disasters, the author viewed a man who had survived a strong tornado and was being interviewed. The man soon broke down and cried; he could not complete the interview. The experience was that devastating!

Tornados readily wipe out trailer courts in cities. Remains from the tornado, such as family mementos may be found miles away. Related to tornados are cyclones and hurricanes. The latter has been very destructive along the southeastern coast of the United States. Island nations, such as Cuba, located fifty miles south from the Florida Keys, are highly susceptible to hurricanes and face immense destruction at yearly intervals of time.

Hail and its Problems

Hail, comprised of ice, may be as large as golf ball size. A heavy rain of hail can wipe out crops of wheat, oats, or barely in a matter of seconds. Small pieces of hail lasting for a few minutes in duration may cause considerable crop damage. Also, glass panes in windows may be damaged through large sized hail balls. When an area in a city has been hit by extensive hail, the supply of glass panes from hardware stores may be in very short supply due to high demands. Fortunately, very few people die or are injured from hail due to the taking of shelter.

Volcanic Eruptions

Volcanic eruptions occur at certain locations such as the Pacific coastal areas. Volcanos may be dormant for centuries and yet the eruption causes much damage. They may also be active in that at any time, basically, an eruption might occur. One rather recent volcanic eruption of major importance occurred in 1943 in Paricutin, Mexico. This volcano reached a height of 1500 feet in just seven months. The volcano began with a hissing sound. Ashes, red hot lava, and red hot stone were hurled to the surface. Lava also poured out of the volcano. Other major volcanic eruptions included:

1. Mount St. Helens in Washington state in 1980. Rock and ash coming from the summit crater reached a height of more than eleven miles into the atmosphere. The interior heat of a volcano has tremendous energy!

2. Mount Pelee' on Martinique island which levelled the town of St. Pierre in 1902, killing 30,000 people. Molten rock (lava) rushed down the hills to bury the city.
3. Mount Vesuvius, in Italy, erupted in 79 AD and a fierce extremely hot lava flow buried the modern city of Pompei with its inhabitants.

There are a plethora of questions for students to find information such as (a) what are plate tectonics? (b) why does lava become extremely hot in the earth's interior? (c) why do volcanic eruptions occur? (d) what is a seismograph and its role in describing earthquake activity?

For studying of current events, students with teacher guidance need to identify the problem clearly, such as what causes hail. After the problem has been adequately delimited, then relevant information from a variety of reference sources need to be used to secure necessary subject matter. An hypothesis needs to be developed in answer to the problem. The hypothesis is tentative and subject to evaluation through further information gathering. The hypothesis may need modification or left as is, depending upon the best knowledge and information possible. Problem solving requires:

1. an attitude of curiosity;
2. being open to new ideas;
3. desiring to change one's thinking based on evidence;
4. critical thinking in separating the relevant from the irrelevant in information gathering;
5. creative thought when coming up with unique ideas and novel ways of doing things;
6. effort in moving from problem identification to conducting thorough research and ending up with a possible solution;
7. skills of assessment throughout the problem solving activity;
8. abilities to use diverse reference sources;

9. developmental reading, writing, oral communication, and listening;
10. perseverance in doing the project.

There are additional natural phenomena for students to study in a quality current events programme in science. These include:

- avalanches and mud slides;
- glaciers and earthquakes;
- ocean waves and coastlines;
- faults and folding.

Science items are continually in the news. Students need to stay abreast of current happenings which affect each human being. Weather reports are always interesting to observe on television. They do present much scientific information such as warm and cold fronts, snow and frost, as well as amounts of precipitation in general. Items dealing with each of the above named discussed sub headings on the harmful effects of nature on human life appear almost daily in the news.

REFERENCES

Bower, B. (April 20, 2002), *"Older Ancestors, Primate Origin Age in New Analysis"*, Science News, 161 (16), 243-244.

Clarkin, Mary (April 21, 2002), *"A Ribbon of Redbud"*, The Hutchinson News, Hutchinson, Kansas, 67504.

Ediger, Marlow (2000), *"Project Methods on Science"*, Becoming, 11 (2), 10-12.

Ediger, Marlow and D. Bhaskara Rao (1996), *Science Curriculum*. New Delhi, India: Discovery Publishing House, Chapter Four.

Ediger, Marlow and D. Bhaskara Rao, (2001), *Teaching Science Successfully*. New Delhi, India: Discovery Publishing House, Chapter Four.

Ediger, Marlow (1994), *"The Unexpected in Science,"* Investigating, 10 (3), 24-25.

Ediger, Marlow (1995), *"Designing Science Units of Study"*, School Science, 33 (1), 14-15.

Ediger, Marlow (1999), *"Problems in Teaching Science"*, Experiments in Education, 27 (7), 112-117.

Jorgenson, Olaf, and Rick Vanosdall (2002), *"High Stakes Testing, The Death of Science?"* Phi Delta Kappan 83 (8), 601-605.

Science Learning and the Student

Each student needs to achieve optimally in science. Each part of the science curriculum needs careful planning. The objectives section is of utmost importance. The objectives determine what students are to achieve. All states in the union need to test students in science during the 2008-2009 school year, in addition to reading and mathematics which is presently being emphasised in testing student achievement. Thus, students in grades three through eight must be tested annually and each must pass, before being promoted to the next grade level. This means that students must study hard and achieve optimally. No longer is social promotion adequate Furthermore, each student must pass the exit test before being granted a high school diploma. State mandated tests are a part of the No Child Left Behind law of 2002 and there are penalties if a school has too many failing students. Thus, if a school does not meet the Adequate Yearly Progress (AYP) standards two years in a row, that individual school is listed as failing and students may then enroll in a school which shows passing results.

It behooves the teacher to choose carefully which objectives students are to achieve. The objectives to be selected need to emphasise knowledge and skills ends which are useful to the student presently as well as in the future.

Science Objectives and the Learner

Which objectives, then, should students achieve in any science unit of study? Vital science facts, concepts, and generalisations need identification and implementation in the classroom. The subject matter identified may then be used in problem solving situations. Thus, within a science unit of study, the students need to choose a problem area which has significance and is relevant. Students may work individually or in a committee for possible solutions to the problem. Multi-media must be available to use in gathering information directly related to the identified problem. Media to be used should include the internet, videotapes, science equipment for experiments and demonstrations. Library books, demonstrations teaching, films, filmstrips, illustrations, among other necessary materials. After searching for viable information, an hypothesis is developed which is directly related the problem. The hypothesis is tentative and is to be tested with additional learning opportunities. Adequate verification is needed to truly come up with scientific information. Scientific experiments and demonstrations are the heart of science in a hands on approach to learning.

Within the framework of problem solving, students need to develop needed skills in thinking critically. To think critically the student needs to be able to analyse subject matter in terms of being factual versus opinion, accurate versus inaccurate, and relevant versus irrelevant.

In addition to critical thought, the student also needs to think creatively, Unique ideas are necessary, in many cases, to solve problems. The "tried and true" might not work as solutions. Thus, novelty and originality of decisions must be made. Flexibility of ideas is then needed in the decision making arena.

Quality attitudes should be an end result of all learning opportunities in ongoing science units of study. These attitudes should include the following:

1. wanting to learn more about the world of science;
2. wanting to get along well with others;
3. wanting to be actively involved in doing science experiments and demonstrations;

4. wanting to become proficient in problem solving;
5. wanting to use flexibility in thinking skills;
6. wanting to increase proficiency in using science equipment;
7. wanting to develop adequate skill in reading, writing, and mathematics, especially as these basics relate to the science curriculum;
8. wanting to integrate all academic disciplines, as needed, into the science curriculum;
9. wanting to work cooperatively with the science teacher as well as peers in the classroom;
10. wanting to do enrichment work in science lessons and units of study.

Role of the Science Teacher

In addition to choosing objectives and aligned learning opportunities, the science teacher needs to use appropriate methodology in the instructional arena. A very important factor in teaching science is to obtain the interests of students. A high quality experiment or demonstration, an illustration, and/or concrete objects, related to the unit title, generally will do much to encourage learner attention in the ongoing lesson. Arousal of interests indicates that students are eager to learn and achieve.

Second, students need to have adequate background information to achieve the new objective(s). With important possessed background information, the student is in a better position to perceive sequence in learning. Relating the old with the new subject matter assists the learner to assimilate ongoing learnings.

Third, students need to attach meaning to new learnings encountered. Understanding of new subject matter is a must! It will become increasingly difficult to understand important facts, concepts, and generalisations if meaningful learning is not in evidence. To attach meaning means for the learner to make complete sense of what is being studied.

Fourth, student motivation is salient. With good motivation, the student may reach out and accomplish. The sky is the limit for the student if he/she is motivated to learn more in science. An enrichment centre might then provide choices for the student to acquire vital learnings. *High Expectations and Challenge* are key ideas to emphasise in the institutional arena. Objectives, however, should be attainable.

Fifth purpose is an important factor in learning. Thus, if students perceive reasons for learning, they should achieve at a higher level. The teacher may state the purpose at the beginning of a learning opportunity or inductively assist students to ascertain reasons for achieving a given objective.

Sixth, learning by discovery as well as teacher directed learning should be emphasised. Ample time needs to be given to productive learning by discovery or inductive learning. With inductive learning, students present hypotheses, for example, in answer to a problem in a science experiment. Brain storming is another approach to inductive learning, if quality criteria are followed, such as:

1. all participate and no one dominate in providing possible answers to a question or problem area;
2. respect for the thinking of others is necessary;
3. no one should dominate the brain storming experience;
4. each answer/hypothesis should be recorded on the chalkboard so that duplication of statements is not in evidence;
5. responses given by students need to be clear and concise;
6. no value statements are made pertaining to each answer/hypothesis given;
7. responses given may be regrouped following the brain storming session in terms of being related answers/ hypotheses.

Seventh, a variety of evaluation devices need to be used to assess student achievement. State mandated tests may be one way. This test should provide feedback on what students have missed so that remedial measures may be taken. Since state mandated tests are given once a year, the science teacher must be a good evaluator along the way and assess continuously. Thus, teacher written tests with high validity and reliability should be used. Essay tests, multiple choice test items, true/false, completion, short answer, and matching tests may be used to assess student achievement. Results from the test need to be used to ascertain where, specifically, students exhibit strengths and where assistance in teaching and learning must be emphasised.

Conclusion

Student achievement in science is an important area of personal development. The world of science surrounds the individual with technological improvements, innovations in ideas, and the natural environment. Thus, in medical practices and human health, in agriculture, in transportation, in structural buildings, in communication, the individual perceives what science has accomplished for the individual. The natural environment can be very favourable for human progress with adequate food and fiber production, as well as detrimental with its natural disasters.

REFERENCES

Astin, P, and C. Buxton (2000) *Science As Inquiry*, Boblinks, 10 (2), 10-15.

Blough, Glenn O., and Julius Schwartz (1984), *Elementary School Science and How to Teach it*. New York: CBS College Publishing.

Condrey, Jean Friend (1996), "*Focus on Science Concepts*", The Science Teacher, 63 (4).

Dewey, John (1916), "*Democracy and Education*", New York: The MacMillan Company.

Ediger, Marlow (1999), *Teaching Science in the Elementary School*. Kirksville, Missouri: Simpson Publishing Company, Chapter Seven.

—— (1995), "*Designing Science Units of Study*", School Science, 33 (1), 14-15.

Melber, Leah M. (2003), "*True Tales of Science*", Science and Children 41 (2), 24-32.

National Research Council (1996), *National Science Education Standards*, Washington, DC: National Academy Press.

Ward, Kathleen, et. al. (1996), "*Constructing Scientific Knowledge*", The Science Teacher, 63 (9).

Wolf, Kenneth (1996), "*Developing An Effective Teaching Portfolio*", Educational Leadership, 53; 34.

29

Guidelines for Teaching Social Studies

The social studies teacher needs to be well versed in teaching subject matter and methods of teaching. He/she must be able to motivate students to learn as much as possible. Students are citizens in society presently as well as in the ongoing future. Social studies objectives have much to offer students in achieving viable knowledge, skills, and attitudinal ends. This curriculum area may well be taught integrating history, geography, economics, anthropology, sociology and political science. Other academic disciplines may be brought into the social studies as it would benefit students to do so. Thus, as an integrated unit on history is being taught, the related literature of that time period may also be emphasised. Which guidelines should the teacher stress in teaching and learning situations?

High Expectations for All Students

Challenging goals need to be in the offing for all students. It is not acceptable for any student to fall through the cracks in social studies, but each needs to achieve as optimally as possible. Objectives need to be carefully selected which challenge but are achievable by students. To become an effective citizen, students need to acquire necessary knowledge, skills and attitudes. The knowledge comes from history and the social sciences presented in a manner which is understandable by learners individually. The teacher must be certain that all are achieving optimally. Each student is living in a society which will become increasingly complex with technology and the knowledge explosion being in evidence.

Securing Student Attention

For high quality instruction to be in evidence, the teacher needs to obtain the attention of each student. This means that the teacher has chosen learning opportunities which engage students. Active involvement of learners then is in evidence, rather than having passive recipients in the classroom. The teacher assists students to work individually/collectively on chosen projects. The making of murals, charts, maps/globes, models, puppets and marionettes, as well as construction items occur in a busy classroom. To do each project, much research needs to be done by the student by using a variety of reference sources. A variety of rich learning experiences should be in the offing. Students may share their findings and ideas with other learners in the classroom setting.

Enrichment centres, too, need to be located in the classroom so that a student may go beyond meeting requirements. Choices may be made as to what to do at any one learning centre. Criteria are there to assess student achievement and progress.

Caring for Students

The social studies teacher needs to portray a model of truly caring for students regardless of socioeconomic level. Each student has tremendous worth as a human being and deserves the best instruction possible. This means, too, that negative behaviour toward others needs to be omitted. Every effort must be made to have a pleasant learning environment. Rudeness, put downs, name calling, and bullying must be curbed. If the undesirable are to remain in the classroom, student achievement will go downhill. Accepting each other must be a major objective in classroom behaviour. In the following areas of individual differences, learners need to develop positive behaviours:

1. interests possessed;
2. charisma and charm;

3. physical height and manual dexterity;
4. weight and flexibility of movement;
5. intellectual and abilities;
6. fluency in oral communication;
7. interaction skills and abilities;
8. hobbies possessed;
9. flexibility in adjusting to others;
10. choices made in the classroom.

Thus any of the above areas, a student may be criticised and belittled. When growing up in a strong farming community, the author as a grade/high school student was criticised for not having interests in farm life. Others had tremendous knowledge and interests in tractors, combines, grain drills, harrows, and the like, but the author could never measure up with interests in repairing implements and the specifics of seeding and fertilizing land for crops to be grown. The feelings of put downs send shivers down one's back. It was truly good to leave a farming community and move to a non-rural area where other positive interests were prized and farming was not even considered to be in the top categories of interests valued! It is important to respect individuals who, in many possible ways, are different from the self.

Building Resilience in Learning

Students need to be resilient as learners in the classroom and in society. When students fail in a given situation, they need to receive assistance to regain/develop self confidence. Too frequently, a student may hurtfully tease a learner for responding incorrectly to a question in class or for a project done incorrectly. The teacher needs to phrase questions which do provide opportunities for learners to respond positively. Many questions do not have the correct answer such as when issues are discussed in the social studies. Situations such as these assist students to feel more resilient. Life's happenings occur which make for difficulties in being resilient such as in the following:

1. death or serious illness of a parent/sibling, or important relative;

2. loss of job(s) of breadwinners in the family;
3. destruction of property due to tornados, hail, or floods;
4. personal illness, particularly if it is long term;
5. failing to meet requirements of the No Child Left Behind Act of 2002.

There are a plethora of major problems which any family may experience. Problems in school should be minimised through tutoring, monitoring, and needed classroom assistance provided to students. Problems need to be diagnosed and remedied. For example in reading in the social studies, the teacher may provide help in word recognition including the use of context clues, phonics, onset/rhyme, and syllabication skills, among others. Comprehension skills may be emphasised through assisting students to read critically, creatively, inferentially, and for problem solving. Adequately, teaching word recognition skills as well as comprehension abilities may well make the difference between success and failure in learning to read well.

Resilience of the student is vital when thinking of all the areas in which a learner may fail, but bouncing back is of utmost importance. This is what resilience is all about.

Working Effectively with Parents

With continued emphasis being placed upon students learning more than formerly, it behooves the teacher to stay abreast of new approaches and methods of instruction. Thus, the teacher of social studies needs to confer with parents as often as necessary. There are a plethora of ways to keep in close contact with parents including:

1. parent/teacher conferences;
2. telephone conferences along with leaving messages on the voice recorder;
3. notices/letters mailed;
4. report cards;
5. e-mail messages sent and received;

Cooperation between the home and school is an ideal to achieve in order to assist the student to progress as optimally as possible. Together, the home and the school may solve problems involving difficulties faced by the learner in the social studies. The following are areas which may cause the student difficulties. These may be ironed out with parental involvement:

1. use of and understanding primary sources;
2. understanding relevant concepts in map and globe use;
3. making use of time lines;
4. relating history (time) and geography (place);
5. organisation of information for a report;
6. participating fully in a discussion;
7. accepting others in doing a project;
8. helping a student when assistance is needed to move on in achievement;
9. being able to make progress with inductive methods of learning;
10. achieving well within a hands on approach in learning.

The above listed ways are a few of the problems which a student may face in the social studies. With teacher and parental support, the student may become stronger in each category of learning. Quality objectives, learning opportunities, and assessment procedures are necessary for student improvement to take place in the social studies.

Meaningful Learnings in the Social Studies

Ongoing learning opportunities must make sense to students. It is difficult to build upon what has been learned if meaning is not there. The social studies teacher needs to be certain that students do attach meaning to what is being taught. Those who do not understand may:

1. turn off during a discussion;
2. refrain from participating in an activity due to inadequate background information;

3. respond incorrectly during a discussion;
4. remain very passive in doing a project;
5. bother others who are willing to be active participants.

Each new learning in social studies provides a building block for the new concept or generalisation being stressed. Parroting back a correct answer which comes directly from the basal textbook might well indicate a lack of meaningful learning. Students should say relevant subject matter desired during a discussion in their very own words. When doing this, they may be better able to understand new subject matter encountered.

Using What has been Learned

Sometimes, the level of application becomes difficult for the student. Facts, concepts, and generalisations have been acquired but making use of these learnings is not being made. Thus, the student has learned selected concepts on latitude, longitude, parallels, and meridians, but applying these concepts in a new situation becomes complex. The teacher then must assist students to apply "latitude" in a multiplicity of ways. This may be done through the student:

1. making a mercator map relating directly to an ongoing unit of study, for example, and labelling the equator, Tropic of Cancer, the Arctic Circle, and the North Pole. The same reference lines may be placed on the map pertaining to the Southern hemisphere, such as the Tropic of Capricorn, the Antarctic Circle, and the South Pole. A few intermediate points may also be located and labelled on the map;
2. listening to a newscast or reading about a current event and locating the distance north/south of the equator, as well as east/west of the Prime Meridian, being emphasised;
3. placing north/south and reference lines, pertaining to major degrees of latitude on a blank map projection;
4. attaching meaning to lines of latitude such as related temperature readings, as well as plant/animal life;

5. practice locating a geographical place with the use of latitude and longitude reference lines.

Each map and globe concept needs to be taught indepth. Using the concept in a variety of meaningful ways increase the chances for students to retain and remember.

Learning Styles of Students

The social studies teacher needs to use learning styles theory to ascertain under which conditions students learn best. A major consideration here pertains to students learning better by the self or with others. A student who learns best within a committee setting should have ample opportunities to do so. Or a student who prefers to work individually on an assignment or enrichment activity should also be permitted to do so. Flexible arrangements in grouping students for instruction need to be in the offing.

There are a plethora of ways of grouping students for instruction and each must be considered in the instructional arena in assisting students to achieve more optimally. The following procedures may then be emphasised:

1. homogeneous or heterogeneous grouping;
2. multiple age or multiple grade grouping;
3. student seeking, selecting, and doing, from among alternative activities;
4. student choice of committee to work on;
5. reading activity or hands on approach in learning.

There are choices then in terms of how students are grouped for instruction; the selection made should assist students to achieve more optimally.

REFERENCES

Banks, James A. (1997), *Educating Citizens in a Multicultural Society*. New York: Teachers College Press.

Curriculum Advice (1994), *Geography for Life; National Geography Standards*. Washington, DC: National Council for Geographic Education.

Emery, Donna W. (1992), *"Children's Understanding of Story Characters"* Reading Improvement, 29 (1), 2-9.

Ediger, Marlow (2002), *"The Teaching of Social Studies"*, Edutracks, 1 (6), 6-11.

Ediger, Marlow, and D. Bhaskara Rao (2001), *Teaching Social Studies Successfully*. New Delhi, India: Discovery Publishing House, Chapter One.

Ediger, Marlow, and D. Bhaskara Rao (2001). *Teaching Science Successfully*. New Delhi, India: Discovery Publishing House, Chapter Two.

Ediger, Marlow, and D. Bhaskara Rao (2000), *Teaching Reading Successfully*. New Delhi, India: Discovery Publishing House, Chapter Two.

National Council for the Social Studies (2001), *Curriculum Standards for Social Studies*. Washington, DC: NCSS, pp. 3-6. Excerpted from the Original by Walter C. Parker, and John Jarolimek.

Parker, Walter C. (2001) *Social Studies in Elementary Education*. Upper Saddle River, New Jersey: Merrill, Prentice Hall, Chapter Four.

Searson, Robert, and Rita Dunn (2001), *"The Learning Styles Teaching Model"*, Science and Children, 38 (5), 22-26.

Wiggins, Grant (1993), *Assessing Student Performance: Exploring the Purpose and Limits of Testing*. San Francisco: Jossey—Bass.

30

Teaching History in the Classroom

Considerable attention is being given to the importance of teaching history. History and its study is vital for students in order to become good citizens in society. Students need to understand the events in time which made for their native land as well as for the world. They may then analyse strengths and weaknesses of their nation in its dealings from the beginning until the present. This is a difficult task for any student on any level of instruction. However, now is a good time to begin, whatever the developmental level of the learner. Indepth study is recommended since this makes for better understanding as compared to survey learnings.

What Makes for a Good History Curriculum?

There are a plethora of dimensions which make for quality lessons and units of study in history. The objectives need to be clearly stated with relevant knowledge, skills and attitudinal ends of instruction being in the offing. Knowledge objectives will be plenteous in number to achieve and need careful screening to implement what is truly worthy. Facts, concepts, and generalisations which are enduring need to be separated from trivia. Vital facts are the building blocks for students in achieving concepts. In return, relating significant concepts make for important generalisations.

History emphasises a study of the past. It assists in understanding sequence of events which have in its totality made for the present. To realise the present, however, students need to realise the struggles, the successes, and the attempt to develop meaning therein. Change then is a key concept for students to understand in ongoing units of study in history. One can trace the history of transportation, for example, from the beginning of time such as walking; using horses, mules, and donkeys; early ships and water canals; trains, cars, trucks, buses, and modern rail transportation. Refinements are always in the offing of transportation methods such as power steering, air bags, automatic drive, or star, and computerised parts, among others in vehicles. Life does not stand still but in changing, modifying, and developing.

It is good to assist students to develop time lines pertaining to changes in history. A drawn illustration together with its accompanying printed event may be neatly placed on a line with sequential dates to show the succeeding event such as:

1. Jamestown colony was founded in 1607.
2. Plymouth Rock colony in 1620.
3. Massachusetts Bay Colony in 1630.

Additional colonies and their beginning in time may be added on the time line when they are being studied sequentially.

In addition to change being a key idea for students to understand in history, learners also need to understand interactions among people and how a society adapts to new situations. The United States has indeed become nation of many nationalities and cultures since its beginning. After World War Two ended, many immigrants arrived from war torn areas of Western Europe. People, too, looked for a better life when leaving their native land and coming to the United States after:

1. the Korean War which ended in 1953;
2. the Vietnamese War which was brought to a halt in 1973.

Many immigrants have come from Mexico when seeking jobs and a better future. Those who speak another language than

English do provide challenges to teachers when providing for individual differences among students. Immigrants do need to communicate in the major language of a nation in order to benefit more fully from its many institutions in society. A multi-cultural curriculum then needs to be in the offing. Contributions from other nations must be recognised and diversity stressed when choosing objectives and learning opportunities to achieve these ends.

Technology and inventions play an important role in history. There are a few survivors living today who remember when the automobile was just arriving on the American scene. These people remember when there were paths for automobile transportation instead of roads! This was as late as the early 1920s. Trucks, also, came into being at that time to haul farm crops and a few manufactured items. Sixty per cent of the population were involved in farming. Much heavy *manual* work went into producing grain, meat, and fiber. The pull type combine, pulled by a tractor, to cut wheat came into being in the early 1930s.

With technology, modern ways of living have produced refrigerators, ranges, dishwashers, computers, television, CD and DVD players, among other items of convenience and utility. Modern farms have self propelled combines, hay balers, tractors with hydraulic lifts, implements such as plows, disks, and grain drills which are readily attached to the tractor. Less than two per cent of the population is presently engaged in farming. Technology has certainly made its inroads in a study of history.

Third, the average life span of the individual has increased much from fifty years to seventy five years, since the beginning of the twentieth century in American society. Progress in medical science has done much to curb heart disease, diabetes, cancer, lung disease, and pain, among others. Polio, a deadly, crippling disease as late as the 1950s has been eliminated. Much money goes into educating the lay public to encourage more healthful living practices.

Fourth, philosophical beliefs have been identified within specific periods of time in history. The early Massachusetts Bay Colony, begun in 1630, tended to stress Puritanism in religious beliefs to govern and rule its colony. The Puritans had left England for the New World to seek religious freedom and economic benefits. They wished to continue to separate themselves from the Church of England. Puritan rules were strict pertaining to punishing those who did not believe and act "correctly". They believed strongly in absolutes in religious beliefs. God determined human history and was angry at those who failed to follow Puritan beliefs. Toward the later Colonial years, religious beliefs had changed much with deism being in strong evidence, especially by farmers of the United States constitution. Deism emphasised the importance of science, human progress, perfectibility, and freedom of expression. They believed in a God who had set the world in motion and then left it up to human beings to progress and move forward. Today, much stress is placed upon experimentalism, as a philosophy of life, with its problem solving approach. Problems need to be identified and solved in the societal arena.

Presently in American society, there is a divided camp between conservatives who favour a very strong form of capitalism, freedom from any form of abortion, complete opposition to same sex marriages, and strong military intervention in foreign affairs. To the somewhat opposite end of the continuum, liberals represent those who are more inclined to emphasise national health care, more money spent on education, taking care of the needy, and more money spent domestically, in general. A strong military is stressed by both sides, conservatives and liberals, of the spectrum.

From the above named trends, among others, objectives need to be selected which harmonise with democracy as a form of government and as a way of life.

Selecting Objectives in Historical Units of Study

Knowledge objectives must be weighted and carefully considered since there is much subject matter which may be taught. History objectives then need to be chosen carefully from among the following periods of time:

1. Colonial America, beginning with the first permanent colony in 1607.
2. Growth and settlements in the colonies up to the American Revolution in 1776.

3. The American Revolution, and a new nation 1776-1815.
4. Expansion, the Westward Movement, and Issues pertaining to Slavery.
5. The Civil War (1861-1865) and Reconstruction (1865-1877).
6. Development of the United States in terms of railroads, manufacturing, and industry.
7. Involvement in World War One (1917-1918) and World War Two (1941-1945) involving sacrifices of life on the battle fields, as well as cost of military equipment used in war.
8. Contemporary America with its many inventions, techniques, and beliefs to make for a better society. However, intermittent involvement in wars included the Korean War (1950-1953), and the Vietnamese War (1962-1973).

From the above named periods of time and unit titles, the history teacher may choose relevant objectives. These knowledge objectives should incorporate vital facts, concepts and generalisations. The following knowledge objectives might be worthwhile for students to achieve pertaining to colonial America:

1. The student will give three reasons why many colonies grew rapidly in the new world.
2. The student will give four reasons which hindered some colonies from growing even more rapidly than they did.

Each objective needs to be clearly stated. The teacher, also, needs to choose learning activities which assist students to achieve the stated objectives of instruction. Periodically, the teacher needs to evaluate with students the correctness and appropriateness of each response.

A few states have state mandated objectives and their accompanying test which measure if students have achieved criteria in social studies for their grade levels in grades three through eight, and also in grade ten as an exit test. Most states, at the present time do not test for student achievement in history and the social studies, but do test in reading and mathematics, as mandated by law. Many educators, believe strongly that history and the social studies should also be mandated by each state for testing purposes. The thinking is that the academic areas being tested receive more attention than those not being tested in state mandated testing.

Knowledge or subject matter objectives should emphasise different levels of cognition and skills involved. Certainly, students should not stay merely with the learning of facts, but also achieve more complex ends such as:

1. understanding what has been taught so that meaning is involved in learning;
2. using that which has been learned;
3. thinking critically as in separating facts from opinions, fantasy from reality, and accurate from inaccurate statements;
4. thinking creatively by coming up with unique ways of solving problems;
5. assessing the values or worth of information being considered.

Quality attitudes also need to be developed within students. These attitudes need to include that students:

1. develop a love for learning;
2. respect and accept each other as human beings having much worth;
3. assist each other, as needed, to achieve objectives;
4. identify problem areas in history and the social studies;
5. analyse subject matter;
6. use subject matter in novel and unique ways to meet specific purposes;
7. apply what has been learned to new situations in the social studies curriculum and in life;
8. want to be a good citizen;

9. place good human relations high on the list of objectives to achieve;
10. participate eagerly and fully in ongoing lessons and units of study.

Learning Opportunities to Achieve Objectives

Learning opportunities to achieve objectives should be engaging, interesting, and purposeful. They should assist students to become motivated individuals. Multimedia approaches should be used to provide for the needs of individual students. Multimedia stresses the concrete whereby students learn from realia and real objects and items. Semi-concrete materials stress the use of CDs, DVDs, illustrations, study prints, transparencies and the overhead projector, video tapes, films, and filmstrips. Pictorial forms are inherent in the semiconcrete. Abstract materials are the most complex for many learners since letters and numerals in symbolic form are used in reading and learning. Thus, textbooks, library books, encyclopaedia entries, work books, written work, and primary sources consisting of letters, diary entries, artifacts, biographies, autobiographies, among others, may be classified as abstract materials of instruction.

To use each of the above concrete, semiconcrete, and abstract materials, diversity of methods may be used to provide for individual differences in the classroom. The following methods of instruction might then be used:

1. learning by discovery or induction;
2. deduction whereby ideas move from a speaker to the classroom audience;
3. problem solving procedures;
4. committees at work, dyads, as well as individual endeavours;
5. peer mediated instruction and teaching;
6. heterogeneous and homogeneous grouping;
7. large group, small group, and individual projects;
8. cross grade grouping;

9. use of learning centres and self selected tasks;
10. enrichment learning which goes beyond assigned lessons.

The teacher of history needs to study students and ascertain under which conditions each learner may achieve most optimally. It is good if a teacher has quality aid service available. Retired teachers may make for a good source of teacher aid service. Properly trained aids may assist the regular teacher by reading historical content aloud to students having problems in reading. They may also listen to students read aloud certain portions of difficult as well as important textbook content. Other tasks for the aid might well involve the following:

1. evaluation of student written work;
2. listen to and assess oral student book reports;
3. make materials for teaching history;
4. assist students with dramatizations involving incidences in history;
5. work one on one with very low achieving students.

Assessment of Student Achievement in History

There are a plethora of quality ways to assess learner achievement. If a state mandates testing in history, hopefully there will be feed back to the teacher on what can be done to assist student achievement. All test items should be valid. Thus with state mandated objectives as a guide, the teacher may use these guidelines in teaching. If the test is aligned with the objectives, the history teacher should have considerable assurance that what is taught will relate directly to items on the lest. This is especially true if the state mandated test has also be pilot tested for reliability either through test/retest, split half, and/or alternate forms of reliability.

Systematic testing, using teacher written tests, may assist the history teacher to ascertain which facts, concepts, and generalisations students have left to achieve. Learning activities might then be provided to minimise student errors made on the test. Testing, according to the writer, should be done to determine how successful the instructional process has been. Testing tc compare students in achievement has very few, if any, benefits. Rather, testing and test results may be helpful as teaching tools and that tool being to find out if additional learning activities need to be provided due to students having missed out on responding correctly to any test item. Test items should be varied, in kind, to provide for diverse learning styles of students. Thus the following kinds of test items may be administered to students:

1. true/false, with corrections made by the learner to change a "false" test item to that of being "true";
2. multiple choice, with each distractor being plausible;
3. completion, with inadequate information given so that a student may respond to a meaningful test item. –, –, and – are in –, is not meaningful to the student in making responses;
4. matching, whereby a student matches column A with column B. There needs to be more items in one column as compared to the other so that the process of elimination may be minimised when students respond to a matching test;
5. essay, in which students may engage in problem solving. These kinds of test items may be quite open ended which truly might encourage problem solving. To make for more objective scoring, a rubric should be carefully designed and used;
6. short answer, in which students respond to a question but the require answer may consist of a phrase or sentence.

Teacher observation may be an excellent way to ascertain student achievement. Quality standards need to be used here. Teacher observation may well be continuous and ongoing.

Themes to Emphasise in the Geography Curriculum

There are major themes in geography which all teachers should incorporate into the social studies. These themes assist students to organise information and relate relevant ideas. Teachers need to study and experiment with using a set of structural ideas to facilitate student learning. Otherwise, learning may comprise of isolated facts, concepts, and generalisations which are difficult to remember, use, and to apply. Then too, what is taught may consist of trivia and the unimportant. These situations can be largely avoided if time is taken to select vital ideas which stress a structure of knowledge. Geography teachers in the social studies need to meet together with university professors of the social sciences to identify salient ideas in the curriculum. The identified ideas may then become objectives for use in teaching and learning situations. A good set of guidelines to use here were developed cooperatively by the National Council for Geographic Education (NCGE, 1994).

Place Geography in the Social Studies

Place geography in the past might have stressed location and memorisation of capitol cities of states and nations. When being a grade school and/high school student, 1934-1946, the author remembers well when mimeographed outline maps within a unit of study, with heavy basal textbook use, were handed out to students. Capitol cities, states and nations, along with major rivers, were to be identified and labelled by the student. In fact in a college course entitled "Principles of Geography", the instructor handed out several outline maps, and we the students were to fill in different information or data thereon such as the location of bays, seas, oceans, major sea ports, and capitol cities of nations, among other items. The author cannot say that this was all in vain, because there are a plethora of salient remembrances here on place geography.

But, the study of place geography might have been enriched with meaningful characteristics. Thus, a study of the Dead sea in the land of Palestine may be enriched with the use of AV materials containing vital facts, concepts and generalisations such as:

- it has no outlet and thus contains 26 per cent salt and other minerals;
- it is receding at an annual rate of 300 yards since almost no water is received from the Jordan River;
- it is desert area with less than five inches of rainfall per year;
- it had ancient civilization nearby such as the ruins of a religious sect known as Qumran with its storerooms, scriptorium, communal kitchen and dining area, along the northwest shore of the Dead Sea;
- it is the place where the Dead Sea scrolls were found.

A multi-media approach in teaching needs to be used so that all students may benefit optimally in geographical learnings.

Location

Location describes the connections of the specific place, such as the Dead Sea, with other places and people. The Dead Sea has interesting connections with other places such as:

- it is connected with the fresh water Sea of Galilee in the north, 67 miles distant, the connector being the Jorden River. Water used for irrigation purposes from the Sea of Galilee has made the Jorden River almost without water as it empties into the Dead Sea;

- the Sea of Galilee is excellent for fishing and used by tourists for commercial water transportation to nearby villages including the ancient site of Capernaum with its restored Jewish synagogue of the third century AD;
- the Sea of Galilee is 660 feet below sea level whereas the Dead Sea is 1300 feet below sea level making the former much more hospitable for human endeavours;
- it receives most of its waters from the melting snow of Mount Hermon, located directly to the north, with an elevation of 14,000 feet above sea level.

Teachers need to assist learners to perceive knowledge as being related and connections need to be made.

Human Environment Interaction

The Dead Sea area is very inhospitable as compared to the Sea of Galilee. Human beings, however, can modify their surroundings to make for a better life. The city of Jericho, located four miles northwest of the Dead Sea, is 800 feet below sea level and would be a desert if it were not for several springs available for irrigation. With irrigation water from Elisha's fountain, Jericho is a beautiful garden spot. Humans over the centuries have built irrigation channels to send water to where it is needed. Jericho, an oasis, then has luscious, bananas, grapefruit, oranges, lemons, limes, and traditional vegetables including carrots, green beans, spinach, and peas. The irrigation channels are built of concrete and serve their purposes well to provide water to where it is needed.

Early in the latter part of the first century BC and the early part of the first century AD, ancients thought of a new approach to secure water, other than from local springs. Caesarea was built by Herod the Great in honour of Caesarea Augustus, ruler of the Roman Empire. Engineers of the Roman Empire devised aqueducts which channelled water from a distance to the desired place. Cities, such as Caesarea might then be built in any area as long as water could be channelled to reach these distant places of human habitation. Caesarea, presently, has a beautiful, well restored, excavated amphitheater. Amphitheaters were used to provide entertainment for people of their day. Caesarea is located along the Mediterranean Sea between Haifa and Tel Aviv.

Regions As Defined By Geographers

A region has homogeneous characteristics within that area of land such as the Dead Sea and Jericho being in a desert. A desert may be defined in terms of its characteristics such as having less than five inches of rainfall per year, among other criteria. The Middle East region on the planet earth can be located on a map and globe. Characteristics of the Middle East include the Mediterranean climate:

- rainfall is present from November to April only, with no rainfall, basically, from April to November;
- limited rainfall makes for desert situations, unless irrigation is possible or an area receives adequate rainfall for the six months which must then last a calendar year. Thus, Jerusalem receives 25 inches annual rainfall amount and has moderate temperature readings due, in part, to being 2500 feet above sea level. Even than, the surrounding Judean Hills begin to look barren after the beginning of July;
- specific agricultural crops are grown in the Mediterranean region including olives, citrus fruits, dates, figs, almonds, sesame seeds, and pomegranates, as well as wheat and barley;
- the bedouin population uses donkeys and camels for transportation. Sheep and goats are raised for a supply of meat along with some cattle. The kinds of livestock raised and used are adapted to semi-desert life;
- cities can be quite modern and sell state of the art equipment and machines. Cairo, Damascus, Tel Aviv, Haifa, Amman, Jidda, and Riyadh are examples of modern cities, in whole or part.

Characteristics such as those listed above separate the Mediterranean region from North and South America, and Australia, among others. When defining the Middle East as a region, there are homogeneous as well as heterogeneous characteristics. Thus, within that region, there are language differences such as Arabic and Turkish, the latter spoken in Turkey. Religious differences also are in the offing such as Islam being dominant (Sunni and Shiaa), Greek Orthodox Christian, as well as Roman Catholic, among other less populous religions (Ediger, 1998).

Human Interaction on the Planet Earth

There is much human interaction within a region such as within the Mediterranean World. People do need to produce goods and services for human use and consumption. Interaction is then needed to provide/distribute food, clothing, and shelter. These may be produced locally or imported. Then too, there is much interaction among people from different regions and continents. Thus, people come to the Mediterranean world for a variety of purposes. For example, in normal times, many tourists come to the Holy Land to visit sites of religious significance including:

- The Church of the Annunciation in Nazareth.
- The walled city of Jerusalem.
- The Church of the Holy Sepulcher in Jerusalem.
- The Dome of the Rock, an octagonal shaped Mosque, with a gold plaited dome, in Jerusalem.
- The Western Wall, the only remnant of the ancient Jewish Temple.
- The Church of the Nativity in Bethlehem.
- The rich history of the city of Hebron.
- Famous Tombs such as of Christ; Mary, Absalom, son of King David; and Joseph, the son of the Patriarch Jacob.
- Jacob's hand dug well in Samaria.

People from the Mediterranean World visit other geographical regions on the planet earth. Some migrate to a different region in looking for improved opportunities such as jobs, professions, safety factors from wars, and education. People are mobile and move to other nations and regions in order to satisfy basic needs (Ediger and Rao, 2001).

Important Factors in Learning

The geography teacher needs to master subject matter as well as use appropriate methods of teaching. Thus, he/she needs to engage students actively in ongoing learning activities. If students then are making relief maps, each needs to be thoroughly involved. Students here may work individually or within a committee, preferably meeting their unique learning styles. As a result of these activities, students should become increasingly interested in place located and other related information containing relevant concepts and generalisations. Placing the Dead Sea (1300 feet below sea level), the Sea of Galilee (660 feet below sea level) and the Jordan River as a connector, assists students to use knowledge in making a relief map.

Second, students need to perceive purpose for learning. Mere busy work is not a purpose, but assisting students to see reasons for making a products map may clarify for learners in which regions specific farm crops are grown. The learning activity should help students to acquire information on why the agricultural products are grown in that particular area. Information on citrus fruits and vegetables grown in the Middle East can be placed on a products map in pictorial form.

Third, students should experience quality sequence in learning. Each idea gained should provide background information for the new objective to be achieved. With objectives to be achieved being related, the student should perceive connections in the geography curriculum. Thus, knowledge about agricultural products grown should provide necessary information on marketing and selling consumer items. Related knowledge and skills are retained for a longer period of time as compared to isolated learnings.

Fourth, students should perceive meaning in teaching and learning situations. Learners who understand subject matter taught will be better able to apply what has been learned as compared to meaningless content acquired. Depth learning should be stressed. A variety of learning activities pertaining to a concept or to a generalisations should help students to attach meaning in achieving objectives.

Fifth, individual differences should be provided for in the multi-cultural geography curriculum. Students individually possess multiple intelligences (see Gardner). The strengths of each student must be respected/accepted and used positively in the classroom setting. For example, a student who does not read well may work within a committee where there is a proficient reader. Those who need assistance in reading may receive this kind of help. Thus, the good reader may work harmoniously with other committee members in doing art work, construction experiences, creative dramatics, and the making of models, which relate directly to the ongoing unit of study in geography.

Sixth, classroom experiences need to stress problem solving activities. Students may identify and secure information from multi-media sources on:

- what caused the Great Rift along the Jorden River;
- what causes folding such as that in the Judean Hills;
- why there is level land in the fertile triangle of the Plains of Esdraelen (20 x 20 x 30 miles in dimension) while the other surrounding land areas are hilly and mountainous.

Conclusion

A student centred geography curriculum needs to contain essential elements. These elements, among others, include quality, challenging, objectives, which are attainable by learners. Learning opportunities need to assist students individually to attain the chosen objectives. Assessment results help to determine if the objectives have been achieved, as well as provide feedback to students and teachers for further learnings needed.

REFERENCES

Ediger, Marlow (1998), *The Holy Land*. Kirksville, Missouri: Simpson Publishing Company.

Ediger, Marlow, and D. Bhaskara Rao (2001), *Teaching Social Studies Successfully*. New Delhi, India: Discovery Publishing House.

Gardner, Howard (1999), *The Disciplined Mind*. New York: Simon and Schuster.

National Council for Geographic Education (1994), *Geography for Life*. Washington, DC: NCGE.

32

Notebooks in the Social Studies

Writing experiences for students in the social studies assists in clarifying ideas and developing understandings in greater depth. Each student needs to keep a notebook to record information gleaned in ongoing units of study. Notebooks are handy sources for review of what has been learned previously. Retention is then aided. Questions may be raised of notebook content leading to indepth learning. Student ownership of recordings made in the notebook is to be encouraged. How should the social studies teacher proceed in student notebook development?

What to Write About

Students need to have subject matter content to incorporate into a notebook. Thus, background information needs to be acquired by the student in order to have something to write about. Interesting social studies units of study might well provide the needed information. Each unit need to be well planned. The objectives must be carefully chosen so that relevant knowledge, skills, and attitudinal ends are in evidence. Learning opportunities to achieve the desired ends must stimulate student learning. The learning opportunities need to be varied and provide for individual differences in the classroom. Assessment procedures to ascertain learner progress must be valid and reliable.

Learning opportunities need to capture student attention and be engaging. A dull social studies curriculum needs to be changed to one which is challenging and achievable. Meaning needs to be inherent in student learning. If students do not understand subject matter taught, they will tend not to be interested in doing written work. Meaning theory must be emphasised in all social studies experiences for students. Also, purpose in learning is salient to stress. With purpose, students perceive reasons for achieving and for doing written work. With purpose, learning is not done for the sake of doing so, but rather to accomplish a goal or objective. In written work, there will be diverse purposes in writing.

Within the above named framework, students need to experience a rich environment for writing. There are a plethora of experiences for written work in the social studies. One kind is to have students indicate what was learned within unit of study. The written work may be divided into daily or weekly writing. The plans need to be flexible to notice student desire to write.

When writing, students need to perceive the relationship of knowledge. Background information has a plethora of relationships. Thus, in the social studies, the student has acquired concepts and generalisations pertaining to history, geography, political science (government), economics, sociology, and anthropology. When new learnings accrue in the social studies, the subject matter is related to previously learnings. By doing this, the student is achieving more of indepth knowledge as well as in skills. Skills stress the importance of using methods of inquiry as each academician does in his/her academic area of speciality. The historian then has specific methods of inquiry such as in using primary and secondary sources in studying relevant ideas of the past. To an historian, a study of change, interaction of culture, people, and ideas are important. Technological and economic changes need to be studied as they affect people. Continuous change occurs on the world scene with borders, power of nations, and alliances.

The geographer uses a variety of maps and globes, among other data sources, to obtain useful ideas in changes pertaining to the natural environment or political boundaries. Thematic approaches become important in that five major themes have been stressed by the National Council for Geographic Education and the Association of American Geographers for student inquiry, knowledge and skills. These five themes are:

1. movement of humans when interacting with the planet earth;
2. regions and how they form and change;
3. human and environment interaction;
4. location and position on an earth's surface;
5. place: physical and human.

The above five named themes should permeate geographical learnings in the social studies.

Political science in the social studies stresses a study of diverse levels of government and their influence on human beings. A major role of government is to solve problems among human beings, involving different levels courts, pertaining to disputes among individuals and groups, so that an orderly society may exist. Taxation, law enforcement, property rules/regulations, and elections, are key concepts to emphasise in political science within the social studies.

Economic concepts for student understanding in the social studies are the following:

1. law of supply and demand;
2. surpluses and unemployment;
3. goods and services;
4. inflation and interests rates;
5. cost of living, salaries, wages;
6. labour unions and corporations;
7. gross national product;
8. opportunity costs;
9. natural resources;
10. human resources.

Anthropology and sociology stress concepts pertaining to the human made part of the environment. Culture, as a concept. stresses products and ideas of human beings such as clothing worn, means of transportation, foods eaten, music developed, recreational activities, religious beliefs, art, drama, architecture, and literature of a given society. Subjectivity is brought into social studies units when studying the works of human beings. The writer has studied the Old Order Amish in society for some thirty years. They possess different beliefs as compared to the dominant group in society. Thus, Old Order women wear long dresses extending to the ankles, sleeves going down to the wrist, and a high neckline. A prayer bonnet is always worn. Clothing colours are plain with no stripes and no checks. Means of transportation in the neighbour involve the use of a horse and carriage, not modern automobiles. Religious services for the group are conducted in homes or in barns, not in a church. The services are conducted in the German language with Pennsylvania Dutch spoken in the home setting and informally among the Old Order Amish, whereas English is spoken in society. Art work is minimised; however, Amish women are very artistic when sewing design blankets for sale. Amish children do some art work. The author has a drawing by an Amish student entitled, "A City Set on a Hill", which is taken from The Sermon on the Mount (Matthew 5-7), "A city set on a hill cannot be hid". Music in Amish churches consist of German Hymns with no musical notes and no musical accompaniment with the use of pianos and organs. The musical score is handed down by oral tradition. Pitch pipes are not used to start a hymn.

Taking Notes in Class

Note taking should reflect basal subject matter content from the academic disciplines making up the social sciences as indicated above. Students then need to have understandings pertaining to what is history, geography, political science, economics, and anthropology/sociology. Balance among these academic disciplines must be emphasised. To study human beings from one or two academic disciplines is not adequate. Each human is a complex being who is influenced by his/her past (history), region (geography), system of government (political science), buying patterns of goods and services (economics), and culture (anthropology/sociology). Individuals do not live in a vacuum, but interact with others in institutions in society.

The teacher needs to demonstrate, for student observation, how notes might be taken over discussion content. For this, purpose, the author suggests that the teacher play a developmentally appropriate cassette dealing with social studies content, presently being studied. The teacher may analyse with student input as to which are the salient ideas in the recording. Each major generalisation should then be recorded on the chalkboard. There might be ten suggested major ideas, forthcoming. The ideas need to be discussed in depth to seek consensus on what should be put down in note taking. When students take notes, they may wish to compare and contrast what was written with that of classmates. This is an intellectually challenging experience. Notes may also be taken covering subject matter from the basal text.

Students using modern technology to obtain vital information from the internet find that note taking is a very valuable skill. The notes taken highlight subject matter needed for the ongoing social studies unit. Notes taken may be summarised with word processor use. Maximum use needs to be made of computer technology since it changes rapidly to offer vital services for consumer use. Unless a person keeps abreast of computer services and use, he/she will remain further and further behind in the wave of the future.

There are many advantages in taking notes. They can be a source for rather instant review of subject matter. Retention of content is a problem for everyone. Each person wishes he/she could remember things better. As information is recorded, it is being rehearsed. Indepth learning is more likely to take place when ideas are recorded. Some kind of use is then being made of knowledge and skills acquired.

An alternative to note taking is to outline subject matter content from the basal. Here, the student needs to arrange ideas read in terms of major generalisations, subtopics, and details. When students work on these parts of an outline, the perceive is sequence of ideas expressed. Not only is sequence stressed, but also critical thinking is in the offing. It takes time and effort to use higher levels of cognition. Critical thinking is stressed when students perceive ideas as being of major and minor importance. This does not mean that subtopics and details are unimportant. Not at all. The subtopics must support the major generalisations and the details need to relate and substantiate the subtopics. Critical thought assists in separating the major from the less salient ideas.

Keeping diary entries helps students to retain and use ideas gleaned from ongoing social studies units of study. Each day a student records ideas pertaining to what has been achieved. The ideas achieved are dated as in keeping a regular diary. So that boredom and the routine does not set in, it is good to change membership as to who keeps the diary entries, be it done individually or in a committee.

Journaling provides opportunities for the student to record personal interests and feelings within a social studies unit. Also, what has been acquired and what is left to learn may also be written in the journal. Journaling and other means of recording ideas provide students with chances to reflect upon a unit. Reflection gives the student opportunities to think of gaps in knowledge obtained as well as in indentifying problems areas for discussion and possible solutions.

Cooperative jouranaling may interest students in that a learner responds to another person's journal entry. The entry may deal with discussing an item studied in the social studies or a personal area of interest in the social studies.

Poetry writing related to the social studies unit being studied opens windows of opportunity for written work in a journal. There are numerous kinds of poems to write. The student, when ready, should choose the poetry type. The student needs to select the subject matter to write about. Rhymed verse may be written such as couplets, triplets, quatrains, and limericks. Free verse need not contain any rhyme and is an open ended poem in length. Haiku and tankas have selected numbers of syllables per line such as haiku has five, seven, five syllables for each of three lines of verse. Add two more lines to the haiku with seven syllables each and a tanka results. Poems written may be strictly personal and not to be shared with others or learners may wish to share the poetry written. Generally, if one student shares his/her poem, the others may desire to do the same.

Charts may also become a part of the notebook. There are a variety of charts which convey information about the present unit being studied. Vocabulary charts may be very useful to develop and provide opportunities for review of selected concepts. Additional charts to be incorporated into a notebook include:

1. a narrative. Here, a student tells the ordered steps of an event;
2. an organisation chart. The student indicates lines of organisation in government such as on the federal level—the President, the Senate and the House of representatives, as well as the members of the Supreme Court;
3. a time line showing major events studied in reference to time;
4. a classification chart which indicates the types of homes, foods eaten, recreational activities, work performed, and transportation of a given culture being studied.

Drawings, diagrams, graphs (line, bar, picture) might become a part of a student's notebook. Here, the student indicates understandings obtained from different social studies units through other means than written work, solely. Students need to reveal knowledge, skills, and attitudes achieved through a variety of methods in a notebook.

REFERENCES

Aiken, Adel G., and Lisa Bayer (2002), *"They Love Words"*, The Reading Teacher, 56 (1), 68-75.

Astleitner, Herman (2002), *"Teaching Critical Thinking Online"*, Journal of Instructional Psychology, 29 (2), 53-76.

Chappuis, Stephen, and Richard J., Stiggins (2002), *"Classroom Assessment for Learning"*, Educational Leadership, 60 (1), 40-41.

Ediger, Malow, and D. Bhaskara Rao (2000), *Teaching Reading Successfully*. New Delhi, India: Discovery Publishing House, Chapter Eight.

Ediger, Marlow (2002), "*Developing a Reading Community*", Edutracks, 1 (4), 16-19.

Ediger, Marlow (2002), "*Social Studies and the Guidance Counselor*", Experiments in Education, 30 (9), 176-181.

Ediger, Marlow (2002), "*Improving Spelling*", Reading Improvement, 39 (2), 69-70.

Gardner, Howard (1983), *Frames of Mind: The Theory of Multiple Intelligences*. New York: Basic Books.

Maslow, A.H. (1954), *Motivation and Personality*. New York: Harper and Row.

Meyer, Richard J. (2002), "*Captives of the Script: Killing Us Softly With Phonics*", The Reading Teacher, 79 (6), 452-461.

National Science Teachers Association (2001), *Classroom Assessment and the National Education Standards*. Washington, DC: the Association, NSTA.

Searson, Robert, and Rita Dunn (2001), "*The Learning Styles Teaching Model*", Science and Children, 38 (5), 22-36.

Citizenship Education in the Social Studies

Citizenship education is vital for all students in a democratic society. If a democracy is to survive and grow, it is imperative that students learn, achieve, grow, and develop into being productive members in society. Each student presently is a member in the societal arena and will assume increasing responsibilities as the years go by in the adult world of ideas and interactions. Now is a good time for students to practice and apply quality standards of good citizenship. Thus, students should not only read about the roles of excellence in being a good citizen, but also through a variety of experiences put into practice that which was studied.

Standards Needing Application

The good citizen adheres to formal and informal criteria which exemplify roles to be played in the societal arena. There are criteria which need to be emphasised within any role implemented by a good citizen. The good citizen then:

1. accepts others as human beings having much value. Accepting means to incorporate others into deliberation situations. People must not be shunned but receive positive inward feelings of being welcome. Cliques and closed entities must realise that omitting others from being welcome violates feelings of belonging;

2. assists others as needed to achieve as optimally as possible. A student may need a little help to move on sequentially in learning. This assistance must be given in a willing way. It is good for the self and for others when this help is provided. An improved self concept should be an end result, especially for the provider of the necessary assistance. Cooperation in academic and social endeavours makes for a wholesome learning environment;

3. has concern for others. The good citizen will guide others to be resilient. There are a plethora of situations which individuals face which distract from achievement and progress. Thus, prolonged illness, death of loved one, estrangement, poverty, job loss, extreme fear of the future, mental problems, among others, distract the student from moving on toward the positive in life. However, these individuals who face the negative should be befriended so that resilience is increasingly possible;

4. faces problems for motivation in life. Within the problematic, resilience is possible, in degrees, if there is adequate, positive support from accepting persons. It is beneficial to all if resilience is in evidence so that all may achieve in diverse facets of development. Resilience emphasises many specifics when bouncing back from an unfortunate situations. These specifics include the following:

   (a) success in ongoing endeavours;

   (b) perceiving value in what is being pursued;

   (c) experiencing developmental learning opportunities;

   (d) seeing challenge in learning, but being able, with effort, to achieve objectives;

   (e) learning to face obstacles in life and realising them as challenges, not frustrational.

5. thinks critically. The student then is able to analyse information. This involves separating the relevant from the irrelevant, the accurate from the inaccurate, and the useful from the non-useful. Analysing information from diverse sources may also involve separating fact from fantasy. Critical thinking is very necessary in the solving of personal and social problems (Ediger and Rao, 2004);
6. thinks creatively. Each student needs to be able to think creatively since old solutions may not work for newly identified problems. To be able to come up with unique solutions is often needed. The creative mind is not frustrated by a problem but identifies it and continually seeks for better ways of doing things. A good citizen perceives new problems in the societal arena and attempts to work to solve a dilemma;
7. works well in a group setting. Very frequently, an individual will be asked to work in a group or collective setting. Committee endeavours require good human relations. Quality group dynamics are necessary to assist in the circulation of ideas within a group. The group is important when making a committee decision, but to do so the rights of individuals need to be respected. Put downs, rudeness, cliques, shunning selected ideas, and having a personal agenda do not harmonise with good standards for doing committee work;
8. need self realisation goals emphasised. Students need to feel they are realising the optimal self. If students do not achieve what is within their individual capacities to do so, the chances are the self is not achieving as much as possible. This might result in minimising what a student is capable of doing. The desire to realise the optimal self may be stated in a plethora of ways. Thus, the student has major objectives in mind which need to be achieved, No one lives unto the self only, but in relationship to others. A student's behaviour does affect others. Talents and abilities need to be recognised and used for the common good. Students' knowledge, skills, and attitudes need to be applied in every way possible;

9. need for recognition. Each person desires to be recognised for accomplishments. He/she has contributions to make toward others in school and in society. These contributions need to be used in diverse situations. Recognition for achievements need to be given. Achievement may go downhill if acknowledgement for positive achievements is not made periodically. Human beings have needs and these must be met if optimal achievement is to be in evidence;

10. desiring to belong to a group in society. Each student must feel that he/she is a part of a group. The feelings of belong are strong within any individual. No one, basically, likes to be minimised, an isolate, or shunned. It is detrimental to be ostracized. The feeling therefrom makes for a lower self concept. Rather, each person must assume responsibilities to make others feel at home in a group setting. Embarrassing others has no place in the belonging dimension of human desires. But, too frequently, one sees individuals who do feel neglected and unwelcome. Students individually need to assume responsibility for welcoming others to truly be a member of a group (Ediger and Rao).

Voting and Citizenship Behaviour in a Democratic Society

Citizens in society need to become actively involved in improving the lot of people in the community. There are problems of poverty, alienation, disenfranchised, homeless, and the uneducated. These need to be identified and provided for in nation of great wealth.

Voting for candidates to hold office should be a major responsibility of all. There are a plethora of decisions which go into selecting candidates for office. Yeich (2002) provides the following guidelines for using newspapers in students making choices as who to vote for and to fulfil many relevant objectives in the social studies:

- Gain a deeper understanding of candidates, issues, and of the election process.

- Study the elections in a context of reality and connectedness to other events.
- pursue informed discussions about politics and current issues.
- Compare coverage of issues and candidates by different newspapers.
- Strengthen inferential and evaluation skills.
- Develop lifetime habits of active participation in the election process and the government.
- Synthesise different sources and writing styles for valuable information.

There are specific facets of curriculum development involving citizenship goals in the social studies. The major goal of citizenship units of study should be to develop quality members in the social arena. The responsibilities are indeed great when assisting young people to become good citizens. They represent life long learning in a rich, socially responsible environment.

The scope of social studies units stressing citizenship should be adequately broad to encompass vital knowledge, skills, and attitudinal objectives. The learning activities for students to achieve these objectives should be meaningful, purposeful, engaging, and provide for individual differences. Each student needs to benefit optimally from these learning activities. Careful attention needs to be given in developing appropriate sequence when students encounter the learning activities to achieve the stated objectives of instruction. Quality sequence in learning might well make for feelings of success within learners. A variety of learning activities should be in the offing so that each student may benefit optimally. Knowledgeable citizens are necessary when making contributions in society. These learning activities may well include the following:

- daily newspapers and weekly news magazines, developmentally appropriate for students;
- videos, VDs, DVDs, among other AV presentations;
- radio and TV newscasts;
- textbook materials to secure background information;

- dramatization of news items;
- problem identification to locate relevant information in its solving;
- bulletin board displays to develop interest in current events;
- project methods in the community to serve the common good.

Evaluation of student achievement is a very salient part of the curriculum. Certainly, good teachers wish to know how well students are achieving in citizenship development. A variety of appraisal techniques should be used to determine student achievement. These techniques should include:

- teacher observation to notice student achievement in acquiring knowledge, skills, and attitudinal objectives for good citizenship behaviour;
- tests written by the teacher involving multiple choice, essay, matching, completion, short answer, and true/false;
- student self evaluation in terms of recommended criteria;
- state mandated tests whereby feedback occurs to notice areas of emphasis for citizenship instruction;
- formal and informal situations to assess learner behaviour and growth in becoming a good citizen.

There are selected concepts important in citizenship education which students need to understand and apply:

- The Bill of Rights consisting of the first ten amendments to the constitution.
- Civil rights which states the rights and responsibilities of citizens.
- Constitutionalism which stresses the powers and limits of federal government.
- Due process of law which states rights of citizens against arbitrary action of the government.

- Freedom of expression refers to freedom of speech, press, assembly, and petition as protected by the first amendment.
- Rule of Law emphasises that every member of society must follow the law. No one is above the law, not even the ruler.
- Separation of powers in government such as the legislative, executive, and judicial.

Suffrage stresses the right to vote (See the National Standards for Civics and Government, 1994).

REFERENCES

Ediger, Marlow, D. Bhaskara Rao (2001), *Teaching Social Studies Successfully*. New Delhi: Discovery Publishing House.

Ediger, Marlow, and D. Bhaskara Rao (2004), *Relevancy in Elementary Curriculum*. New Delhi: Discovery Publishing House.

National Standards for Civics and Government (1994), Calabasas, CA: Centre for Civic Education, 151-156.

Yeich, Colette (September, 2020), "*Using Newspapers to Teach About the Election, Social Education*, 66 (5), 281-283.

Additional Reading

Bhaskara Rao, Digumarti (1994). *Scientific Aptitude*. New Delhi: Ashish Publishing House. ISBN 81-7024-658-X.

Bhaskara Rao, Digumarti (1995). *Animal Kingdom*. New Delhi: Discovery Publishing House. ISBN 81-7141-274-2.

Bhaskara Rao, Digumarti (1995). *Batracology*. New Delhi: Discovery Publishing House. ISBN 81-7141-279-3.

Bhaskara Rao, Digumarti (1997). *Scientific Attitude*. New Delhi: Discovery Publishing House. ISBN 81-7141-381-1.

Bhaskara Rao, Digumarti (1996). *Scientific Attitude vis-à-vis Scientific Aptitude*. New Delhi: Discovery Publishing House. ISBN 81-7141-308-0.

Bhaskara Rao, Digumarti (2004). *Scientific Attitude, Scientific Aptitude and Achievement*. New Delhi: Discovery Publishing House. ISBN 81-7141-781-7.

Bhaskara Rao, Digumarti (2004). *Educational Administration*. New Delhi: Discovery Publishing House. ISBN 81-7141-842-2.

Bhaskara Rao, Digumarti, editor (1996). *Encyclopaedia of Education For All*, 5 volumes. New Delhi: APH Publishing Corporation. ISBN 81-7024-759-4 (set).

Vol. I *Education For All: The World Conference*. ISBN 81-7024-760-8

Vol. II *Education For All: The EPA-9 Summit*. ISBN 81-7024-761-6

Vol. III *Education For All: Quality Education For All*. ISBN 81-7024-762-6.

Vol. IV *Education For All: Planning and Monitoring*. ISBN 81-7024-763-4.

Vol. V *Education For All: The Indian Scenario*. ISBN 81-7024-764-0.

Bhaskara Rao, Digumarti, editor (1996). *Global Perceptions on Peace Education*, 3 volumes. New Delhi: Discovery Publishing House. ISBN 81-7141-319-6.

Bhaskara Rao, Digumarti, editor (1996). *National Policy on Education*, 2 volumes. New Delhi: Anmol Publications Pvt. Ltd. ISBN 81-7488-323-1.

Bhaskara Rao, Digumarti, editor (1997). *Care the Child*, 2 volumes. New Delhi: Discovery Publishing House. ISBN 81-7141-394-3.

Bhaskara Rao, Digumarti, editor (1997). *Education for the 21st Century*. New Delhi: Discovery Publishing House. ISBN 81-7141-389-7.

Bhaskara Rao, Digumarti, editor (1997). *Reflections on Scientific Attitude*. New Delhi: Discovery Publishing House. ISBN 81-7141-319-6.

Bhaskara Rao, Digumarti, editor (1997). *Success Story of a Primary Education Project*. New Delhi: APH Publishing Corporation. ISBN 81-7024-850-7.

Bhaskara Rao, Digumarti, editor (1997). *World Food Summit*. New Delhi: Discovery Publishing House. ISBN 81-7141-386-2.

Bhaskara Rao, Digumarti, editor (1998). *Adolescence Education*. New Delhi: Discovery Publishing House. ISBN 81-7141-432-X.

Bhaskara Rao, Digumarti, editor (1998). *Community and School Nutrition Education*. New Delhi: Discovery Publishing House. ISBN 81-7141-435-4.

Bhaskara Rao, Digumarti, editor (1998). *District Primary Education Programme*. New Delhi: Discovery Publishing House. ISBN 81-7141-396-X.

Bhaskara Rao, Digumarti, editor (1998). *Earth Summit*, 2 volumes. New Delhi: Discovery Publishing House. ISBN 81-7141-435-4.

Bhaskara Rao, Digumarti, editor (1998). *National Policy on Education: Towards an Enlightened and Humane Society*. New Delhi: Discovery Publishing House. ISBN 81-7141-426-5.

Bhaskara Rao, Digumarti, editor (1998). *Reforming School Education*. New Delhi: Discovery Publishing House. ISBN 81-7141-403-6.

Bhaskara Rao, Digumarti, editor (1998). *Teacher Education in India*. New Delhi: Discovery Publishing House. ISBN 81-7141-406-0.

Bhaskara Rao, Digumarti, editor (1998). *World Summit for Social Development*. New Delhi: Discovery Publishing House. ISBN 81-7141-420-6.

Bhaskara Rao, Digumarti, editor (2000). *Education For All: Achieving the Goal*, 3 volumes. New Delhi: APH Publishing Corporation. ISBN 81-7648-152-1 (set).

Vol. I *The Global Consensus*. ISBN 81-7648-155-6.

Vol. II *Mid-Decade Review Reports of Regional Seminars*. ISBN 81-7648-154-8.

Vol. III *Issues and Trends*. ISBN 81-7648-155-6.

Bhaskara Rao, Digumarti, editor (1999). *International Encyclopaedia of AIDS*, 11 volumes. New Delhi: Discovery Publishing House. ISBN 81-7141-522-6 (set).

Vol. 1 *Introduction to HIV/AIDS*. ISBN 81-7141-523-7.

Vol. 2 *HIV/AIDS-Issues and Challenges*, 2 parts. ISBN 81-7141-524-5.

Vol. 3 *HIV/AIDS-Socio Economic Realities*. ISBN 81-7141-524-3.

Vol. 4 *HIV/AIDS-Law Ethics and Human Rights*, 2 parts. ISBN 81-7141-526-1.

Vol. 5 *AIDS and NGOs*. ISBN 81-7141-527-X.

Vol. 6 *AIDS and Home Care*. ISBN 81-7141-528-8.

Vol. 7 *STD Case Management*. ISBN 81-7141-529-6.

Vol. 8 *HIV/AIDS Prevention and Care-Teaching Modules for Nurses and Midwives*. ISBN 81-7141-530-X.

Vol. 9 *HIV Prevention Education for Educational Institutions*. ISBN 81-7141-531-8.

Vol.10 *Instructional Modules for AIDS Education*. ISBN 81-7141-532-6.

Vol.11 *School Health Education to prevent AIDS and STD-A Package for Curriculum Planners*. ISBN 81-7141-533-4.

Bhaskara Rao, Digumarti, editor (2000). *International Encyclopaedia of Science and Technology Education*, 11 volumes. New Delhi: Discovery Publishing House. ISBN 81-7141-548-2 (set).

Vol. 1 *Science and Technology Education*. ISBN 81-7141-568-7.

Vol. 2 *Science Education in Developing Countries*. ISBN 81-7141-569-9.

Vol. 3 *Organizational Structure of Science*. ISBN 81-7141-570-9.

Vol. 4 *Science Education in Asia and the Pacific*. ISBN 81-7141-571-7

Vol. 5 *Science and Technology Education For All*. ISBN 81-7141-572-5.

Vol. 6 *Values, Ethics, Talent and Girls in Science and Technology Education*. ISBN 81-7141-573-3.

Vol. 7 *Popularization of Science and Technology Education*. ISBN 81-7141-574-1.

Vol. 8 *Science, Power and Society*. ISBN 81-7141-575-X.

Vol. 9 *Information Technology*. ISBN 81-7141-576-8.

Vol. 10 *Teacher Training in Science and Technology Education*. ISBN 81-7142-577-6.

Vol. 11 *Teacher Training in Science and Technology: A Curriculum Framework*. ISBN 81-7141-578-4.

Bhaskara Rao, Digumarti, editor (2001). *Distance Education in Different Countries*. New Delhi: APH Publishing Corporation. ISBN 81-7648-229-3.

Bhaskara Rao, Digumarti, editor (2001). *Decentralised Management of Education: Management of Education in Panchayati Raj and Municipal Bodies*. New Delhi: Discovery Publishing House. ISBN 81-7141-617-9.

Bhaskara Rao, Digumarti, editor (2001). *Electrochemistry for Environmental Protection*. New Delhi: Discovery Publishing House. ISBN 81-7141-619-5.

Bhaskara Rao, Digumarti, editor (2001). *Global Educational Studies*. New Delhi: Discovery Publishing House. ISBN 81-7141-616-0.

Bhaskara Rao, Digumarti, editor (2001). *Global Synthesis of Educational Assessment*. New Delhi: Discovery Publishing House. ISBN 81-7141-613-6.

Bhaskara Rao, Digumarti, editor (2000). *International Encyclopaedia of Human Rights*, 7 volumes in 13 parts. New Delhi: Discovery Publishing House. ISBN 81-7141-567-9 (set).

Vol. 1 *International Instruments of Human Rights*, 2 parts. ISBN 81-7141-569-4.

Vol. 2 *Regional Instruments of Human Rights*. ISBN 81-7141-604-7.

Vol. 3 *Human Rights and the United Nations*, 2 parts. ISBN 81-7141-605-5.

Vol. 4 *Fact Files of Human Rights*, 3 parts. ISBN 81-7141-606-3.

Vol. 5 *Study Stories of Human Rights*, 3 parts. ISBN 81-7141-607-3.

Vol. 6 *International Meetings on Human Rights*, 2 parts.ISBN 81-714-608-X.

Vol. 7 *Professional Training in Human Rights*. ISBN 81-7141-609-8.

Bhaskara Rao, Digumarti, editor (2001). *Jomtein Decade of Education*. New Delhi: Discovery Publishing House. ISBN 81-7141-618-7.

Bhaskara Rao, Digumarti, editor (2001). *Nuclear Materials: Issues and Concerns*, 2 volumes. New Delhi: Discovery Publishing House. ISBN 81-7141-611-X.

Bhaskara Rao, Digumarti, editor (2001). *World Conference on Education for All*. New Delhi: APH Publishing Corporation. ISBN 81-7141-274-9.

Bhaskara Rao, Digumarti, editor (2001). *World Conference on Higher Education*. New Delhi: Discovery Publishing House. ISBN 81-7141-610-1.

Bhaskara Rao, Digumarti, editor (2001). *World Conference on Science*. New Delhi: Discovery Publishing House. ISBN 81-7141-612-8.

Bhaskara Rao, Digumarti, editor (2003). *Inspiring Experiences in Teacher Education*. New Delhi: Discovery Publishing House. ISBN 81-7141-656-X.

Bhaskara Rao, Digumarti, editor (2003). *International Studies in Education*, 3 volumes. New Delhi: Discovery Publishing House. ISBN 81-7141-647-0.

Bhaskara Rao, Digumarti, editor (2003). *Military Conversion: Impact on Science and Technology*. New Delhi: Discovery Publishing House. ISBN 81-7141-578-4.

Bhaskara Rao, Digumarti, editor (2003). *United Nations Millennium Summit*. New Delhi: Discovery Publishing House. ISBN 81-7141-632-2.

Bhaskara Rao, Digumarti, editor (2003). *World Assembly on Aging*. *New Delhi*: Discovery Publishing House. ISBN 81-7141-637-3.

Bhaskara Rao, Digumarti, editor (2003). *World Conference on Human Rights*. New Delhi: Discovery Publishing House. ISBN 81-7141-661-6.

Bhaskara Rao, Digumarti, editor (2003). *World Education Forum*. New Delhi: Discovery Publishing House. ISBN 81-7141-639-X.

Bhaskara Rao, Digumarti, editor (2003). *Education, Employment and Human Resource Development*. New Delhi: Discovery Publishing House. ISBN 81-7141-681-0.

Bhaskara Rao, Digumarti, editor (2003). *Successful Schooling*. New Delhi: Discovery Publishing House. ISBN 81-7141-677-2.

Bhaskara Rao, Digumarti, editor (2003). *European Education and Teachers*. New Delhi: Discovery Publishing House. ISBN 81-7141-702-7.

Bhaskara Rao, Digumarti, editor (2003). *Teachers in a Changing World*. New Delhi: Discovery Publishing House. ISBN 81-7141-694-2.

Bhaskara Rao, Digumarti, editor (2004). *International Encyclopaedia of Learning to Live Together*, 4 volumes. New Delhi: Discovery Publishing House. ISBN 81-7141-848-1.

Vol. 1 *International Conference on Learning to Live Together.*

Vol. 2 *Globalization and Living Together.*

Vol. 3 *Curriculum for Learning to Live Together.*

Vol. 4 *Science Education for the Contemporary Society.*

Bhaskara Rao, Digumarti, editor (2004). *International Guidelines on Open and Distance Teacher Education*. New Delhi: Discovery Publishing House. ISBN 81-7141-777-9.

Bhaskara Rao, Digumarti, editor (2004). *Adult Learning in the 21st Century*. New Delhi: Discovery Publishing House. ISBN 81-7141-797-3.

Bhaskara Rao, Digumarti, editor (2004). *Educational Practices: Research and Recommendations*. New Delhi: Discovery Publishing House. ISBN 81-7141-835-X.

Bhaskara Rao, Digumarti, editor (2004). *General Secondary Education In the 21st Century*. New Delhi: Discovery Publishing House. ISBN 81-7141-885-6.

Bhaskara Rao, Digumarti, editor (2004). *Reforming Secondary Education*. New Delhi: Discovery Publishing House. ISBN 81-7141-843-0.

Bhaskara Rao, Digumarti, editor (2004). *Human Rights Education*. New Delhi: Discovery Publishing House. ISBN 81-7141-882-1.

Bhaskara Rao, Digumarti, editor (2004). *United Nations Decade for Human Rights Education*. New Delhi: Discovery Publishing House. ISBN 81-7141-887-2.

Bhaskara Rao, Digumarti and B.S.V. Dutt, editors (2003). *Education: Programmes and Policies*. New Delhi: APH Publishing Corporation. ISBN 81-7648-470-9.

Bhaskara Rao, Digumarti, C.A.P. Swamy and B.S.V. Dutt (1997). *Self-Evaluation in Student Teaching*. New Delhi: Discovery Publishing House. ISBN 81-7141-374-9.

Bhaskara Rao, Digumarti and D. Naresh Kumar (2004). *School Teacher Effectiveness*. New Delhi: Discovery Publishing House. ISBN 81-7141-782-5.

Bhaskara Rao, Digumarti and D. Sridhar (2002). *Job Satisfaction of School Teachers*. New Delhi: Discovery Publishing House. ISBN 81-7141-652-7.

Bhaskara Rao, Digumarti, C. Sridevi and K. Vijaya (1995). *Achievement in Social Studies*. New Delhi: Discovery Publishing House. ISBN 81-7141-281-5.

Bhaskara Rao, Digumarti and Digumarti Pushpa Latha (1994). *Achievement in Biology*. New Delhi: Discovery Publishing House. ISBN 81-7141-264-5.

Bhaskara Rao, Digumarti and Digumarti Pushpa Latha (1995). *Achievement in English*. New Delhi: Discovery Publishing House. ISBN 81-7141-283-1.

Bhaskara Rao, Digumarti and Digumarti Pushpa Latha (1994). *Achievement in Science*. New Delhi: Discovery Publishing House. ISBN 81-7141-280-70.

Bhaskara Rao, Digumarti and Digumarti Pushpa Latha (1995). *Achievement in Mathematics*. New Delhi: Discovery Publishing House. ISBN 81-7141-278-5.

Bhaskara Rao, Digumarti and Digumarti Pushpa Latha (2004). *Education for Women*. New Delhi: Discovery Publishing House. ISBN 81-7141-873-2.

Bhaskara Rao, Digumarti and Digumarti Pushpa Latha, editors (1998). *International Encyclopaedia of Women*, 5 volumes. New Delhi: Discovery Publishing House. ISBN 81-7141-410-9 (set).

Vol. 1 *Status of World's Women*. ISBN 81-7141-494-X.

Vol. 2 *Women, Education and Empowerment*. ISBN 81-7141-498-1.

Vol. 3 *Women Challenges and Advancement*. ISBN 81-7141-497-4.

Vol. 4 *Women and Family Health*. ISBN 81-7141-497-4.

Vol. 5 *Women and International Action*. ISBN 81-7141-498-2.

Bhaskara Rao, Digumarti, Digumarti Pushpa Latha and Digumarthi Harshitha, editors (2001). *Biological Warfare*. New Delhi: Discovery Publishing House. ISBN 81-7141-597-0.

Bhaskara Rao, Digumarti, Digumarti Pushpa Latha and Digumarthi Harshitha, editors (2001). *Women as Educators*. New Delhi: Discovery Publishing House. ISBN 81-7141-602-0.

Bhaskara Rao, Digumarti and Digumarthi Harshitha (2004). *Adjustment of Adolescents*. New Delhi: APH Publishing House. ISBN 81-7648-836-8.

Bhaskara Rao, Digumarti and Digumarthi Harshitha, editors (2001). *Education in India*. New Delhi: APH Publishing House. ISBN 81-7648-207-2.

Bhaskara Rao, Digumarti, Digumarti Pushpa Latha and Digumarthi Harshitha, editors (2001). *Assessing Learning Achievement*. New Delhi: Discovery Publishing House. ISBN 81-7141-601-2.

Bhaskara Rao, Digumarti, Digumarti Pushpa Latha and Digumarthi Harshitha, editors (2001). *Energy Security*. New Delhi: Discovery Publishing House. ISBN 81-7141-598-9.

Bhaskara Rao, Digumarti, Digumarthi Harshitha and K.R.S. Sambasiva Rao, editors (1999). *Advanced Biotechnology*. New Delhi: Discovery Publishing House. ISBN 81-7141-516-4.

Bhaskara Rao, Digumarti and K.R.S.Sambasiva Rao, editors (1996). *Current Trends in Indian Education*. New Delhi: Discovery Publishing House. ISBN 81-7141-311-0.

Bhaskara Rao, Digumarti and D. Naresh Kumar (2004). *School Teacher Effectiveness*. New Delhi: Discovery Publishing House. ISBN 81-7141-782-5.

Bhaskara Rao, Digumarti and E. Sreekanth Babu (2004). *Educational Interests of School Students.* New Delhi: Discovery Publishing House. ISBN 81-7141-837-6.

Bhaskara Rao, Digumarti and K. Vijaya (1995). *A Text Book Evaluation.* Ambala Cantt: The Associated Publishers.

Bhaskara Rao, Digumarti and M.A. Fayaz (2004). *Problems of Primary School Drop-outs.* New Delhi: Discovery Publishing House. ISBN 81-7141-834-1.

Bhaskara Rao, Digumarti and N.V.M. Mohana Rao (2002). *Problems of Mentally Handicapped Children.* New Delhi: Discovery Publishing House. ISBN 81-7141-645-4.

Bhaskara Rao, Digumarti and S. Chandra Mohan (2002). *Sports Management.* New Delhi: APH Publishing House. ISBN 81-7648-467-9.

Bhaskara Rao, Digumarti and S.A. Khader (2004). *Problems of Private School Teachers.* New Delhi: Discovery Publishing Corporation. ISBN 81-7141-838-4.

Bhaskara Rao, Digumarti and S.A. Khader (2004). *School Education in India.* New Delhi: Discovery Publishing Corporation. ISBN 81-7141-849-X.

Bhaskara Rao, Digumarti and Sk. Johni Basha (2004). *Teachers' Population Education Awareness.* New Delhi: Discovery Publishing House. ISBN 81-7141-832-5.

Bhaskara Rao, Digumarti, V.V. Rao, V.V. Lakshmi and V.V. Krishna, editors (1999). *Status and Advancement of Women.* New Delhi: APH Publishing Corporation. ISBN 81-7648-169-6.

Babu, P.C., author and Digumarti Bhaskara Rao, editor (2004). *Flowers of Wisdom.* New Delhi: Discovery Publishing House. ISBN 81-7141-695-0.

Amala, P.A. and Anupam, P., authors and Digumarti Bhaskara Rao, editor (2004). *History of Education.* New Delhi: Discovery Publishing House. ISBN 81-7141-860-0.

Bhagya Lakshmi, L., author and Digumarti Bhaskara Rao, editor (2000). *Reading and Comprehension.* New Delhi: Discovery Publishing House. ISBN 81-7141-543-1.

Bhasha, S.A., author and Digumarti Bhaskara Rao, editor (2004). *Methods of Teaching Geography*. New Delhi: Discovery Publishing House. ISBN 81-7141-807-4.

Bhuvaneswara Lakshmi, Gadde, author and Digumarti Bhaskara Rao, editor (2000). *Attitude Towards Science*. New Delhi: Discovery Publishing House. ISBN 81-7141-541-6.

Bhuvaneswari Lakshmi, G., author and Digumarti Bhaskara Rao, editor (2004). *Methods of Teaching Life Science*. New Delhi: Discovery Publishing House. ISBN 81-7141-804-X.

Bhuvaneswari Lakshmi, G. and K. Subba Rao, authors and Digumarti Bhaskara Rao, editor (2004). *Methods of Teaching Biology*. New Delhi: Discovery Publishing House. ISBN 81-7141-914-3.

Chowdary, S.B.J.R. and Naga Raju authors and Digumarti Bhaskara Rao, editor (2004). *Mastery of Teaching Skills*. New Delhi: Discovery Publishing House. ISBN 81-7141-861-9.

Devraj, T.A.S., author and Digumarti Bhaskara Rao, editor (1997). *Trace Analysis of Uranium and Thorium*. New Delhi: Discovery Publishing House. ISBN 81-7141-375-7.

Durga Rani, K., author and Digumarti Bhaskara Rao, editor (2000). *Educational Aspirations and Scientific Attitudes*. New Delhi: Discovery Publishing House. ISBN 81-7141-555-5.

Dutt, B.S.V. and Digumarti Bhaskara Rao (2001). *Empowering Primary Teachers*. New Delhi: Discovery Publishing House. ISBN 81-7141-615-2.

Dutt, B.S.V., author and Digumarti Bhaskara Rao, editor (2004). *Comparative Education*. New Delhi: Discovery Publishing House. ISBN 81-7141-912-7.

Ediger, Marlow and Digumarti Bhaskara Rao (1996). *Science Curriculum*. New Delhi: Discovery Publishing House. ISBN 81-7141-321-8.

Ediger, Marlow and Digumarti Bhaskara Rao (2000). *Teaching Mathematics Successfully*. New Delhi: Discovery Publishing House. ISBN 81-7141-552-0.

Ediger, Marlow and Digumarti Bhaskara Rao (2001). *Teaching Science Successfully*. New Delhi: Discovery Publishing House. ISBN 81-7141-600-4.

Ediger, Marlow and Digumarti Bhaskara Rao (2001). *Teaching Social Studies Successfully*. New Delhi: Discovery Publishing House. ISBN 81-7141-596-2.

Ediger, Marlow and Digumarti Bhaskara Rao (2002). *Philosophy and Curriculum*. New Delhi: Discovery Publishing House. ISBN 81-7141-631-4.

Ediger, Marlow and Digumarti Bhaskara Rao (2002). *Improving School Administration*. New Delhi: Discovery Publishing House. ISBN 81-7141-633-0.

Ediger, Marlow and Digumarti Bhaskara Rao (2002). *Elementary Curriculum*. New Delhi: Discovery Publishing House. ISBN 81-7141-658-6.

Ediger, Marlow and Digumarti Bhaskara Rao (2003). *Language Arts Curriculum*. New Delhi: Discovery Publishing House. ISBN 81-7141-657-8.

Ediger, Marlow and Digumarti Bhaskara Rao (2003). *Psychology and Curriculum*. New Delhi: Discovery Publishing House. ISBN 81-7141-691-8.

Ediger, Marlow and Digumarti Bhaskara Rao (2003). *Teaching Language Arts Successfully*. New Delhi: Discovery Publishing House. ISBN 81-7141-678-0.

Ediger, Marlow and Digumarti Bhaskara Rao (2003). *School Curriculum and Administration*. New Delhi: Discovery Publishing House. ISBN 81-7141-709-4.

Ediger, Marlow and Digumarti Bhaskara Rao (2003). *Teaching Mathematics in Elementary Schools*. New Delhi: Discovery Publishing House. ISBN 81-7141-687-X.

Ediger, Marlow and Digumarti Bhaskara Rao (2003). Teaching Science in Elementary Schools. New Delhi: Discovery Publishing House. ISBN 81-7141-698-5.

Ediger, Marlow and Digumarti Bhaskara Rao (2003). *School Curriculum and Administration*. New Delhi: Discovery Publishing House. ISBN 81-7141-709-4.

Ediger, Marlow and Digumarti Bhaskara Rao (2003). *Elementary Curriculum Improvement*. New Delhi: Discovery Publishing House. ISBN 81-7141-740-X.

Ediger, Marlow and Digumarti Bhaskara Rao (2004). *School Organisation*. New Delhi: Discovery Publishing House. ISBN 81-7141-843-0.

Ediger, Marlow and Digumarti Bhaskara Rao (2004). *Relevancy in Elementary Curriculum*. New Delhi: Discovery Publishing House. ISBN 81-7141-845-9.

Ediger, Marlow, B.S.V. Dutt and Digumarti Bhaskara Rao (2003). *Teaching English Successfully*. New Delhi: Discovery Publishing House. ISBN 81-7141-707-8.

Elizabeth, M.E.S., author and Digumarti Bhaskara Rao, editor (2004). *Methods of Teaching English*. New Delhi: Discovery Publishing House. ISBN 81-7141-809-0.

Harshitha, D. author and Digumarti Bhaskara Rao, editor (2004). *Methods of Teaching Information Technology*. New Delhi: Discovery Publishing House. ISBN 81-7141-805-8.

Indira Devi, author and J. Prasanth Kumar and Digumarti Bhaskara Rao, editors (2004). *Values in Language Text Books*. New Delhi: APH Publishing Corporation. ISBN 81-7141-833-3.

Jalaja Kumari, C., author and Digumarti Bhaskara Rao, editor (2004). *Methods of Teaching Educational Technology*. New Delhi: Discovery Publishing House. ISBN 81-7141-810-4.

Jayasree, Kandi, author and Digumarti Bhaskara Rao, editor (1999). *Correlates of Socialisation*. New Delhi: Discovery Publishing House. ISBN 81-7141-517-2.

Jayasree, Kandi, author and Digumarti Bhaskara Rao, editor (2004). *Methods of Teaching Science*. New Delhi: Discovery Publishing House. ISBN 81-7141-801-5.

John Babu, Chikati, author and T.J.R. Prasad, G.M. Madhukar and Digumarti Bhaskara Rao, editors (1996). *Problem Solving in Mathematics*. New Delhi: APH Publishing Corporation. ISBN 81-7648-273-0.

Joseph Raju, B and G.A. Anitha, authors and Digumarti Bhaskara Rao, editor (2004). *Population Education*. New Delhi: Sonali Publications. ISBN 81-88836-31-3.

Lalitha, T., author and K.S. Prabhakaram, D.S.N. Sastry and Digumarti Bhaskara Rao, editors (2004). *Educational Philosophic Beliefs*. New Delhi: Discovery Publishing House. ISBN 81-7141-765-5.

Madhu Bala, Jampala, author and Digumarti Bhaskara Rao, editor (2004). *Adjustment Problems of Hearing Impaired*. New Delhi: Discovery Publishing House. ISBN 81-7141-831-7.

Madhu Bala, Jampala, author and Digumarti Bhaskara Rao, editor (2004). *Methods of Teaching Exceptional Children*. New Delhi: Discovery Publishing House. ISBN 81-7141-802-3.

Marja, Talvi and Digumarti Bhaskara Rao, editors (1996). *Educational Leadership and Social Changes*. New Delhi: Discovery Publishing House. ISBN 81-7141-320-X.

Nageswara Rao, S.and M. Srihari, authors and Digumarti Bhaskara Rao, editor (2004). *Guidance and Counselling*. New Delhi: Discovery Publishing House. ISBN 81-7141-840-6.

Nageswara Rao, S. and P. Sridhar, authors and Digumarti Bhaskara Rao, editor (2004). *Methods and Techniques of Teaching*. New Delhi: Sonali Publications. ISBN 81-88836-33-8.

Nirmala Jyothi, M., author and Digumarti Bhaskara Rao, editor (2003). *Non-detention System in School Education*. New Delhi: Discovery Publishing House. ISBN 81-7141-654-3.

Padma Tulasi, G., author and Digumarti Bhaskara Rao, editor (2004). *Methods of Teaching Elementary Science*. New Delhi: Discovery Publishing House. ISBN 81-7141-871-6.

Pala Prasada Rao, V., author and K. Nirupa Rani and Digumarti Bhaskara Rao, editors (2004). *Methods of Teaching Elementary Science*. New Delhi: Discovery Publishing House. ISBN 81-7141-871-6.

Prabhakaram, K.S., author and Digumarti Bhaskara Rao, editors (1998). *Concept Attainment Model in Mathematics Teaching*. New Delhi: Discovery Publishing House. ISBN 81-7141-424-9.

Prasanth Kumar, J., author and Digumarti Bhaskara Rao, editor (1998). *Effectiveness of Distance Education System*. New Delhi: Discovery Publishing House. ISBN 81-7141-437-0.

Prasanth Kumar, J., author and Digumarti Bhaskara Rao, editor (2004). *Methods of Teaching Civics*. New Delhi: Discovery Publishing House. ISBN 81-7141-806-6.

Prasanth Kumar, J., author and G. Sundara Rao and Digumarti Bhaskara Rao, editors (2000). *Open University Student Support Services*. New Delhi: Discovery Publishing House. ISBN 81-7141-550-4.

Raja Kumari, M.A. and D.R.S. Sundari, authors and Digumarti Bhaskara Rao, editor (2004). *Special Education*. New Delhi: Discovery Publishing House. ISBN 81-7141-846-5.

Raja Kumari, M.A. and D.R.S. Sundari, authors and Digumarti Bhaskara Rao, editor (2004). *Methods of Teaching Educational Psychology*. New Delhi: Discovery Publishing House. ISBN 81-7141-820-1.

Ramatulasamma, K., author and Digumarti Bhaskara Rao, editor (2002). *Job Satisfaction of Teacher Educators*. New Delhi: Discovery Publishing House. ISBN 81-7141-655-1.

Rama Krishnaiah, D., author and Digumarti Bhaskara Rao, editor (1998). *Job Satisfaction of College Teachers*. New Delhi: Discovery Publishing House. ISBN 81-7141-438-9.

Rama Kumar Ratnam, M.V., author and Digumarti Bhaskara Rao, editor (1998). *Dukkha: Suffering in Early Buddhism*. New Delhi: Discovery Publishing House. ISBN 81-7141-653-5.

Rama Krishna Prasad and P. Vide Sagar, authors and Digumarti Bhaskara Rao, editor (2004). *Methods of Teaching Physical Education*. New Delhi: Discovery Publishing House. ISBN 81-7141-868-6.

Rama Seshaiah, P. author and Digumarti Bhaskara Rao, editor (2004). *Methods of Teaching Home Science*. New Delhi: Discovery Publishing House. ISBN 81-7141-916-X.

Ramesh, Ganta and Digumarti Bhaskara Rao, editors (1998). *Environmental Education: Problems and Prospects*. New Delhi: Discovery Publishing House. ISBN 81-7141-423-0.

Ranga Rao, R., author and Digumarti Bhaskara Rao, editor (2004). *Methods of Teacher Teaching*. New Delhi: Discovery Publishing House. ISBN 81-7141-812-0.

Rathaiah, Lavu and Digumarti Bhaskara Rao, editors (1996), *International Innovations in Education*. New Delhi: Discovery Publishing House. ISBN 81-7141-359-5.

Rathaiah, Lavu and Digumarti Bhaskara Rao (1997). *Achievement Correlates*. New Delhi: Discovery Publishing House. ISBN 81-7141-385-4.

Ravi Krishna, M., author and Digumarti Bhaskara Rao, editor (2004). *Examination System*. New Delhi: Discovery Publishing House. ISBN 81-7141-824-4.

Ravi Kumar, M., author and Digumarti Bhaskara Rao, editor (2004). *Methods of Teaching Computer Science*. New Delhi: Discovery Publishing House. ISBN 81-7141-823-6.

Reddy, Sudhakar Y., author and Digumarti Bhaskara Rao, editor (2003). *Creativity in Adolescents*. New Delhi: Discovery Publishing House. ISBN 81-7141-659-4.

Reddy, M. S., author and Digumarti Bhaskara Rao, editor (2004). *Creativity in College Students*. New Delhi: Discovery Publishing House. ISBN 81-7141-697-7.

Rudramamba, B., author and Digumarti Bhaskara Rao, editor (2003). *Problems of Teaching*. New Delhi: APH Publishing Corporation. ISBN 81-7648-462-8.

Rudramamba, B. and V. Lakshmi Kumari, authors and Digumarti Bhaskara Rao, editor (2004). *Methods of Teaching Economics*. New Delhi: Discovery Publishing House. ISBN 81-7141-900-3.

Sanjeeva Rao, P.C., author and Digumarti Bhaskara Rao, editor (1996). *A Text Book of Geology*. New Delhi: Discovery Publishing House. ISBN 81-7141-313-7.

Satya Narayana, V., author and Digumarti Bhaskara Rao, editor (2001). *Physical Education, Social Attitudes and Leadership Qualities*. New Delhi: Discovery Publishing House. ISBN 81-7141-593-8.

Satya Narayana, P.V.V. and G. Krishna, authors and Digumarti Bhaskara Rao, editor (2004). *Curriculum Development and Management*. New Delhi: Discovery Publishing House. ISBN 81-7141-813-9.

Siva Lakshmi, G.V. and G.L. Subbaiah, authors and Digumarti Bhaskara Rao, editor (2004). *Methods of Teaching Environmental Science*. New Delhi: Discovery Publishing House. ISBN 81-7141-839-2.

Srinivas, M. and I. Prasada Rao, authors and Digumarti Bhaskara Rao, editor (2004). *Methods of Teaching History*. New Delhi: Discovery Publishing House. ISBN 81-7141-803-1.

Srinivasulu Reddy, M. and K.R.S. Sambasiva Rao, authors and Digumarti Bhaskara Rao, editor (1999). *A Text Book of Aquaculture*. New Delhi: Discovery Publishing House. ISBN 81-7141-482-6.

Srinivasa Rao, Mandalapu, author and Digumarti Bhaskara Rao, editor (2003). *Achievement Motivation and Achievement in Mathematics*. New Delhi: Discovery Publishing House. ISBN 81-7141-674-8.

Sunil Kumar, K. and K. Rama Krishana, authors and Digumarti Bhaskara Rao, editor (2004). *Methods of Teaching Chemistry*. New Delhi: Discovery Publishing House. ISBN 81-7141-913-5.

Sunita, E. and R. Sambasiva Rao, authors and Digumarti Bhaskara Rao, editor (2004). *Methods of Teaching Mathematics*. New Delhi: Discovery Publishing House. ISBN 81-7141-915-1.

Swarupa Rani, T. and J.R. Priyadarshini, authors and Digumarti Bhaskara Rao, editor (2004). *Educational Measurement and Evaluation*. New Delhi: Discovery Publishing House. ISBN 81-7141-859-7.

Vanaja, M., author and Digumarti Bhaskara Rao, editor (1999). *Inquiry Training Model*. New Delhi: Discovery Publishing House. ISBN 81-7141-515-6.

Vanaja,M., author and Digumarti Bhaskara Rao, editor (2004). *Methods of Teaching Physics*. New Delhi: Discovery Publishing House. ISBN 81-7141-867-8

Valeri V. Koustiouk, author and Digumarti Bhaskara Rao, editor (2002). *A Text Book of Cryogenics*. New Delhi: Discovery Publishing House. ISBN 81-7141-642-X.

Vamsi Krishana, V., author and Digumarti Bhaskara Rao, editor (2004). *School Psychology*. New Delhi: Discovery Publishing House. ISBN 81-7141-880-5.

Veena Kumari, Balusu and Digumarti Bhaskara Rao (1996). *Operation Black Board*. New Delhi: APH Publishing Corporation. ISBN 81-7024-711-X.

Veena Kumari, B. author and Digumarti Bhaskara Rao, editor (2004). *Methods of Teaching Social Studies*. New Delhi: Discovery Publishing House. ISBN 81-7141-899-6.

Veena Kumari, Balusu, author and Digumarti Bhaskara Rao, editor (2000). *Psycho-Social Correlates of Achievement*. New Delhi: Discovery Publishing House. ISBN 81-7141-547-4.

Venkata Rao, P. and Digumarti Bhaskara Rao (1989). *A Text Book of Zoology-Junior Intermediate*. Guntur: Vignan Publishers.

Venkata Rao, P. and Digumarti Bhaskara Rao (1989). *A Text Book of Zoology-Senior Intermediate*. Guntur: Vignan Publishers.

Venkateswara Reddy, L. and Lakshmi Narayana, M., authors and Digumarti Bhaskara Rao, editor (2004). *Methods of Teaching Rural Sociology*. New Delhi: Discovery Publishing House. ISBN 81-7141-811-2.

Venkateswara Rao, V., author and Digumarti Bhaskara Rao, editor (2004). *Problems of Education*. New Delhi: Discovery Publishing House. ISBN 81-7141-841-4.

Venkateswara Rao, V., V. Vijaya Lakshmi and V. Vamsi Krishna, authors and Digumarti Bhaskara Rao, editor (2004). *Education For All*. New Delhi: Sonali Publications. ISBN 81-88836-30-3.

Venkateswara Rao, V., V. Vijaya Lakshmi and V. Vamsi Krishna, authors and Digumarti Bhaskara Rao, editor (2004). *Education in India*. New Delhi: Sonali Publications. ISBN 81-88836-858-9.

Venkateswara Reddy, L. and Lakshmi Narayana, M., authors and Digumarti Bhaskara Rao, editor (2004). *Education for Dalits*. New Delhi: Discovery Publishing House. ISBN 81-7141-872-4.

Venkateswarlu, K. and S.J. Basha, authors and Digumarti Bhaskara Rao, editor (2004). *Methods of Teaching Commerce*. New Delhi: Discovery Publishing House. ISBN 81-7141-808-2.

Venugopala Rao, K., author and Digumarti Bhaskara Rao, editor (2000). *Teacher Morale in Secondary Schools*. New Delhi: Discovery Publishing House. ISBN 81-7141-551-2.

Vidya, C., author and Digumarti Bhaskara Rao, editor (1996). *A Text Book of Nutrition*. New Delhi: Discovery Publishing House. ISBN 81-7141-309-9.

Vijaya Bharathi, D., author and Digumarti Bhaskara Rao, editor (2000). *Educational Philosophies of Swami Vivekananda and John Dewey*. New Delhi: APH Publishing House. ISBN 81-7648-309-9.

Vijaya Lakshmi, D., author and Digumarti Bhaskara Rao, editor (2004) *Basic Education*. New Delhi: Discovery Publishing House. ISBN 81-7141-881-3.

Books in Telugu Language

Bhaskara Rao, Digumarti (1986). *Dhrushya Sravana Bodhanapakaranalu (Audio Visual Teaching Aids)*. Guntur: Nagarjuna Publishers.

Bhaskara Rao, Digumarti (1993). *Jeevasashtra Bodhana (Teaching of Biology)*. Guntur: Nagarjuna Publishers.

Bhaskara Rao, Digumarti (1995). *Vignanasasthra Bodhana (Teaching of science)* Guntur: Nagarjuna Publishers.

Bhaskara Rao, Digumarti (1997). *Vidya Manovignana Seshtram (Educational Psychology)*. Guntur: Creative Press.

Bhaskara Rao, Digumarti (1998). *DSC Study Material*. Guntur: Nagarjuna Publishers.

Bhaskara Rao, Digumarti (1998). *Upadhyayudu Vidya. (Teacher and Education)* Guntur: Nagarjuna Publishers.

Bhaskara Rao, Digumarti (1998). *Vidya Drukpadalu (Perspectives of Education)*. Guntur: Nagarjuna Publishers.

Bhaskara Rao, Digumarti (1999). *EdCET Teaching Aptitude*. Guntur: Nagarjuna Publishers.

Bhaskara Rao, Digumarti (2001). *Bharata Samajamulo Upadyayudu Vidya (Teacher and Education in Emerging Indian Society)*. Guntur: Sri Nagarjuna Publishers.

Bhaskara Rao, Digumarti (2001). *Bhoutika Sastra Bodhana Paddathulu (Methods of Teaching Physical Science)*. Guntur: Sri Nagarjuna Publishers.

Bhaskara Rao, Digumarti (2001). *Jeeva Sastra Bodhana Padhathulu (Methods of Teaching Biology)*. Guntur: Sri Nagarjuna Publishers.

Bhaskara Rao, Digumarti (2001). *Vidya Manovignana Sastram (Educational Psychology)*. Guntur: Sri Nagarjuna Publishers.

Bhaskara Rao, Digumarti (2003). *Patasala Yajamanyam/Paripalana (School Management and Administration)*. Guntur: Sri Nagarjuna Publishers.

Gopala Krishna, G., A. Ramkrishna, K. Subba Rao and Bhaskara Rao, Digumarti (2004). *Jeevasashtra Bodhana Padhatulu (Methods of Teaching of Biological science)*. Guntur: Sri Nagarjuna Publishers.

Krishna Murthy, V., K.S. Sudheer Reddy and Digumarti Bhaskara Rao (2004). *Vidya Manovignana Sastra Adharalu (Foundations of Educational Psychology)*. Guntur: Sri Nagarjuna Publishers.

Lalini, V., V. Dayakara Reddy, M. Srihari and Digumarti Bhaskara Rao (2004). *Vidya Adharalu (Foundations of Education)*. Guntur: Sri Nagarjuna Publishers.

Subba Rao, K.P., P. Ayodhya and Digumarti Bhaskara Rao (2004). *Patasala Yajamanyam-Vidhya Vyavasthalu (School Management and Systems of Education)*. Guntur: Sri Nagarjuna Publishers.

Sudhakar, V., B. Ravindra Babu, D.S. Kumar and Digumarti Bhaskara Rao (2004). *Vidya Sanketika Sastram-Computer Vidya (Educational Technology and Computer Education)*. Guntur: Sri Nagarjuna Publishers.